BREAD AND ROSES

Bread and Roses

Gardening Books from 1560 to 1960

VOLUME TWO

Martin Hoyles

Pluto  Press

First published 1995 by Pluto Press
345 Archway Road, London N6 5AA

Copyright © Martin Hoyles 1995

The right of Martin Hoyles to be identified as the author
of this work has been asserted by him in accordance with
the Copyright, Designs and Patents Act 1988.

British Library Cataloguing in Publication Data
A catalogue record for this book is available from the British Library

ISBN 0 7453 0802 3 hbk

Library of Congress Cataloging in Publication Data
Hoyles, Martin.
    Gardeners delight: gardening books from 1560 to 1960 / Martin
Hoyles.
    240 p. 23 cm.
    Includes bibliographical references and index.
    ISBN 0 7453 0802 3
    1. Horticultural literature–History. 2. Gardening–Bibliography.
I. Title.
SB318.3.H69   1994
635–dc20   94-2332
                                                              CIP

Designed and produced for Pluto Press by
Chase Production Services, Chipping Norton, OX7 5QR
Typeset from author's disk by
Stanford Desktop Publishing Services, Milton Keynes
Printed in the EC by T.J. Press, Padstow

Contents

For Asher with love

Introduction

'If I wrote grammars, if I wrote on agriculture; if I sowed, planted, or dealt in seeds; whatever I did had first in view the destruction of infamous tyrants.'
William Cobbett, *The Political Register*, XXXV, 14 August 1819

'Study books, study gardens, and study wild nature, but use your own brains.'
Harry Roberts, *The Book of Old-Fashioned Flowers* (1901)

Over the last four centuries gardening books in English have been written and read by people from all walks of life. Volume 1, *Gardeners Delight*, illustrated this range of writers and readers, their knowledge and experience, and looked at the common theme of pleasure which runs through the works. It examined gardening's religious roots and the writers' continual emphasis on morality; and it explored the relationship between age and gardening, especially the growth of school gardening and the contrasting stereotype of the aged gardener.

Gardening literature is a microcosm of the history of the last 400 years and reveals much about our culture and politics. This volume explores some of this history further, both thematically and chronologically, looking particularly at the political issues of gender, race and class in gardening books. Over 2,000 works have been consulted for this study.

The political implications of gardening are well summed up by Christopher Hill in *The English Bible and the Seventeenth-Century Revolution* (1993): 'To hear it proclaimed from the stage that "Adam was a gardener" could provoke thoughts subversive of degree and hierarchy.'

The demand for 'Bread and Roses' (from the 1912 women textile workers' strike in Lawrence, Massachusetts) embodies the desire to unite use and beauty. In gardening literature the pleasure of gardening is often linked with its usefulness. Gerard, in his *Herball* (1597), stresses the need to grow plants both for food and medicine, as well as for beauty: 'The delight is great, but the use greater, and joyned often with necessitie.

1

Double Marigold

Double Eglantine   *Turnip*

Illustrations from Gerard's Herball *(1597).*

In the first ages of the world they were the ordinary meate of men, and have continued ever since of necessary use both for meates to maintaine life, and for medicine to recover health.'

In the seventeenth century the enthusiasm for orchards, expressed by writers such as Samuel Hartlib and Ralph Austen, is based on the principle that they combined beauty and use. For Austen, they also have both a natural and a spiritual dimension. In 1653 he wrote two works on orchards (considerably expanded in 1657), which he published in the same book, dedicated to Hartlib. One is called *A Treatise of Fruit-Trees*, on the material or practical side of growing fruit trees; the other, *The Spirituall Use of an Orchard, or Garden*, is about the moral or spiritual parallels, which he calls 'similitudes'.

He insists, however, that 'both the Naturall, and Spirituall part, is but one Treatise', and begins the second part's Preface to the Reader with these words: 'When we have gone through all the workes and labours to be performed in the Orchard, & have received thereby a rich recompence of Temporall Profits & Pleasures in the use of the Trees and Fruits, we may (besides all that) make a Spirituall use of them, and receive much Profit and Pleasure thereby.'

In Hartlib's *Legacie ... of Husbandry* (1651), written largely by Richard Weston, a royalist who had fled to Holland, the many merits of orchards are listed: 'They affoard fuel for the fire, and also shades from the heat, physick for the sicke, refreshment for the sound, plenty of food for man, and that not the worst, and drink also even of the best, and all this without much labour, care, or cost, who therefore can justly open his mouth against them?'

In the eighteenth century these two aspects of gardening tended to be separated, a practice supported by Humphry Repton: 'The country gentleman can only ornament his place by separating the features of farm and park; they are so totally incongruous as not to admit of any union but at the expence either of beauty or profit.' In *Observations on the Theory and Practice of Landscape Gardening* (1803) he argues that the park should contain uniform verdure, undulating lines, light and shade, animals wandering freely. On the other hand, the farm, with its motley and discordant hues, should be subdivided by straight lines of fences, the trees in its hedges cut, its animals yoked to the plough or 'closely confined to fatten within narrow enclosures'.

To illustrate his case, Repton recalls the financial failure of William Shenstone who attempted to combine beauty and use on his estate at The Leasowes, near Birmingham. Shenstone was a minor eighteenth-century poet who spent all his money trying to create the perfect landscape garden on his farm. It became very fashionable, being visited by such notables as Horace Walpole and Samuel Johnson, and was

*Frontispiece, entitled 'A Garden Mingling Beauty and Utility',
from Richard Sudell's* Secrets of Successful Gardening *(1939).*

constantly quoted by contemporary writers. Repton, however, comments: 'I have never walked through these grounds without lamenting not only the misapplication of good taste, but that constant disappointment which the benevolent Shenstone must have experienced in attempting to unite two objects so incompatible as ornament and profit.' He concludes that there can be no union of 'laborious exertion and pleasurable recreation'.

There were exceptions to this eighteenth-century ideology. One is provided by William Speechly, gardener to the Duke of Portland. In *A Treatise of the Culture of the Vine* (1790) he maintains that hot-houses are not just to be seen as luxuries, but that they are also useful and profitable. Consequently, he argues, the tax on glass should be removed, as fuel and glass are the main expenses in managing hot-houses: 'The former article is of small consideration in counties where coals abound, but glass is become a truly serious affair; and indeed it were much to be wished, that glass employed in gardens should be exempt from duty; for please consider, by the aid of this useful material in gardening, our markets would be more plentifully supplied with many kinds of fruit, and also with rare and wholesome vegetables, at a much earlier season than in the natural way they can possibly be; and these, let me observe, are not to be considered as articles of luxury.'

Speechly emphasises the satisfaction involved in raising exotic species. Entrepreneurial business and aristocratic pleasure are combined: 'But in regard to the variety of plants, generally cultivated in stoves, &c. I may properly add, that, independently of profit, every denomination of Forcing-houses is capable of affording to a speculative mind, a source of rational pleasure and real satisfaction.'

Another exception to the eighteenth-century orthodoxy comes from Charles Marshall, Vicar of Brixworth in Northamptonshire. In *An Introduction to the Knowledge and Practice of Gardening* in 1796, he argues for the combination of kitchen and flower garden. Even if they are to be separate, the kitchen garden should still 'be adorned with a sprinkling of the more ordinary decorations, and chiefly those of the most powerful sweet scents, as roses, sweet-briars, and honey-suckles, in order to counteract the coarser effluvia of vegetables, or of dead leaves'.

In the nineteenth century the debate continued. Cobbett argues, in *The English Gardener* (1829), that 'it is most miserable taste to seek to poke away the kitchen-garden, in order to get it out of sight. If well managed, nothing is more beautiful than the kitchen-garden.' But William Paul (1876) clearly wants use and beauty kept distinct: 'The kitchen-garden should be separated from the flower garden by a wall, palings or hedge.'

SAGE
(*Salvia officinalis*)

CHIVES
(*Allium schœnoprasum*)

Illustration by Hilda Coley, from Eleanour Sinclair Rohde's
Herbs and Herb Gardening, *first published in 1936.*

One of Reginald Blomfield's main arguments against the eighteenth-century landscape garden is that it separated use and beauty. Blomfield was an architect who stressed the formal qualities of garden design, as opposed to William Robinson's 'natural' approach. In *The Formal Garden in England* (1892) he writes: 'The double purpose of a garden – for use and pleasure – has been forgotten in landscape gardening. You either get a kitchen garden useful but ugly, or a pleasure garden not useful, and only redeemed from ugliness by the flowers themselves.' He quotes approvingly Lawson's *The Country Housewife's Garden* of 1617, in which the author states that you should not neglect beauty in the kitchen garden.

In the twentieth century the gardening writers Thomas and Wythes agree. They write in *Vegetable Growing Made Easy* (1913): 'Why should it be supposed that beauty must of necessity be divorced from utility? Culinary crops are not necessarily unlovely – for witness, take the silvery grace of a well-grown plant of Globe Artichoke, which in its own way can scarcely be equalled.'

E.T. Cook (1902) compares the utilitarian times in which he lives with the more public-spirited Middle Ages: 'In our days, when rush and hurry and the pressure of business, and the worship of bare utility fill the minds of most men, there are many who have almost forgotten the gracious aspects of the more leisurely life.' He advocates planting shade-giving trees in towns and villages, where they 'would be a comfort and a pleasure to many hard-working folk, and might be the means of converting unsightliness into beauty'. Similarly the frontispiece of Richard Sudell's *Secrets of Successful Gardening* (1939) is entitled A Garden Mingling Beauty and Utility.

Social History

It is evident from these examples that gardening books contain far more than just information about gardening. As Eleanour Rohde writes in *Herbs and Herb Gardening* (1936): 'The old herbals and gardening books are a source of profound interest not only to gardeners and botanists but also to artists, folklorists, ethnologists, and philologists.'

They are also of interest to historians. The first chapter of this book aims to set gardening books in their political and historical perspective. The presentation is in a series of cameos, picking out certain key historical moments, such as the seventeenth-century Commonwealth or the Second World War. They illustrate the unexpected effects such political events have on gardening writing and the ideological debates they can provoke. In both these periods, for example, there was an

emphasis on cultivating fruit trees in the garden: in the former as a
political project to create another Eden and in the latter as an economic
defence against Hitler's blockade.

The other chapters look at the issues of gender, class and race. The
archetypal gardener is certainly male, harking back to Adam. But women
have always gardened, often being regarded as the experts in particular
areas, for example herbs and flowers. There has been a strong tradition
of separate spheres of gardening for men and women, which is why Jane
Loudon's challenge to it in the middle of the nineteenth century is so
radical.

The story of Adam and Eve contrasts the pleasurable work in the garden
of Eden with the hard labour which is necessary outside it. Two points
are critical when discussing gardening as work. One is that unalienated
labour is pleasant; the other is that the division of labour means that
some people are largely confined to boring, mechanical, physically
exhausting tasks, which are necessary for them to earn a living. Both
are clearly relevant to gardening books, some of which are aimed at wage
labourers and others at amateur gardeners. Many books, particularly those
in the tradition of the eighteenth-century encyclopaedias and diction-
aries, are intended for both kinds of reader.

Perhaps the most difficult areas to deal with are those of race and
nationalism. They are constant themes in English gardening books
and on one level fit in with wider social expressions of patriotism and
imperialism. Clearly the eighteenth-century landscape garden can be
seen as the epitome of ruling-class power and status, and the export of
this style worldwide a reflection of Britain's imperial influence. It is
certainly important to note the emphasis throughout the century on
planting oak trees in country estates in order to supply timber to build
ships for the British navy. Likewise economic botany is an example of
British capitalist exploitation of worldwide natural resources. The
colonial importation of plants in the nineteenth century affected both
gardening style and horticultural literature.

But the mythology surrounding the English cottage garden is more
difficult to explain. In one sense it continues the tradition of the free-
born Englishman, going back to before the Norman invasion. It reflects
the idea of an Englishman's home (and garden) as his castle, a symbol
of the privacy and reserve of the English, as expressed by G.A. Jellicoe
in his Foreword to Lanning Roper's *Royal Gardens* (1953): 'The desire
for seclusion is part of the British temperament and nowhere is this
characteristic so well illustrated, for instance, as in the enclosed front
gardens of all English and Scottish homes. These gardens are a peculiarity
of an independent island race, in which every man would like to think
that his home were his castle and the front gate his drawbridge.' The

destruction of these village gardens through enclosure is not so often mentioned, however, nor their forced abandonment during the industrial revolution.

Nevertheless it is hard not to succumb to the enticement of 'England's green and pleasant land'. We want to believe the 'foreign gentleman' quoted by Daniel Defoe at the beginning of the eighteenth century, in *Tour of the Whole Island of Great Britain*, who is recorded as commenting 'that England was not like other countries, but it was all a planted garden'.

1

Digging for Victory:
History and Politics in
Gardening Books

*'There is much more than meets the eye in English Gardens. Even
the most insignificant have their story to tell, for every stage of
English history is reflected in them. They have gradually changed
through the centuries, and each phase of our political development, our foreign policy, our wars, and our discoveries has left
its mark on our gardens.'*

Alicia Amherst, *Historic Gardens of England* (1938)

*'It is only one more of the regrettable results of the barbarous
way in which the Reformation was carried out in England, that
the gardens shared the fate of the stately buildings round whose
sheltering walls they flourished.'*

Alicia Amherst *London Parks and Gardens* (1907)

*'The Great War has so altered our views in many respects that
whereas formerly the vegetable plot was one which we hurried
past, giving but a cursory glance at its contents, we now desire
to give it prominence.'*

Frances Wolseley *Gardens: Their Form and Design* (1919)

*'In the present century Britain has been engaged in two great wars,
conducted on novel lines, with novel weapons; the total effect
of which on gardening in this country is bound to be immense.
Already one sees a great reduction in the number of large gardens
in private hands. The cultivation of flowers except on the smallest
scale, is discouraged, and large estates all over the country are
being split up for building development.'*

Harry Roberts *English Gardens* (1944)

With some notable exceptions, histories of gardens and gardening tend to isolate their subject from the social and political movements of the day. This is particularly true of accounts of eighteenth-century landscape gardens which often use art and architecture as points of reference rather than contemporary events. However, major social upheavals, such as the Civil War and the Restoration in the seventeenth century, had an impact on gardening practice and theory, and contradictory accounts of the same events can often be attributed more to later historians' political views than to the original sources.

THE COMMONWEALTH

It is a commonplace of most gardening histories that Puritans were not interested in gardening for pleasure, that the Parliamentarians cut down trees and destroyed gardens, and that only with the Restoration did gardening flourish again.

In *Gardens of Celebrities and Celebrated Gardens* (1919), for example, Jessie MacGregor maintains that 'Horticulture made no advance during the Civil War and the Commonwealth'. (She does acknowledge, however, that General Lambert was famous for cultivating tulips.) Likewise, in *English Countryside and Gardens* (1947), Montagu Allwood declares: 'The period from the outbreak of the Civil War to the Restoration is more or less blank.' In *The Story of Our Gardens* (1958), Dorothea Eastwood writes: 'Until the disturbing appearance of Cromwell, the first half of the seventeenth century were great days for gardeners.' She goes on to lump together the Tradescants, who were royalist plant hunters, and Ralph Austen, a radical Puritan, saying that 'they thought of little else but their beloved flowers, now grown, not for medicine or for seasoning, but for their beauty's sake'. She later refers to the 'joyful day of Charles' return'.

The Destruction of Gardens

The destruction of gardens during the Commonwealth was deplored by many later writers. W. Angus's *The Seats of the Nobility and Gentry in Great Britain and Wales* (1787) is a book of illustrations of country estates, accompanied by a brief commentary. The history of Theobalds in Hertfordshire, where James I died in 1625, is recalled: 'This Palace was plundered in 1651, and defaced so as to become from a princely Residence, a Village, and the Park was converted into Farms.' Angus draws his political conclusion: 'In its Neighbourhood resided Richard Cromwell, the abdicated Protector, in a very private Manner, from 1660 to 1712, when he died in the 86th Year of his Age. A striking Lesson how much Obscurity and Peace are to be preferred to the splendid Infelicity of guilty Ambition.'

In the nineteenth century, T. James similarly attacks the Roundheads, in *The Poetry of Gardening*: 'As for old Noll, I am certain, though I have not a jot of evidence, that he cared no more for a garden than for an anthem; he would as lief have sacrificed the verdant sculpture of a yew-peacock as the time-honoured tracery of a cathedral shrine; and his crop-eared soldiery would have had as great satisfaction in bivouacking in the parterres of a "royal pleasaunce" as in the presence-chamber of a royal palace. It were a sorrow beyond tears to dwell on the destruction of garden-stuff in those king-killing times.'

It is important, however, to realise the significance of the famous gardens of the early seventeenth century which were destroyed during the Civil War. In 1605 Inigo Jones (1572–1652) was first employed by James I to design the sets for court masques, and in 1615 he was appointed Surveyor of the King's Works. He went on to design gardens and was behind the reforms carried out in royal gardens such as Greenwich and St James's. Some of these he reconstructed on stage, where the garden was always presented as an emblem of the divine right of kings to rule both their subjects and nature. 'No Wonder', writes Roy Strong, in his contribution to *The Garden* (1979), 'that the Parliamentarians included the destruction of gardens along with that of the art collections as part of their programme to obliterate the ancient images of monarchy. Deliberately destroyed or abandoned, their contents sold off, down went Hampton Court, Nonsuch, Theobalds, St James, Whitehall and the rest of them. When Charles II returned in 1660 royal gardening had to begin again.'

A more positive view of the Commonwealth period is expressed by George Johnson in *A History of English Gardening* (1829), where he acknowledges Cromwell's achievements: 'Cromwell was a great improver of Agriculture and the useful branches of Gardening.'

Richardson Wright (*The Story of Gardening*, 1934) likens Cromwell's policy to Soviet collective farming: 'Once Cromwell was in the saddle, luxury gardening diminished and economic gardening increased. What Russia under the Soviets is doing today in agriculture, England did under the Commonwealth. Farms were enlarged and many more opened to the plough. Better farming methods were studied and introduced by the aristocracy and the gentry. A greater interest was shown in fruit and economic plants.'

Reginal Blomfield, in *The Formal Garden in England* (1892), describes this period as 'comparatively speaking, a blank in the history of the arts', in which category he includes gardening. He quotes approvingly John

Evelyn's comments in 1666 on the destruction of the royal garden at Nonsuch by the Parliamentarians: 'There stand in the garden two handsome stone pyramids, and the avenue planted with rowes of faire elmes; but the rest of these goodly trees both of this and Worcester Park adjoyning, were felled by those destructive & avaricious rebels in the late war, which defaced one of the stateliest seats his Majesty had.'

In fact, much of Nonsuch survived the Commonwealth. In *A History of Garden Art* (1913), Marie Luise Gothein points out the irony of its post-Restoration fate: 'But the estate that escaped the Commonwealth fell a victim to baser greed, for Charles II presented it after the Restoration to his mistress, the Countess of Castlemaine, and she, having learned a lesson from Parliament, parcelled out the royal estate and sold it.'

Parliamentarians

Carew Hazlitt, writing in 1892 (*Gleanings in Old Garden Literature*), shows more sympathy towards the Parliamentarians. He says of John Lambert, at one time the second most powerful man in the land after Cromwell: 'General Lambert, who was lord of the manor of Wimbledon in 1656, was very fond of his garden at that place, and grew, it is said, the finest tulips and gilliflowers procurable. It is to his passion for this pursuit that he owed his place on a pack of satirical cards published during the Commonwealth, where the Eight of Hearts bears a small full-length of him, holding a tulip in his right hand, with "Lambert Kt. of ye Golden Tulip" beneath. He had withdrawn into what was then the country from political life; but, amid his recreations as a florist, was doubtless watching the opportunity for a return to the field of his professional work. Next to Monk he was probably the most able of the generals of the Commonwealth and Protectorate, and it was an error on the part of Cromwell to have estranged him. But to his temporary retirement we owe this little glimpse of his taste for a pursuit more genial and more humane than that of war.'

Mollie Sands also provides a balance to the generally negative view of this period: 'There was indeed some gardening progress during the Commonwealth, in spite of the disturbed nature of the times.' In *The Gardens of Hampton Court* (1950) she goes on to refer to Hartlib and Austen, concluding: 'The chief improvements were in fruit-growing and in market-gardening.'

In 1641 Hartlib wrote a brief utopian work, entitled *A Description of the Famous Kingdome of Macaria*, in the form of a dialogue between a scholar and a traveller. In Macaria the parliament has five councils and the one responsible for husbandry orders that 'the twentieth of every mans goods that dieth shall be employed about the improving of lands, and making of High-wayes faire, and bridges over Rivers; by which meanes the whole Kingdome is become like to a fruitfull Garden.' Hartlib looks to books to help the development of democracy: 'The Art of Printing will so spread knowledge, that the common people, knowing their own rights and liberties, will not be governed by way of oppression.' As in the later American and French revolutions, the aim is universal happiness, 'so wee and our posterity shall bee all happie'.

Peter Cornelisson, another radical supporter of the Commonwealth, had a similar vision. In *A Way Propounded* (1659) he sets out a proposal for a commune of cooperative living, in which both men and women 'shall govern by turns'. It would include 'Gardiners having skill in gardening, for roots, plants, and orchards, for fruit, flowers and hearbs, as well medicinal, for our Physitians, as other'.

The digger and leveller Gerrard Winstanley uses garden imagery to put forward his political views: 'You shall find I speake of the Garden of Eden, which is the spirit of man, not the spirit of Beasts. And in that Garden there are weeds and hearbs.' In *Fire in the Bush* (1650) he distinguishes between the sinful weeds and the virtuous herbs: 'There is likewise in the garden of Eden (mans heart) sweet flowers and hearbs; As Joy, Peace, Love, humility, self-denyall, patience, sincerity, truth, or equitie.' Winstanley attacks enclosures by land-owners, looking forward to the day when their 'bloody and theeving power be rooted out of the land'. In *A Declaration from the Poor Oppressed People of England* (1649), signed also by 44 others, he criticises the academic establishment in a manner reminiscent of Culpeper: 'The secrets of the Creation have been locked up under the traditional Parrat-like speaking, from the Universities, and Colledges for Scholars.'

Like Hartlib and Winstanley, Austen was also a supporter of the Commonwealth and a man of egalitarian principles. In the second edition of *The Spirituall Use of An Orchard, or Garden of Fruit-Trees* (1657) he uses the fact that the 'Husbandman makes use of ordinary, and common Tooles' to observe that 'God (for the most part) useth meane and ordinary men, and meanes, for effecting of the greatest works in the world'. He continues with a similar levelling comparison: 'When God roots up, or cuts down high, green, flourishing trees, but barren of good fruits, and plants choice trees in their stead, though low, and despised in the eyes of the world, this is, that he may dwell among them and walke among them.'

Austen refutes the assumption that Puritans do not enjoy life: 'O say not we shall loose our pleasures if we turn to be precise, and religious.' He writes passionately about the beauty of gardens and in 1676 bears witness to the increased planting of orchards in the middle of the century: 'Men have Planted more Fruit-trees within 30 or 40 yeares last past, then in severall hundred of yeares in former ages; as is manifest by Orchards that are planted.'

The notion that the Puritans could not enjoy themselves later became ubiquitous, and Nan Fairbrother cannot understand how Ralph Austen could have been both a Puritan and a gardener. In *Men and Gardens* (1956) she writes of 'his divided mind' and calls his book, *The Spirituall Use of an Orchard*, 'a pathetic attempt to reconcile his opposing enthusiasms'. She refers to 'strangely twisted consciences' and asserts that 'the gentle light of reason could not reach the dark and deformed spirits of the Puritan zealots'.

Public Enclosure

In *A Treatise of Fruit-Trees* (1653) Austen argues very reasonably for the planting of orchards to deliver the poor 'multitudes from Idlenesse, Beggery, Shame, and consequently, Theft, Murther, and (at last) the Gallows'. He wants to see an organised system of enclosure to benefit the poor: 'For in divisions, and inclosures of Wast, and Common Grounds, (by Persons appoynted for that purpose,) why should not the Poore have their share, and proportion, as well as their rich Neighbours, and that to them, and their heires for ever; yea, let the Poore be first provided for.'

Anthony Lawrence (1677) also argues for enclosures to plant orchards, which would benefit everyone: 'And thus, many Commons, which have been hitherto little better than waste-ground, may in a short time become populous Villages, and well provided of all necessaries.' He refers to the protests against enclosure, arguing that fair enclosure will turn protesters into supporters: 'Here is work enough, and stuff enough, to engage all the Ring-leaders of the tumultuous Rabble, to call in all their Parties, and to stickle as stoutly for Inclosures as ever they did formerly to hinder them.'

Earlier, in 1649, Walter Blith, who was a captain in the New Model Army, had addressed a book to 'those of the High and Honourable Houses of Parliament', putting a similar case for enclosed land to be shared by all. In *The English Improover, or a New Survey of Husbandry* he proposes that the new hedgerows be planted also with fruit trees, providing both fuel and sustenance, so they 'will not only be most profitable, but most delightfull'. The third edition of his book came out in 1652, entitled *The English Improver Improved*, 'all clearly demonstrated from Principles of Reason, Ingenuity, and late, but most Real Experiences'. It is dedicated to the 'The Lord Generall Cromwell' and the frontispiece is headed 'Vive

La Republick'. Blith is quick to distance himself, however, from the diggers and levellers. The leaders of the levellers had been executed at Burford in 1649. He is not 'of the Diggers minde', nor does he agree with 'the Levell Principles of Parity or Equally'. His appeal is to all sections of society, from the nobility to the meanest commoner: 'But this Parity is all I indeavour, to make the poor rich, and the rich richer, and all to live of the labour of their owne hands.'

Blith believed in public investment in mining and in the nationalisation of land, favouring 'publique service' over 'base privacy of Spirit'. Landlords are attacked for reaping all the benefits of land improvements and Blith puts forward a proposal to double the extent of woodlands through new plantations. The author supports only 'such Enclosures as prevents Depopulation, & advanceth all Interests', and argues for 'the great Advance of Land by divers Orchards and Garden Fruits'.

THE RESTORATION

After the defeat of the Commonwealth these utopian ideals are no longer so evident in gardening literature. Richard Blome claims in 1686 that 'there is no greater Improvement to be made on Ground, than the planting it with Fruit Trees'. But unfortunately 'the Rustick People will not easily be perswaded to go out of their old way, nor be one Peny charge in expectation of a future Gain'. Blome's harsh solution, set out in *The Gentlemans Recreation*, is for landlords to force people to plant fruit trees in the hedgerows every year as a condition of their tenancy.

One of those to benefit from the Restoration was Andrew Mollet, who became 'Master of His Majesty of Englands Gardens in His Park of St. James's'. In *The Garden of Pleasure*, published in 1670 and dedicated to the King, he praises 'our invincible Monarch, Charles the Second', who 'hath made notable Changes, and added more Royal Decorations since the 10 years of His happy Restoration, then any of His Ancestors ever thought on in the space of a whole Age'.

John Evelyn was also pleased to see the Restoration of Charles II, who was his friend. The King visited him at Sayes Court in 1663 and presumably saw his bees. In his 'Manuscript on Bees', part of his unfinished *Elysium Britannicum* which he began around 1659, Evelyn writes that bees 'are of all Creatures, the most affected to Monarchy, and the most Loyal, reading a Lecture of obedience to Rebels in every man's garden'.

Evelyn's *Sylva* (1664), the first work to be published by the Royal Society, is dedicated to the King. In the book Evelyn deplores the loss of the nation's trees, cut down to be used for ship-building, glass-works and

SYLVA,

Or A DISCOURSE Of
FOREST-TREES,
AND THE
Propagation of Timber
In His MAJESTIES Dominions.

By *J. E.* Efq;

As it was Deliver'd in the *ROYAL SOCIETY* the xv[th] of *October*, CIƆIƆCLXII. upon Occafion of certain *Quæries* Propounded to that *Illuftrious Affembly*, by the *Honorable* the Principal *Officers*, and *Commiffioners* of the *Navy*.

To which is annexed

POMONA Or, An *Appendix* concerning *Fruit-Trees* in relation to *CIDER*; The *Making* and feveral ways of *Ordering* it.

Publifhed by exprefs Order of the ROYAL SOCIETY.

ALSO

KALENDARIUM HORTENSE; Or, *Gard'ners Almanac*; Directing what he is to do *Monethly* throughout the *Year*.

―――――*Tibi res antiquæ laudis & artis Ingredior, tantos aufus recludere fonteis.* Virg.

NVLLIVS IN VERBA

LONDON, Printed by *Jo. Martyn*, and *Ja. Allestry*, Printers to the *Royal Society*, and are to be fold at their Shop at the *Bell* in S. *Paul's* Church-yard, MDCLXIV.

Title page of John Evelyn's Sylvia (1664).

iron furnaces. He proposes a massive programme of tree planting 'for the benefit of His Royal Navy'. The Parliamentarians of the Commonwealth are 'greedy rebells', 'prodigious spoilers', 'unhappy Usurpers' and 'injurious Sequestrators', 'whose furious devastation of so many goodly Woods and Forests have left an Infamy on their Names and Memories not quickly to be forgotten'. By the second edition, in 1669, more than a thousand copies had been sold, and Evelyn claims that this had resulted in the planting of 'two millions of timber-trees'. By 1825 the book was in its ninth edition. Blanche Henrey writes in her 1975 survey of horticultural literature that 'no other work on arboriculture exerted a greater influence on forestry in this country than Evelyn's "Sylva", and certainly no other book on the subject was so often quoted.'

John Beale

The year 1660 led to the settling of old scores and the reversal of fortunes. John Evelyn, the royalist, became famous; Ralph Austen, the republican, was ignored. Others, such as John Beale, simply changed sides. In *Herefordshire Orchards, A Pattern for all England* (1657), written as 'an Epistolary Address to Samuel Hartlib', Beale praises his native Herefordshire: 'From the greatest persons to the poorest cottager, all habitations are encompassed with Orchards and Gardens; and in most places our hedges are inriched with rowes of fruit-trees.' He adds that 'in every village there is some excellent republican'. In 1660, however, Beale became vicar of Yeovil, in 1662 a fellow of the Royal Society and in 1665 chaplain to Charles II.

The civil wars had been a traumatic experience for Beale, as he reveals in a letter to Robert Boyle in 1663: 'About the beginning of these civil wars, I was overwhelmed in melancholy and grief, to see the publick confusions and ruins, (my nearest alliances, and dearest friends, being engaged, and many lost on both sides.) This broke out into the blind piles, stoppage of my stomach, hypochondriacal torments, jaundices ...'

After the Restoration Beale tries to play down the importance of Ralph Austen, preferring his friend Lawrence: 'I dare say, that Anthony Lawrence can do more for propagation of orchards in five years, than Mr. Austen hath done in fifty-two years, as he numbers them.' Lawrence, on the other hand, tried to rehabilitate Austen after his death in 1676. In a letter written in 1677 to Henry Oldenburg, secretary to the Royal Society, Lawrence asks why the author of *A Treatise of Fruit-Trees* has been so neglected: 'I conceive, that it was meerly by Incogitance, that that Industrious Author, Mr. Austen, hath not been hitherto mentioned in your Tracts amongst others who have handled the same Arguments.' He goes on to give Austen a glowing reference: 'This plain Writer, who pretends to no glory in Rhetoric, hath by his labours and Experiments done more good for Oxford, and thence for England, than is yet done by many gaudy Gallants, who spend more in a day, than this honest Nursery-man can spare in a year.'

SEVENTEENTH-CENTURY PUBLISHING

Blanche Henrey, in *British Botanical and Horticultural Literature Before 1800*, puts the 'dividing line' in the seventeenth century at 1650, not 1660, in other words at the beginning of the Commonwealth, not at the Restoration: 'Compared with the years 1600–50, the second half of the seventeenth century in England witnessed a great increase in the number of gardening books published.' It is difficult, for example, to find a single new gardening book published in the 1630s.

An Overview of book production during this period can be found in Frank Mumby's *Publishing and Bookselling* (1930): 'The story of the book trade through the reign of Charles I is largely a record of restriction and persecution.' He describes the Star Chamber decree of 1637 as ushering in 'the darkest age in the history of the English book trade since Caxton', though by 1641 it was a dead letter, as censorship broke down.

Christopher Hill (1993) writes of 'the printing explosion of the 1640s': 'For the first time in English history anyone could get into print who could persuade a printer that there was money in his or her idea. Significant numbers of persons (including women) who had had no university education, often no grammar school education even, found no obstacles to publication.'

Publication of pamphlets in particular increased dramatically during the next two decades. During this period the bookseller George Thomason collected around 23,000 newsbooks and pamphlets, which mainly bypassed the bookshops and were sold on the streets. The number of printers in London rose from 23 to 60, though the Licensing Act of 1662 reduced it again to 20.

The vast majority of the publications of this period were religious and political. William London's *A Catalogue of The most vendible Books in England* (1657), for example, contains hundreds of books, half of which are on divinity. Among the other subjects, he lists nine books on gardening including, with dates of first publication, works by Hyll (1577), Platt (1608), Butler (1609), Lawson (1618), Markham (1631, a revision of an earlier book by Heresbach, translated by Googe in 1577), Blith (1649), Hartlib (1651) and Austen (1656). The ninth is an anonymous work entitled *Bread for the Poore*. London comments ironically: 'Though there be a complaint that the world seems opprest with Books, yet do we daily want them.'

By Easter 1660 he had published *A Catalogue of New Books*: 'By way of Supplement to the former. Being Such as have been Printed from that time.' They include a translation by John Evelyn of *The French Gardiner* (1658), herbals by Robert Lovell (1659) and Nicholas Culpeper (1659), Adolphus Speed's *Adam out of Eden* (1659) and *The History of the Propagation and Improvement of Vegetables* (1660) by Robert Sharrock, who was a Fellow of New College, Oxford, and became Archdeacon of Winchester in 1684.

In *The Happy Man* (1954) Maren-Sofie Rostvig writes of the 'sudden vogue for gardens which arose during the Commonwealth and The Restoration'. Likewise, Edmund Rack, one of the contributors to Alexander Hunter's *Georgical Essays* (1803), backs up the view that the 1640s and 1650s were a time of general improvement in husbandry. In his essay, entitled 'On the Origin and Progress of Agriculture', he praises the advances made during this period: 'The time in which Hartlib flourished, seems to have been an era when the English husbandry rose to great perfection, compared with that of former ages; for the preceding wars had impoverished the country gentlemen, and of course made them industrious.' He also sees a corresponding decline at the end of the Commonwealth: 'At the Restoration, they generally became infected with that intoxication and love of pleasure which succeeded. All their industry and knowledge were exchanged for neglect and dissipation; and husbandry descended almost entirely into the hands of common farmers.'

THE EIGHTEENTH-CENTURY LANDSCAPE GARDEN

The formal gardening style persisted in England at the end of the seventeenth century, and gardens in country estates were influenced by both French and Dutch gardens. Even so, William Temple claims aspects of English gardening to be the best in the world. In his essay 'Upon the Gardens of Epicurus; or, of Gardening in the Year 1685', he considers gardening in England to have 'been so mightily improved' that 'perhaps few Countries are before us; either in the Elegance of our Gardens, or in the number of our Plants; and I believe none equals us in the Variety of Fruits, which may be justly called good; and from the earliest Cherry and Strawberry, to the last Apples and Pears, may furnish every Day of the circling Year'.

The eighteenth century gradually saw England achieve military supremacy over France and at the same time establish its own distinctive form of gardening which was to become famous throughout the world. Gardening books of the time reflect both aspects of English hegemony. At the beginning of the century England was fighting France in the War of the Spanish Succession. In 1710 William Salmon published *The English Herbal*, dedicated to Queen Anne, in which he praises her conquests in idealistic fashion: 'Your Triumphs are not in the Ruin of Nations and Kingdoms, not in Victories of Blood and Cruelty, not for Dominions and Sovereignty; but to give Freedom and Ease to Mankind, and set the World at Liberty.'

In this period John James is also concerned to establish English horticultural supremacy. In *The Theory and Practice of Gardening* (1712), which he translated from the French, he argues that, if the advice in the book is followed, 'we may hope to see, ere long, our English Pleasure-Gardens in greater Perfection, than any the most renowned, in France, or Italy, since our Woods and Groves, our Grass and Gravel, which are the great Subjects of this Work, are allowed to surpass in Verdure and natural Beauty, whatever is to be found in those Countries'.

His prediction about English gardening style superseding the French came true, but not in the way he imagined. In 1715 Stephen Switzer wrote the first English gardening book to advocate the new landscape style. Switzer came from Hampshire and trained at Brompton Park under London and Wise. In *The Nobleman, Gentleman, and Gardener's Recreation* he acknowledges the magnificent French garden designs 'which certainly yet very much excel ours, notwithstanding those considerable Advantages we have by Nature beyond what they have'.

These natural advantages of the English climate were used to create a new ruling gardening style, which became known abroad as the English garden.

There were disadvantages, too, in England's cool climate, but these could be overcome by native gardening ingenuity and skill. In *The Practical Gardener* (1769) James Garton claims that by using hot-beds 'we are enabled to rear many products of warmer climates, and in England the table is furnished with the several products of the garden, during the winter and spring-months, better than they are in any other country in Europe'.

Switzer also acknowledges the limitations of a cool climate, but the new landscape style could draw on English strengths, particularly its grass and trees. He draws the connection between English oak trees and English supremacy over the French, in more ways than one: '"Tis true, we do not abound so much as they do with Oranges, and some other delicious Fruits, but in their room we have the more durable and serviceable Blessings of Oak, besides fructiferous Trees, proper enough for our Use, and that which abundantly commands them all, I mean our Ships and the Balance of Trade.'

Oak Trees, the Navy and the Balance of Trade

Many gardening writers of this period were concerned about oak trees, the navy and the balance of trade. In 1728 Batty Langley wrote *A Sure Method of Improving Estates, by Plantations of Oak, Elm, Ash, Beech and Other Timber-Trees, Coppice-Woods*. The book is dedicated to Viscount Torrington, First Lord of the Admiralty, and to 'those who are by his most Gracious Majesty entrusted with the Care and Directions of his

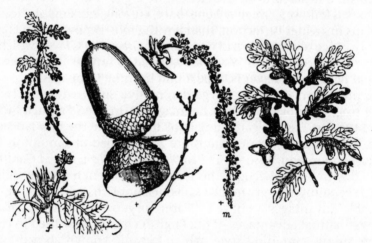

'Quercus pedunculata. The common, or peduncled, British Oak.'
From John Loudon's An Encyclopaedia of Trees and Shrubs *(1842).*

Royal Navy; the Bulwark and Glory of Great-Britain'. The author, like Evelyn in the seventeenth century, makes it clear that if the planting of timber is neglected, British power and commerce will decline.

Another seventeenth-century author, Ralph Austen (1657), can be heard complaining of the scarcity and high cost of wood. He attacks the lack of timber for building ships and houses, but also the fact 'that the poorer sort of people make lamentable mone for want of fire, in cold long winters, whereas by diligent planting there would be fuell enough for all people'. He wants children to be encouraged to plant trees: 'If Schoole-boyes and others while they are young, set upon planting Okes, Ashes, Elmes and other trees, they may probably (as others have done) make use of them for building, sale &c. even themselves in their owne persons, unto exceeding great profit.'

In the eighteenth century Batty Langley expresses another recurring worry, namely that we are 'already much oblig'd to foreigners'. If we have to buy timber for shipping from abroad "tis to be feared, that this glorious, and now powerful flourishing Nation, that governs the Seas, must submit to every Invasion that's made, for want of its wooden Walls of Defence'. He goes on to quote Evelyn, that the Spanish Armada of 1588 had instructions 'that if when landed, they should not be able to subdue our Nation, and make good their Conquest, they should yet be sure not to leave a Tree standing in the Forest of Dean ... lest the English build them Ships, and Men of War'. Finally he makes the point that 'besides this Necessity of national Security', the 'Advantages and Pleasures' of planting trees are also very great.

Ironically, where the Spanish failed, the English may have succeeded, for the Forest of Dean was overused for domestic purposes and for the iron industry. By the early eighteenth century, according to the historian A.L. Morton, it 'was already showing signs of exhaustion'. Smelting with coal instead of wood was eventually established on a commercial basis in the middle of the century, since by that time the fuel situation had become desperate.

This reliance on oak for the navy is confirmed by Moses Cook in 1676:

> Oak-Walls our Seas and Island do inclose,
> Our Best Defence against our Forreign Foes.

Richard Blome, in *The Gentlemans Recreation* (1686), also vouches for the superiority of English oak: 'The Oak hath the preheminence of all others, for its strength and Durableness; and for that reason is made use of for building of Ships, for which the English Oak excels all other Nations.' In *The Whole Art of Husbandry* (1707) John Mortimer claims that, for building houses and ships, 'our English Oak exceeds that of all other Parts'.

Writing during the same period as Batty Langley, Richard Bradley (1717) is similarly worried about the shortage of oak trees. He gives detailed accounts showing how profitable growing timber can be, in the hope that land-owners will take it up. Later, in *A General Treatise of Husbandry and Gardening* (1724), he claims responsibility for the 'planting of several Millions of Ever-green Oaks in England'.

In his *Gardeners Dictionary*, the best-known gardening book of the eighteenth century, Philip Miller too warns of the consequences of wasting timber: 'Unless a speedy stop be put to it, the government will be greatly distressed for their marine.' He writes to encourage the

Frontispiece, engraved by J. Mynde after a design by John Joshua Kirby, from
The Modern Druid *(1747), by James Wheeler. The Latin title means*
'The Ornament and Protector of Britain'.

growing of indigo, coffee, chocolate and sugar in the colonies, which would help the balance of trade 'greatly to the advantage both of Great-Britain and her colonies'. His book is dedicated 'To the Most Noble Hugh, Duke and Earl of Northumberland, Earl Percy', who is called, among many other titles, 'Vice Admiral of all America'.

Miller also writes that oak trees are 'very proper for a Wilderness in large Gardens, or to plant in Clumps in Parks', as well as in larger plantations. He gives the following advice to his readers, many of whom were members of the aristocracy, as is clear from his list of subscribers: 'The expence of such Plantations is but small, especially where Labour is cheap, and the Profits which must arise from them, to the Successors of those who are so beneficent to their Posterity, as to lay out a small Share of their Fortune this Way, will be very great.'

A telling illustration of the connection between oak trees and British rule of the seas is to be found in James Wheeler's *The Modern Druid* of 1747. The frontispiece shows a tall straight oak in the centre, with Britannia to the right, against the background of a sea full of British men-of-war. Wheeler was a nurseryman in Gloucester and his book is subtitled as giving instructions 'for the much better Culture of Young Oaks'. It is dedicated to 'the Nobility and the Gentry of Great Britain, Proprietors of Woods, Chaces, Wasts, Parks, or Pastures, or any kindly Soils Productive of the Oak'. The author describes the oak as 'that most valuable and August Tree'. He maintains that 'it is the Source of all the Riches and Strength of Britons, and a ministerial Defender of our Lives and Liberties against Foreigners'.

Profit and Pleasure

Oaks are not only profitable, however, but also add to the natural beauty of an estate, giving pleasure to those walking or riding round them. Woods also provide 'the only nurseries of game', which Wheeler sees as a source of great pleasure in country life. He refers to the British innovation of preferring 'serpentine Rivers, before large strait canals' and expounds the new planting orthodoxy which opposes 'Resemblance – Rule – Regularity' and anything that smacks of 'Stiff – Starch'd – Studied order'. The trees should not be 'planted in strait lines, saving where walks, or vista's are intended; but after a natural manner: Art therein appearing best in masquerade'. He adds an ironic comment on the idea that this style was copied from the Chinese: 'But had I not found the opinion current, of such precedent being borrowed from the Chinese, I should rather have thought we had taken it from the Deity's own manner, of planting woods, and modeling the starry heavens.'

In 1755 Edward Wade wrote *A Proposal for Improving and Adorning the Island of Great Britain; for the Maintenance of our Navy and Shipping*, in which he attacks absentee landlords and clergy for neglecting to plant trees: 'We have never had a less Quantity of large Timber for the Use of the Royal Navy than at present.' The price of oak had recently doubled and imports increased: 'Even Oak Timber and Plank, for the Use of our Shipping, is imported from Foreign Countries, and it is said we cannot do without it.'

Wade proposes a scheme for planting trees in every parish, which will not only provide employment and relief for the poor, but will also 'make this Island the richest, most powerful, and most delightful Spot upon Earth'. As a result we will be able to 'defend our own Territories, and to interfere with greatly more Power and Efficacy than at present in the general Affairs of Europe'. He concludes with the nationalist rallying cry of the eighteenth century: 'Slaves have no Heart or Spirit to go about such a Work, Free-born Britons have.'

This theme of planting trees for national security was taken up by many eighteenth-century gardening writers, including William Hanbury in *An Essay on Planting*, written in 1758, during the Seven Years' War; James Justice, in *The British Gardener's Calendar* (1759); William Forsyth in *Observations on the Diseases, Defects, and Injuries in All Kinds of Fruit and Forest Trees* (1791); and William Pontey, planter and tree pruner to the Duke of Bedford, in *The Profitable Planter* (1800).

The literal reliance on oak trees for maritime supremacy is mirrored by the symbolic use of the oak as representing the British character. In 'Unconnected Thoughts on Gardening' (1764) William Shenstone draws the parallel: 'All trees have a character analagous to that of men: Oaks are in all respects the perfect image of the manly character: In former times I should have said, and in present times I think I am authorized to say, the British one.'

By the second half of the eighteenth century tree plantation did increase dramatically, partly as a result of prizes and medals awarded to land-owners by the Society for the Encouragement of Arts, Manufactures and Commerce. In 1758 the Duke of Beaufort received the first gold medal for sowing acorns in 23 acres at Hawksbury in Gloucestershire. In 1776 another medal was awarded to the Earl of Moray for planting 7,646,000 oaks, firs and other trees. These awards continued to be made up until 1835. The number of trees planted as a result of this campaign has been estimated at over 50 million, including 15 million oaks.

'Capability' Brown helped in this process with his clumps of trees and encircling belts of woodland. Although he made use of existing trees, Brown was also responsible, along with other landscape architects, for many new plantations. When Fisherwick in Staffordshire, for instance, was remodelled, the park was planted mainly with oak. Brown assured the owner, Lord Donegall, that 100,000 trees had been put in, which in due course might fetch £100,000.

Walter Nicol, in *The Scotch Forcing Gardener* (1797), emphasises this financial incentive: 'Let us hope no one would place a clump, or run a stripe at random, without considering – of its *use* in the first instance – of its *value* afterwards.' He is particularly concerned with training oak trees for 'crooked timber' to produce 'cuts fitted for ribs or knees', this being 'a matter of the greatest importance to the ship-builder and mariner'. The author concludes: 'Detached or hedge-row trees, those standing on the borders of plantations, or in open woods, rather then in close groves or thickets, are most proper for this purpose.'

Similarly, in *The Planter's Guide* of 1828, Henry Steuart praises Brown's planting in clumps and the similar landscape style of Thomas White in Scotland, as it produced trees of 'great size and beauty'. He too writes of the economic value of planting in this way: 'While in no part so deep as to impede the salutary action of the atmosphere, the circular or oval figure of the clumps, and their free exposure to the elements, furnished them with a far greater proportion of good outside Trees.'

Oliver Rackham, in *The History of the Countryside* (1986), warns us not to take at face value the constant scare stories of a shortage of timber. He claims that the naval dockyards were 'short of funds, not of trees', describing how HMS *Victory*, built in 1759–65, was 'put together from great numbers of the smallest, and therefore cheapest, practicable oaks'. Despite his reservations, however, Rackham admits that by 1780 the increase in ship-building began to catch up with the supply of trees. By 1809 the naval dockyards were importing oak from Albania. He also points to how British ship-building became a major consumer of timber through the 'growth of intercontinental trade and the arms race from the later eighteenth century onwards. The output of timber-built ships between 1800 and 1860 was probably equal to that in all the rest of history put together.' He adds significantly: 'Much shipbuilding timber, especially in large sizes and special shapes, came from hedges and parks, not from woodland.'

Oak was not the only wood used for building ships; the Duke of Atholl also planted larches for this purpose. In the winter of 1819, for example, he had 1,102,367 larches planted, at the rate of 30,440 daily. It took 30 men 36 days to do the work. In 1823 Henry Phillips writes in his *Sylva Florifera*: 'The present Duke of Atholl has had the satisfaction of seeing a frigate of thirty-six guns built entirely of larch timber of his own planting, which we believe is more than any other individual in the universe can boast of. It was launched from the stocks at Woolwich, about three years back, being named the Atholl.'

Aesthetics and Economics

The usual account of the English landscape garden sees it as a return to nature. The debate is conducted in terms of aesthetics, concerning the relationship between art and nature, regularity and irregularity, straight line versus serpentine. Where politics enters the discussion it is usually to draw the comparison between Britain's political constitution and its gardening style, contrasting them both with austere and autocratic foreign ways.

Twentieth-century use of oak. Advertisement from the
Popular Gardening Annual *(1928), edited by H.H. Thomas.*

A reading of eighteenth-century gardening literature, however, also reveals the relationship between gardening style and economic and military power. 'Capability' Brown's clumps and belts of trees were not only aesthetically pleasing, but were also used to build stronger ships to fight the French. The process was reciprocal, for money made from foreign military campaigns helped finance the vast upheavals in landscape design.

The growing use of iron and steel during the next 200 years meant that oak was no longer so vital to the national interest. According to W.H. Rowe in *Tree and Shrub Growing*, the 'new demand was for coniferous wood, rather than oak, and this could be imported in large quantities at very cheap rates'. Writing in the 1940s, he complains about the neglect of British forestry and this reliance on imports: 'Two wars have very fully demonstrated the folly of this and a heavy price has been paid. National security demands that our devastated woodlands shall be replaced. In 1919 the Forestry Commission was established and has achieved much, but there is still a very great deal to be done.'

The oak still remained a potent nationalist symbol, however, and could also be used to comment on internal politics. Reginald Arkell, writing from Gloucestershire during the rise of fascism in Europe, draws a parallel: 'The king of all trees is the oak. It typifies our English character and countryside, in that it is of slow growth and great strength, while its roots descend to a great depth. Like England, it is infested with parasites.' In *A Cottage in the Country* (1934) the author goes on to make his political point, though it is not clear whether his target is racial or social. 'Like some strong and simple people', he argues, the oak supports 'a lot of hangers-on, who are content to draw upon the vitality of their victims. "Poor old chap," you will say; "what a shame that all these worthless creatures should be allowed to batten on your energy and strength!" And, if you are in a reflective mood, the incident may suggest a fable and a moral I will not pursue.'

After the war Montagu Allwood still extols the oak tree's role in maintaining English naval supremacy. He writes in *English Countryside and Gardens* (1947): 'No tree has helped to shape the destiny of a nation more than oak – well named the Hercules of the forest. It constituted the Wooden Wall of England; Hearts of Oak ensured our dominion of the sea, until that duty was relinquished to iron.'

English Hegemony

In *A Book About Roses* Dean Hole refers to the hegemony of the English landscape garden and how it spread throughout the world, particularly in Russia: '"I am now," wrote the Czarina to Voltaire in the year 1772, "wildly in love with the English system of gardening, its waving lines and gentle declivities;" and so was all the gardening world.' Alfred Smee supports this view, writing in 1872 that the English style was 'copied to a greater or less extent by every other European nation'.

This still seems to be the generally accepted view, with the landscape park having been aestheticised and removed from its economic and political context. No discussion today of the famous eighteenth-century gardens relates them to the navy and the balance of trade.

At the beginning of the new landscape garden movement, Gilbert West illustrates how these gardens were intended to demonstrate the superiority of English culture and power. His poem *Stowe, The Gardens of the Right Honourable Richard Viscount Cobham*, published in 1732, is full of classical allusions, comparing Britain to ancient Greece and Rome. Cobham had made a fortune out of Marlborough's wars against France and he spent it on the buildings and gardens at Stowe which celebrated English military might and became famous throughout Europe. The landscape contained obelisks to General Wolfe and Captain Grenville. Inside the Temple of Concord and Victory, which Thomas Whately (1770) calls 'one of the noblest objects that ever adorned a garden', the walls were decorated with representations of victories such as the taking of Quebec, Montreal, Louisberg and Pondicherry. In 1744 Benton Seeley produced a guidebook to the park and in 1748 a French one was published.

Gilbert West describes the statues in the gardens celebrating British imperialism, though couched in terms of liberty:

> Hail! Gods of our renown'd Fore-Fathers, hail!
> Ador'd Protectors once of England's Weal.
> Gods, of a Nation, valiant, wise, and free,
> Who conquer'd to establish Liberty!

The tradition culminates in George I, 'the good old King in Armour clad':

> His Mind, sincere, benevolent and great,
> Nor aw'd by Danger, nor with Pow'r elate;
> For Valour much, but more for Justice known,
> Brave in the Field, and Good upon the Throne.

Later it is George III who is seen as protector of our freedom, according to John Gibson, who practised medicine in London and was a surgeon in the Royal Navy. In *The Fruit-Gardener* (1768) he writes: 'Liberty, supported by the best of kings, and caressed by the freest people on earth, is the peculiar privilege, and forms the happiness of true Britons.'

During the Napoleonic wars, in *A Poetical Introduction to the Study of Botany* (1801), Frances Arabella Rowden expresses similar views, seeing Britain as a place

> Where native freedom, peace, and plenty, smile,
> For George and Charlotte guard Britannia's isle.

In a poem on the oak tree, the country's tall woods are described as 'Where England's safety and her riches lie'. They are the source of the nation's military power:

> Oh! let our navy still triumphant reign,
> And rule the mighty monarch of the main.

The usual comparison is with the competing European power of France. The ideology stresses English liberty as opposed to French authoritarianism. As Hunt and Willis put it in their history of the English landscape garden (1975): 'It was an endorsement of liberty and tolerance against tyranny and oppression; democracy against autocracy.'

The reality was a little different. In 1723 George I's prime minister, Robert Walpole, introduced the Black Act to protect country estates from poaching, which became a capital offence if the persons committing the crime were armed and disguised, their faces blackened. In 1748 two men were caught raiding Cobham's deer-park at Stowe and were sentenced to death. Cobham celebrated the occasion by placing statues of the two men in his park, a deer across their shoulders.

The landscape garden was hailed by those in power, however, as a national triumph. In 1755, for example, John Shebbeare claims that the new irregular English gardens have a universal appeal to all human minds. The French excelled the Italians, who were 'the first improvers of gardens', but the English now 'carried the taste of that embellishement much higher', surpassing both Italy and France.

In his *Essay on Modern Gardening* written in 1770, Horace Walpole also compares the new English style to that of the French: 'Good sense in this country had perceived the want of something at once more grand and more natural.' He recognises that other countries will try and copy it, but without the same success as in its native land: 'We have discovered the point of perfection. We have given the true model of gardening to the world; let other countries mimic or corrupt our taste; but let it reign here on its verdant throne, original by its elegant simplicity, and proud of no other art than that of softening nature's harshnesses and copying her graceful touch.'

A revolution was necessary to introduce the new style, which is equated with 'truth', and there are political and social reasons why it cannot generally be adopted in other European countries: 'Truth, which after the opposition given to most revolutions, preponderates at last, will probably not carry our style of garden into general use on the continent. The expence is only suited to the opulence of a free country, where emulation reigns among many independent particulars.'

The same line of thought is expressed by Richard Steele in *An Essay Upon Gardening* (1793). Referring to the formal gardens of 70 years earlier as 'deformities of Garden Tonsure', he records that 'such barbarisms began to subside, and make way for true and natural elegance'. Again the comparison is drawn between Britain's political constitution and its gardening style, contrasting them with the pale imitations of foreigners: 'In this Island we now seem to have discovered, and to hold up to others, the TRUE MODEL OF GARDENING. LET OTHER COUNTRIES MIMIC TASTE, AS THEY MIMIC LIBERTY!! But here, by softening the rigours of Nature, and minutely attending to her delightful traits, let Britain reign triumphant IN SIMPLE GRACEFUL ELEGANCE!'

In 1823 Henry Phillips records how the style was copied in Europe: 'Early in the eighteenth century, the formal and heavy style of gardening which had for some time prevailed, was changed by the united efforts of the English poets and painters of the day. By their pure taste and united efforts, they gave birth to that classical style of planting which has since been so much admired and imitated throughout the most refined parts of Europe.' In the same year John Papworth writes in his *Hints on Ornamental Gardening* of the English garden as 'a model, imitated by every country in Europe'.

By the second half of the eighteenth century voices were being raised against the new landscape garden, but still often in terms of national culture. Writing as early as 1753, in a magazine called *The World*, Francis Coventry criticises the obsession with irregularity and serpentine shapes, seeing these recent developments as 'fatal proofs of the degeneracy of our national taste'.

Interpreting the Landscape Garden

In *The Genius of the Place* (1975) the garden historians Hunt and Willis recognise the connection between gardening and political history. In their discussion of the English landscape garden they try to correct the tendency to treat the history of gardening as separate from social and political matters: 'The evidence reveals that it is not simply a history of design and stylistic change: the creation of gardens is determined by intellectual, social, economic, political and artistic forces, which in their turn are mirrored in gardens.'

In their own work, however, Hunt and Willis concentrate almost entirely on intellectual and artistic forces. No mention is made of the vast enclosure movement which deprived poor people of common land, nor of the relocation of villages in order to create these landscape gardens, nor the vicious anti-poaching laws which were enforced. The land-owners who carried out these acts are referred to as 'enlightened patrons like Cobham', or people with 'imagination and learning' such as Henry Hoare. Witnesses such as John Clare or Oliver Goldsmith or George Crabbe, who deal with material events and present a different account, are never called.

Similarly, David Jarrett touches on the issue of enclosures in *The English Landscape Garden* (1978) and then says that it is not his intention to stress these 'anti-social or flippant aspects of the eighteenth century landscape garden'. He goes on to praise Lancelot Brown: 'Whatever his dependence upon aristocratic patronage, there must have been something grandly uncompromising about "Capability" Brown which allowed him to transform the English landscape garden ... these gardens are works of art, and as such they can speak directly to us and liberate us – however interested we may be in history and topography – from time and space. It is with the artistic effect that I am concerned ultimately.'

This is a recurring view in gardening writing: that the aesthetic can be divorced from the political and social. It is well exposed by the American art historian Ann Bermingham in *Landscape and Ideology* (1986). She quotes Uvedale Price who wrote *An Essay on the Picturesque* in 1794. Price was opposed to Brown's landscapes because they were artificial and represented a vast transformation of nature. He preferred a picturesque landscape which was the result of a long process of maturation.

In 'Capability' Brown's designs Price sees 'something despotic in the general system of improvement – all must be laid open – all that obstructs levelled to the ground – houses, orchard, gardens, all swept away'. He condemns such tyranny: 'He who destroys dwellings, gardens and enclosures, for the sake of mere extent and parade of property, only extends the bounds of monotony, and of dreary selfish pride; but contracts those of variety, amusement and humanity.'

Ann Bermingham argues, however, that Price's anger was 'no libertarian's outrage at the injustice that attended enclosure and the creation of extensive gardens. The old aesthetic of the old landscape garden was disreputable not because it throve on these injustices but because it made them too obvious at a time when such injustices were being met with popular force in France.'

When discussing an uncle, who wisely took the local inhabitants into consideration in his gardening plans, Uvedale Price shows his real motives: 'Such attentive kindnesses are amply repaid by affectionate regard and reverence; and were they general throughout the kingdom, they would do much more towards guarding us against democratic opinions "Than twenty thousand soldiers, arm'd in proof."' In other words it was part of a general anti-Jacobin strategy. In Price's view

'Capability' Brown's massive intervention in the landscape was in danger of provoking opposition from democratic forces.

These forces were very active at the end of the eighteenth century, as the English historian E.P. Thompson points out in *The Making of the English Working Class*: 'Enclosure-riots, the breaking of fences, threatening letters, arson, were more common than some agrarian historians suppose.' The period 1792–6 was one of 'extraordinarily intensive and far-reaching' agitation: 'It was not an agitation about France, although French events both inspired and bedevilled it. It was an English agitation, of impressive dimensions, for an English democracy.'

Uvedale Price was responding to Humphry Repton's *Sketches and Hints on Landscape Gardening*, published earlier in the year 1794. Repton was not so worried about agitation. He makes clear what he thinks of democracy when discussing fashion, claiming that the 'mass of mankind act without thought, and like sheep follow a leader through the various paths of life'. No doubt with the French Revolution in mind, he considers that in some countries 'it would be dangerous to display any external ornaments of grandeur, but rank and affluence are not crimes in England'. He goes on to maintain that the English expect to see differences in wealth reflected in people's estates. England is safeguarded by its balanced form of government: 'The neatness, simplicity, and elegance of English gardening, have acquired the approbation of modern times, as the happy medium betwixt the wildness of nature and the stiffness of art; in the same manner as the English constitution is the happy medium betwixt the liberty of savages, and the restraint of despotic government.'

William Cobbett was not so complimentary about English government, writing of this period as a time 'when the madness for enclosure raged most furiously'. He describes the 30 cottages and gardens around Horton Heath in Hampshire, the apple trees and black-cherry trees, the stalls of bees and the animals which grazed the common. According to his calculation the 150-acre common produced 'more than any neighbouring farm of 200 acres!'

Edward Hyams is one of the few modern gardening writers who describe the enclosure movement of this period as criminal. In *English Cottage Gardens* (1970) he calls it a 'gigantic crime, by far the grandest larceny in England's history'. He estimates that between 1760 and 1867 England's ruling class 'stole seven million acres of common land, the property and livelihood of the common people of England'.

This was also the time when England began its hegemony over the rest of the world. Sieveking (1899) points to the significance of the defeat of the French in the Seven Years' War and the Treaty of Paris in 1763. It was the date when 'the English style of gardening passed into France and the ideas of the new school were perhaps even more successfully applied by that most susceptible nation.' In 1761 the French philosopher Rousseau published *Julie ou la Nouvelle Héloïse*, advocating a return to nature, and in 1762 he wrote *Émile*, recommending that education should take place through practical experience in the countryside. Ironically it was a Scot, Thomas Blaikie, who designed many of the most famous 'Jardins Anglais' in France between 1776 and the Revolution.

THE NAPOLEONIC WARS

By the end of the eighteenth century there was renewed war between France and England, following the French Revolution. Robert Thornton's *Temple of Flora* (1812) mentions two of the battles which took place, and in a section entitled 'The Blue Egyptian Water Lily (Nymphaea Coerulea)', he writes of Napoleon: 'It was surely a most extraordinary sight, to observe the proud conqueror of Egypt presiding over a literary association to promote science, and most attentively listening to, and applauding, a discourse read by Julius Caesar Savigni, on those sacred NYMPHAEAS which embellish the shores of Egypt; little did HIS arrogant soul imagine, that, at that time, on the buoyant wave was floating the thunder of the British Arms, which Providence had destined to annihilate his proud army, and take from it its famed standard, impiously called "Invincible".'

The desire to escape from this political conflict, however, is typified by the much-quoted example of the Empress Josephine's interest in plants during the Napoleonic Wars. Mrs Earle, for example, in *Pot-Pourri from a Surrey Garden* (1897), refers to this period when the trade in plants was seen to be above politics and war: 'I am told there is still an order preserved in our Admiralty that, when French ships were captured in the war, any plants or seeds that were on board for Madame Bonaparte were to be expedited. That was a gracious order; and gardening in those days meant so much more than it does now. A flower blooming then was an interesting event all over Europe, and the gentle perfume of it rose and permeated through the smoke and din of the Napoleonic wars.'

At Malmaison, on the outskirts of Paris, Josephine kept no less than 250 varieties of roses, tracing her name in the parterres with the rarest of them. Her garden was so extravagantly stocked that at her death she had debts of more than two million francs.

In her article 'Knight to Empress' (1991), Christian Lamb claims that Napoleon was not pleased with Josephine's creation of an informal English garden. Nevertheless he sent her boxes of plants and seeds from his campaigns, including the seed of mignonette, *Reseda odorata*, from Egypt. Lamb goes on to quote the *Gentleman's Magazine* of 4 November 1811: 'Curious plants to the amount of £700 value have lately been shipped from Portsmouth for the ci-devant Empress Josephine [referring to her recent divorce from Napoleon]. They are the produce of a nursery garden at Hammersmith from which she also got a supply in 1803 for the amount of £2,600.'

In *The Book of the Garden* (1932) Arthur Stanley also writes of this period as one which showed 'that the brotherhood of gardening makes friends of foes'. He refers to the gardening truce and praises the French for their culture of roses even while they were at war: 'While the French and English were fighting each other a free passport was granted to "Mr. Kennedy of Hammersmith" to go and come as he pleased in order that he might supervise the planning and planting of the gardens at Josephine's chateau. In the culture of the modern rose Frenchmen led the way, and we have to thank France for M. Vibert's attention to the rose when other gardeners, French and English, were busy at Waterloo.'

Not only combatant gardeners suffered during the wars. The same fate could befall any who got in the way of the advancing armies. Catherine Gore in *The Book of Roses; or The Rose Fancier's Manual* (1838) mentions a French rose grower whose collection of roses was 'cut up by the English troops in 1814'.

According to T. James, in *The Flower Garden* (1842), this period was not conducive to gardening: 'The early part of the nineteenth century presents a great coolness in the garden mania with which the eighteenth was so possessed; and it was hardly till after the peace that public attention again took this direction.' He presumes this to be 'a natural reaction of the public mind, after the turmoil of a foreign war, to fall back upon the more peaceful occupations of home.'

Lewis Castle agrees with this view. In *Flower Gardening for Amateurs* (1888) he points to the increased interest in gardening after the war: 'The battle of Waterloo closed a troublous period, and from that time the advance in horticulture was phenomenal.'

In *Flora Historica* (1824) Henry Phillips writes of the effect Napoleon's defeat had on the European trade in plants: 'The Dahlia was but little known in England until after the year 1814, when the peace enabled our nurserymen to obtain an additional supply both of roots and seed from France, where the cultivation of these plants had been more attended to than in this country.'

Phillips is not so reliable, however, when dealing with home affairs. His *History of Cultivated Vegetables* (1822) was dedicated to the King and his predecessor, under whose patronage 'the arts of Agriculture and Horticulture have advanced towards perfection with a rapidity unparalleled in the history of any other nation, ancient or modern'. The author continues in euphoric mood: 'These arts have banished famine from the land, blessed the poor with plenty, beautified the country ...' In fact, the years following the battle of Waterloo had seen falling wages and high prices, which produced increasing class conflict, resulting in bread riots and other political demonstrations. The Peterloo Massacre had taken place only two years before Phillips was writing. Eighty thousand people had assembled in Manchester to demand the repeal of the Corn Laws. Eleven people were killed by the yeomanry and about 400, including over 100 women, were wounded.

NINETEENTH-CENTURY CLASS CONFLICT

Victorian optimism in the growth of capitalism is celebrated in *The New Practical Gardener and Modern Horticulturist*, edited by James Anderson between 1872 and 1874. Anderson had inherited his parents' farm near Edinburgh when he was only 15 years old, so he knew about business from an early age. He does, however, express nostalgia for the slower pace of earlier times: 'Business in horticultural matters is like business in other matters; it has assumed quite a different tone in these days. No apathy, no rest during business hours, no hoping, no dreaming; but enthusiasm and ingenuity and push, as greatly different in character as the railway is from the old stage coach. Gardeners, too, of the right stamp are animated by the same feelings, and carried along in the onward march of progress.'

Not everyone, however, was equally convinced about this onward march of progress. In May 1866 the first International Horticultural Exhibition took place on the site of the dismantled Crystal Palace. Three and a half acres of Hyde Park were put under canvas. A few months later, a massive demonstration took place in the same park, demanding the vote for working-class men. The demonstrators pulled down half a mile of railings and trampled on the flowerbeds. It was a traumatic event for those in power and contributed to the introduction of the Reform Act of 1867. In the Introduction to the 1932 edition of Matthew Arnold's *Culture and Anarchy* (1869) J. Dover Wilson writes: 'It is scarcely too much to say that the fall of the Park railings did for England in July 1866 what the fall of the Bastille did for France in July 1789.'

Matthew Arnold was horrified by this violation of the park and in his book he makes constant reference to it. His solution to the open class conflict which had been displayed was to suggest that a combination of enlightened people from all three main classes should encourage the spread of 'sweetness and light'.

Many gardening writers in the nineteenth century thought gardens could help in this process, considering them to be a cure for the class conflict caused by the industrial revolution. Public parks and gardens, for instance, were often viewed as places where friendly mixing of the classes could take place.

For Elizabeth Watts, horticultural societies fulfilled a similar function, as they 'create sociality, and cement acquaintanceships'. In *Vegetables and How to Grow Them* (1866) she states: 'In creating a kindly feeling between rich and poor too, local horticultural meetings do much.' She is particularly concerned with the 'frugal poor' and gives advice as to what kind of prizes to give cottagers: 'A set of silver teaspoons becomes an heirloom in a decent poor man's house. Books, too, are often very much prized, provided they are good in type and useful in character.'

Samuel Reynolds Hole (1819–1904) is another example of a gardening writer who favoured this paternalistic approach. He was born near Newark where he was both vicar and squire and became Dean of Rochester in 1887. In *A Book About the Garden and the Gardener* (1892) he quotes the famous hymn 'All Things Bright and Beautiful':

> The rich man in his castle,
> The poor man at his gate
> He made them, high or lowly,
> And ordered their estate.

He sees the village flower-show as confirming this social order: 'It induces, first of all, that communion of classes which teaches men, more forcibly than schools or sermons can, to recognize their place and duty ... Orchids, delicately reared in heat, are gathered under one tent with the hardy wild flowers of the field; the luscious grape from my lord's vinery rests upon the same table with the gooseberry, hirsute and corpulent; and as the question is, not which of these is more beautiful or better than its neighbour, but which is best of its kind, which has been most carefully and wisely cultivated; so when men meet together, lawmakers and brickmakers, coronets and "billycocks", the consideration for each to take home with him is this, not whether he is richer in purse or higher in grade than another, because God has put all men in their places, but whether he is useful and good *in himself*. It concerns every man, and vitally, to reflect, not whether he is a duke or a ditcher, for that is pre-ordained and fixed, but whether his dukery or his dike are in the best available condition.'

Mary Eliza Haweis, on the other hand, was not too keen on contact between the classes. In *Rus in Urbe: or Flowers that Thrive in London Gardens and Smoky Towns* (1886) she discusses 'many a fashionable old "square" which refuses to throw open the central garden to the children of the poor – and very properly, I think as a mother, whilst there are no back gardens to the houses; for high-wrought rich children require an outlet from the prim nursery as much as poor children from the fever-den – and the classes cannot mix whilst the habits of the poor remain what they are. The fleas in the grass alone forbid that: I am speaking from experience.'

Neither was Mrs Boyle (E.V.B.) very eager to mix with the working class. In *Seven Gardens and a Palace* she deplores the 'loud-voiced crowds' visiting Hampton Court in the summer of 1896, 'to whom, if indeed perchance they know it, the name of Wren is nought. The sense of quiet and good taste which belonged to the days of old, when everything was more or less in keeping as it were, is forgotten.' She acknowledges that 'the people of a great nation should have ample resource for holiday playgrounds provided', but the problem is that this produces in Hampton Court a 'depressing sense of "People's Palace"'. It is not so easy, she thinks, for working-class culture to be improved simply by visiting famous gardens: 'Is it not rather a dream than a happy reality – the belief that this going through beautiful gardens, picture-galleries, or noble buildings, will in itself work out an education or enlarge and elevate the minds of the many? Must it not be that the mind of a multitude set upon their day's outing needs long cultivation and preparedness to receive such teaching? And does a Board-school provide it?'

Radical Tradition

The socialist ideas of the second half of the nineteenth century are rarely reflected in horticultural literature, though there are a couple of authors at the turn of the century who represent the radical tradition of gardening writing. Mrs Earle (1836–1925), born Maria Theresa Villiers, came from a Whiggish family and was known as 'Radical T', being proud of her descent from Oliver Cromwell. As a teenager she bought John Bright's radical paper, the *Morning Star*, and her self-taught liberal education included reading J.S. Mill, Darwin, George Eliot and William Morris. In 1864 she married Captain Earle. They were both 'free-thinkers' and agnostics, contributing to the controversial Cremation Society.

Pot-Pourri from a Surrey Garden (1897) is hardly a revolutionary book, however, though the author does complain about the reactionary period in which it was written. She is referring to the period known as the Great Depression, ending with a severe defeat for the Liberals at the general election of 1895: 'Just now even the enthusiastic and the young are trying to live in the past – a whole generation conservative in its youth. I suppose it is all right, but it seems to lack the generous impulses of the generation nourished on the teachings of Mill and Bright. How true it is that Liberalism is not a principle, but an attitude of mind!'

In another passage, attacking the recent fashion for bedding-out, she likens this gardening style to the Tory party: 'Yet twenty years ago this sort of garden was like Tory politics, or Church and State, and seemed to represent all that was considered respectable and desirable. I shall never forget the bombshell I seemed to fling into a family circle when I injudiciously and vehemently said that I hated parks and bedded-out gardens.'

J.D. Sedding's design for a garden, with clipped yew hedges and flowerbeds, from Garden-Craft Old and New *(1891).*

In *More Pot-Pourri from a Surrey Garden* she recommends growing Funkias on 10 September 1898, and explains how to grow Tigridias on 13 September. In between these two entries, on 11 September, are her thoughts about the Battle of Omdurman and the lack of opposition to the war in the Sudan: 'Never in all my life do I remember what might be called the aggressive, grasping, ruling spirit of the typical John Bull to have been so united and so universal. War and the pity of it, and the question why it has to be, which was so strong a feeling and which had such large numbers of supporters in the old Crimean day and even in the Indian Mutiny time, seems now simply non-existent.'

In *Gardening for the Ignorant* (1912) she even quotes the anarchist Kropotkin with approval, particularly his chapter on market gardening and fruit growing.

John Sedding's *Garden-Craft Old and New* was also published in the last decade of the nineteenth century. Sedding was one of the original members of the Art Workers' Guild and in the Introductory Memoir to the book, E.F. Russell writes: 'He shared to the full the ardour of his Socialist friends, in their aspirations for that new order of more just distribution of all that makes for the happiness of men.'

Although his book does not mention socialism, Sedding tries to dispel the myth that the Puritans were not interested in gardening for pleasure: 'Even the Puritan, for all his gloomy creed and bleak undecorated life, is Romanticist here; the hater of outward show turns rank courtier at a pageant of flowers: he will dare the devil at any moment, but not life without flowers. And so we have him lovingly bending over the plants of his home-garden, packing seeds to carry with him into exile, as though these could make expatriation tolerable.'

Like many in the Arts and Crafts movement, Sedding's model is the past rather than a revolutionary future: 'The old-fashioned garden, whatever its failing in the eyes of the modern landscape-gardener (great is the poverty of his invention), represents one of the pleasures of England, one of the charms of that quiet beautiful life of bygone times that I, for one, would fain see revived.'

THE FIRST WORLD WAR

The First World War revealed the dependence of Britain on Germany for the supply of many herb-based drugs. This is noted in the Preface of Ada Teetgen's *Profitable Herb Growing and Collecting*, published in 1916: 'The knowledge that Germany and Austria formerly supplied this country with many herbs, and the patriotic desire that such should not be the case after the war is over, has no doubt had its influence.' Along with the desire for profit, this motive persuaded women throughout the country to take up herb growing. Under the auspices of the Women's Farm and Garden Union, the Herb Growers' Association came into being: 'Their idea is to instruct cottagers how to make the best use of their gardens through the formation of classes and clubs in villages.'

Teetgen's book is addressed to 'those thoughtful people in the country to whom the economic aspect of the question appeals as a patriotic one – to those who would rescue an essentially home market and industry from German competition. If this is not accomplished now, when peace is declared the trade in our own weeds may flow back again into its old channels, and German and Austrian peasants will reap profits which ought to be going into the pockets of our own rural folk.'

Bird's-Eye View of the House and Garden

Illustration by C. Walter Hodges from R.A. Foster-Melliar's
My Garden by the Sea *(1936).*

In *My Garden by the Sea* (1936) R.A. Foster-Melliar recounts how all his lawns were dug up during the war, all flowers destroyed, and the garden 'devoted to growing food and drugs'. Weeds such as couch grass and dandelions had a medicinal use, as did marigolds and foxgloves: 'It appeared that the dark empire across the water had dominion over drugs, and our supply being cut off, we had perforce to extract them from our native flora.' He goes on to show how anti-German feeling affected the name of a rose: 'We were all slightly hysterical in those days, even going so far as to rename Frau Karl Druski, the loveliest (if scentless) white rose, calling it something else – but what, I have forgotten.'

Britain was also dependent on Germany for certain fertilisers, as pointed out by M.G. Kennedy Bell in *A Garden Timepiece* (1925): 'Before the war, practically all potash salts came from Germany, from vast saline deposits at Strassfurth. But now that Alsace-Lorraine has happily come back to French rule again, these are the "French Potash Mines", and the Agricultural Information Bureau issue a warning that when ordering Potash, a guarantee should be asked that the Potash Salts supplied are obtained from the French mines.'

Buy British

In a later book M.G. Kennedy Bell makes reference to the balance of payments and the issue of imports, which had been so crucial during the war. As north London's expert on bees, she was chosen by the BBC to deliver a course of lectures on bee-keeping. In *The Joys of Bee-Keeping* (1932) she writes: 'On every hand we hear the cry, "Buy British Goods" ... "Support British Industries" ... Yet we import thousands of pounds worth of honey into England every year, that could perfectly well be produced at home.'

The same theme crops up in Geoffrey Henslow's books, regarding the parlous state of fruit-growing in England. In *Garden Development* (1923), for example, he writes: 'The orchards of this country are far from being a credit to us, and the very heavy imports of apples and pears when they are with us at the height of their season is a national disgrace.'

Hall and Crane repeat the complaint in *The Apple* (1933), recording that apples imported into Great Britain in 1931 amounted to 380,000 tons, with a value of £7,879,000, compared to the average English production of about £2,500,000. This is despite the fact that 'labour is cheaper than it is with our competitors', and that English apples are considered by the authors to be so superior: 'Granting the English pre-possession for a firm-fleshed apple with a touch of briskness and tang behind its sweetness and spiciness, the superiority of the English apples *here* is outside disputation. As for cooking apples, the supremacy of the best English sorts either for baking or in a pie is merely a question of whether or not you have any taste in such matters.'

This issue of home-grown produce had already been raised in the nineteenth century. In 1879 James Pink, with his mind on the possible danger of an economic blockade, tried to encourage potato cultivation. In *Potatoes: How to Grow and Show Them* he recalls the privations caused

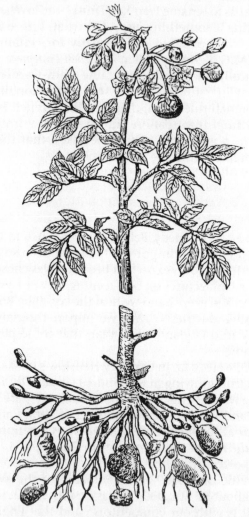

THE WILD POTATO,
As grown by GERARD, and figured in his ' Herbal,' published 1597.

From James Pink's Potatoes: How to Grow and Show Them *(1879).*

by the Napoleonic Wars: 'History proverbially repeats itself, so that we have only to call to mind the distress that was prevalent in England during the early part of the present century, when our commerce suffered so severely on account of the French war, and when in the years 1808–9 – the corn laws being in full force – flour rose to the enormous price of 28s. per bushel, and bread riots took place in several parts of the kingdom; and, as it is quite possible the day may come when England will, to a certain extent, be thrown on her own resources, we cannot help asking ourselves, if distress was so prevalent and food so scarce when the population was only half what it is at present, what would be the result now the country is so densely populated.'

In the same year, in *The London Market Gardens*, C.W. Shaw writes: 'Some have recommended our railway embankments, which, at a rough estimate, represent nearly 200 square miles, to be planted with Apple trees, Pears, or Cherries.' The reason it has not happened, he suggests, is that cheap imports make it uneconomic.

A few years later, in the preface to *The Kitchen and Market Garden*, Shaw's publisher protests against this reliance on foreign produce: 'The supply of our markets with good vegetables and salads is being now to a large extent undertaken by foreigners. There is no good reason why it should be so. If we take advantage of all our opportunities, we ought at least to supply our own markets with vegetables and salads without foreign aid.'

A similar point about food imports is made in S.T. Wright's 'How to Grow Strawberries' (1888), a small pamphlet which sold at twopence, as part of 'The Fruit-Grower's Library'. The aim of the series was to popularise fruit-growing 'in order, amongst other objects, that our English horticulturists may cope with the American, Canadian, and continental fruit-growers, who yearly draw £8,000,000 from this country for garden produce'.

Edward Hobday expreses the argument with slightly more xenophobia. In *Fruit Culture for Profit* (1883) he warns his compatriots: 'The demand for fruit for our ever-growing town population is constantly increasing, and it must be borne in mind that, unless we are up and doing, the foreigner, with his greater aptitude for minutiae in his work, his greater care in small things, will step in and reap the profit.'

Edith Bradley and May Crooke, in *The Book of Fruit Bottling* (1907) also warn us about 'the foreigner' and his profits. The authors think 'we are a fruit-loving and fruit- and vegetable-eating nation!' But 'we are hopelessly behind' in fruit bottling: 'Truly, it is time to "Wake up, England!" and in this case we might say, "Wake up, women of England!" because this is essentially a branch of work suitable in every way for women to do.' They draw attention to the increasing imports of fruit and vegetables between 1901 and 1904 and give their reasons why we should bottle more fruit: 'First, to be independent of the foreigner; and, second, to spend English money in England – let it turn over many times here before the foreigner has it.'

Growing Vegetables

The First World War saw a great growth in allotment gardens as a result of the food shortage. Vita Sackville-West (1944) refers to the year 1917, 'when there was only about three weeks' food supply in the whole country', and she recounts how the first Women's Land Army was created. It numbered 23,000 by 1918.

Vegetables and fruit had to take precedence over flowers. Writing in the middle of the war, William Rowles makes this clear in *The Food Garden* (1917): 'English homes would lose the greater part of their charm without the flower garden, but the hard times of to-day and the possibly harder times we may expect in the near future, urge on us the importance of giving food a preference over flowers. We need not wholly banish flowers, but we must first of all see that our home is provided with all that it requires in the way of garden produce.'

Walter Wright points specifically to the importance of potatoes to the progress of the war: 'But for her abnormal Potato crop of over 50,000,000 tons in 1915, Germany would have been greatly hampered in carrying on the great war.' Apart from their use as food, potatoes also produced alcohol and ether which were used for dissolving gun-cotton for explosive purposes. In *A Book About Potatoes and Other Vegetables* (1917) the author illustrates Germany's superiority in this field, as it produced an average of 45 million tons of potatoes a year, compared to Britain's 7 million.

Wright had founded the National Potato Society of Great Britain in 1903, and had been striving ever since to 'awaken his fellow countrymen to the importance of the crop'. It took the crisis of the First World War to justify his efforts. In 1916 Germany had a very small crop of potatoes, about 21 million tons, and 'this weakened her greatly, alike in maintaining the sustenance of her people and in the manufacture of high explosives'.

Samuel Graveson typifies many gardeners at this time who changed over to vegetable cultivation, to produce potatoes: 'For nearly a year now my villa garden has had to run itself, whilst we – my wife and I – have devoted our energies with ever growing interest to the planting and cropping of our vegetable plot.' In *Our Vegetable Plot* (1918), costing sevenpence, he writes of his 'idea of taking up vegetable culture as a contribution to the national service we were all called upon to undertake'. In January 1917 he decided to cultivate a waste piece of ground: 'The ground was half frozen, the skeletons of enormous weeds lay upon its surface or stood about it like the wrecked forests of the Somme battle-field.' Because of government restrictions he had difficulty obtaining seed potatoes, which were distributed through local councils, 'for prices were soaring alarmingly, and there was every indication of a famine of both seed and ware potatoes'. At the end of April 1917 there was still frost and snow on the ground: 'The outlook was dark by reason of the war and the German submarine campaign.' He concludes by seeing a positive side to the effects of the war: 'The submarine has affected us Britishers in many ways: perhaps history will bracket the years of its menace with the discovery of the fertility of the land of England by countless thousands of town-bred men and women.'

In *The Amateur Gardener* (1948) Arthur Hellyer recalls the same period: 'I still recollect vividly my introduction to gardening. It was in 1915 or 1916 when I was no more than a small boy. My family, in common with tens of thousands of others, started to dig up the lawn and grow vegetables as our own small answer to the U-boat menace.'

W.W. Pettigrew describes, in his *Handbook of the City Parks and Recreation Grounds* (1929), how the Manchester Parks Department produced crops during the war. They grew tomatoes in the propagating houses and provided amateur gardeners with seedlings and advice: 'Potatoes, oats and wheat were grown to a considerable extent at Heaton Park, Debdale Park and Carrington Nurseries, and thousands of cabbage, cauliflower and celery plants were reared and sold at a nominal charge to the public, who at that time were taking up allotment gardening all over the city.' He claims in *Common-Sense Gardening* (1925) that 'allotment holders by their successful efforts undoubtedly saved the food situation in this country'.

A curious fashion developed in public parks during the war. Pettigrew refers to it in his *Municipal Parks* (1937): 'Many public authorities vied with each other in an endeavour to secure captured weapons and disused tanks from the War Office to set up in their parks.' The practice, however, did not long outlive the war, as reaction set in and people sought to forget the carnage. The weapons were removed 'even although the military were prone to describe this action as being unpatriotic'. There was a similar occurrence in 1857 when guns from the Crimean War were displayed in parks.

Pettigrew also writes of rehabilitating disabled soldiers: 'At the conclusion of the War the Parks Department, at the request of the Ministry of Agriculture, undertook the training of disabled soldiers in horticulture, and a camp was established at the Carrington Nurseries, where 140 ex-soldiers were taught horticultural and agricultural work.'

Effects of the War

No one could accuse Frances Wolseley of ignoring the First World War. Her book *In a College Garden*, published in 1916, is full of references to the impact of the war: 'It seems incredible to think that only on the other side of a narrow silver stretch of sea, which alone protects our land, a bombardment is taking place more prolonged and deadlier than any battles that have ever been before in the whole world's history.' From where she lives in Glynde, Sussex, she can hear 'the boom of siege-guns away in Flanders'.

Inflation has increased enormously: 'All requisites, manures, food-stuffs are doubled in price.' The war, however, has shown the value of women gardeners. At her horticultural college they were growing extra lettuces because of the war and each week the students took a cart full of vegetables to sell in the nearby village. As yet there was a glut of unsold produce, but she realised that vegetables might be badly wanted later on.

Even after the war, Frances Wolseley still emphasised the importance of the kitchen garden. In *Gardens: Their Form and Design* (1919) she argues that such a garden could be dug up by a small plough, adding that a man might need the assistance of a crippled soldier or a woman to guide the pony. She also refers to the destruction of many French gardens during the war.

Many English gardens were also destroyed – by English soldiers. Jessie MacGregor's *Gardens of Celebrities and Celebrated Gardens* (1919) is illustrated by her own drawings, but some gardens she found no longer worth drawing: 'Though facilities were kindly given me to draw in the garden of Gray's Inn, laid out, it is said, by Bacon himself, I found that they had been so sorely cut up and worn by the perpetual drilling of thousands of troops, that on aesthetic grounds I was compelled to leave them out.' The same thing had happened at Fulham Palace gardens where 'the War had transformed the once beautiful park ... into a vast drilling ground'.

In *The Small Garden* (1918) Mary Hampden also draws our attention to the effects of the war and writes bitterly of 'the iris that we must still call German'. In the Foreword she offers the book to many people, young and old, among whom are those

Who, abandoned by paid gardeners, must manage in their stead,
Who are practising patriotic economy by paying fewer wages, and setting
    workers free,
Who think it always legitimate to patronise national industries,

Who are keeping situations open for soldiers,
Who are filling gaps to which soldiers will not return,
Who are caring for soldiers' gardens,
Who are partly crippled, wounded, invalided, or have come home to rest,
Who are training child-gardeners,
Who are hopefully planning how to make the Empire spiritually and materially
    fairer in days of Peace.

In *The Garden of Experience* (1921) Marion Cran contrasts the 'careless days of peace before 1914' with 'the bogey of starvation gibbering at us' during the Great War. She describes a 'jamless, butterless, meatless breakfast table where the porridge was served dry and the coffee black'. Her response to the lack of milk was to buy a goat. Even the china took on a 'hybrid appearance as we had to replace it with other patterns, for the Germans had overrun the Luneville potteries in France and we were no longer able to obtain the pretty ware which had pleased our eyes for years'.

Not everyone, however, suffered deprivation in the First World War. Katherine Everett came from Ireland during the war to work as a gardener-companion for Nelly Baring, a cousin of Gertrude Jekyll who lived at Burley in the New Forest. In Everett's memoirs, *Bricks and Flowers* (1949), she recalls how Baring's gardeners had been reduced from three to one. The remaining gardener was 'devoted to vegetable-growing and really disliked flowers' and he is described as 'a bit of a fool'. One greenhouse was maintained throughout the war, as Everett records: 'My employer remained exacting, and said she couldn't live without hothouse flowers all the winter.' The rich could still manage to avoid privation: 'During the first Great War there was no austerity for those who could afford enough and cared enough to secure luxuries.'

After the war the political map of Europe was redrawn. As on similar occasions throughout history, this led to some confusion when locating the geographical origin of plants. A.W. Darnell's solution, in *Winter Blossoms from the Outdoor Garden* (1926), is to stick with the old order: 'It may be mentioned that in the matter of localities in Europe, pre-war political divisions have in all cases been adhered to, as in the great majority of cases it is easier to locate the habitat of a given species on the pre-war standard Atlas than those recently published based on the decisions of the Treaty of Versailles.'

The First World War brought about a massive increase in state control and bureaucracy. This was presaged by Alice Martineau's call for state intervention in the sphere of gardening. She argues in *The Herbaceous Garden* (1913) that the government should have the power to purchase gardens for the benefit of the public: 'Recreation grounds and parks are provided for the people of big towns, why should not gardens be provided for the purpose of educating that portion of the public who really improve the face of the land by their gardening?' She gives an example of the French government's more progressive attitude in taking over the garden at Bagatelle. Unlike Kew, where 'there is *never* anyone to explain things', here everything is done to encourage a love of gardening: 'You are made to feel when you enter that it exists solely for your pleasure and instruction. The Director and gardeners are there primarily for the purpose of imparting information to the casual inquirer.'

Changes in Gardening Style

Gardening style was fundamentally affected by the war. The move from Victorian bedding-out to herbaceous borders was accelerated. Fewer people could afford the bills for the heated greenhouses that were necessary to rear tender bedding plants. Coal was needed for the war effort and labour was not available. Owners of large gardens had to make a virtue of necessity, as Mrs Stebbing notes in *The Flower Garden and How to Work In It* (1917): 'The War has brought many changes in the garden. Whether from the need of economy or, later, owing to the difficulty of obtaining labour in the garden, people have discovered that they can really do a great deal of the work themselves.'

In her second book, *The Secrets of Many Gardens* (1924), Alice Martineau comments on the effects of the 'terrible' war: 'The gardens that depended for their beauty on a modern style of bedding-out, which included relays of plants brought on in greenhouses, have suffered terribly.' She points to the economic reasons, though these are clearly relative, as she still manages every year to buy a few thousand bulbs for naturalising: 'There is no need to dwell on the curtailment of labour following the curtailment of income. We gardeners know it only too well, and those who faced the problem before 1914 and took measures accordingly may now congratulate themselves.'

One of these far-sighted gardeners was Alice Martineau herself. She explains how she changed her bedding-out garden, converting it to herbaceous borders with shrubs and self-seeding annuals: 'I arranged it when war broke out so that it need never be entered by any gardener, just a woman to weed and to mow the grass which borders the stone-paved paths.'

In *Beautiful Flowering Shrubs* (1920) G. Clarke Nuttall points to the growth in the use of shrubs prior to the war: 'Before the Great War the introduction of new shrubs into this country was a matter engaging the special attention of florists and plant collectors, while owners both of large and small gardens were beginning to realise the possibilities that lay in this direction. Though a temporary check has been given – for the fullest economic production of potatoes and carrots became the subject nearest a gardener's heart – yet it is hoped that in not far distant and happier days – flowering shrubs may once more come into their own.'

The process accelerated after the war, according to R.C. Notcutt, the famous Woodbridge nurseryman: 'Towards the end of the nineteenth century and at the beginning of the twentieth, flowering shrubs also began to gain in popularity and since the war this has been still more marked.' In *A Handbook of Flowering Trees and Shrubs for Gardeners* (1926) he emphasises their labour-saving properties: 'Once shrubs have been properly planted the cost of upkeep is small compared with that of plants which must be housed in the winter in heated greenhouses. In fact, a garden of flowering shrubs goes a long way towards solving the labour difficulty.'

According to A.T. Johnson, the new economic conditions also led to a different approach to weeds. Writing in 1927, he refers to the signs of the times, for as 'labour became more difficult, wages higher and money scarcer, how much more tolerant we have become in our attitude towards the weed'. In his view, however, it is not so much the result of economic factors, as the 'trend towards greater simplicity, naturalness and better art which came to rescue our gardens some years ago'.

House and Garden

Between the two world wars there was a house-building boom that gave many families a garden for the first time. In the 20 years up to 1939, nearly 4 million new houses were built in England and Wales, about one-third of the housing stock. Most of these new homes had a private garden. The principle of 'twelve to the acre' was applied, a lower density than previously and also lower than that operating after the Second World War. In *Common-Sense Gardening* (1925) Pettigrew praises this policy: 'Fortunately the housing schemes which are being carried out by public authorities all over the country are so designed as to give greater opportunities than ever to the average householder to cultivate a few flowers about his home.'

E.H.M. Cox makes the same point in *The Evolution of a Garden* (1927): 'Suddenly, when the war ended and the acute housing shortage could be dealt with, there came into being thousands of suburbs and garden cities, where the city worker lives in a house surrounded by a garden. For the first time in their lives most of the dwellers in these suburbs and garden cities have been able to cultivate ground over which they have complete control owing to fixity of tenure; they can give free scope to their imagination and to their love of plants.'

According to John Weathers, in *My Garden Book* (1924), the war had a 'baleful effect' on gardening. But he also thinks it increased its popularity: 'Happily the taste for Gardening acquired under war conditions has been retained by a very large number to whom the cultivation of their gardens is no longer a necessity, but a source of pleasure and happiness.'

In *Trees and Shrubs in my Garden* (1938) T.H.G. Stevens also refers to the change in housing policy: 'The days of the streets of houses all under one roof, without gardens, or with gardens so small that nothing could grow in them, have gone, and literally millions are now living in new houses with a small but interesting garden attached to each. Millions of people have suddenly become garden conscious, and are wondering what to plant.'

A similar phenomenon was noticed after the Second World War. George Taylor observes in *The Little Garden* (1948) that, after 50 years of travelling round the country as a horticulturist, he has 'never met with anything approaching the enthusiasm for gardening that prevails to-day'. In *Natural Gardening* (1958) J.E.B. Maunsell links it to new house-building: 'There are some 300,000-odd new houses (and gardens) being acquired every year by potential gardeners.'

As early as 1939, however, Helen Nussey was sounding a warning. When flats replaced houses, the gardens often disappeared. Comparing the 'gardens of the humbler folk within the walls' of London in the sixteenth century, she writes: 'The gardens in fact must have been very like hundreds of those of the present day in our London boroughs which are, alas, being swept away to make room for flats under our model housing schemes.'

SECOND WORLD WAR

Some gardening writers manage totally to ignore contemporary political events, while others refer to how their gardening is affected by them. Nineteen thirty-three was a fateful year. But the rise of Hitler does not impinge on *My Garden Diary* (1934) by Maude Haworth-Booth. What concerns her is the weather: 'Alas, there has been no rain for weeks and weeks.' With hindsight it is incongruous to hear her say: 'This year, 1933, is I think a red-letter year for roses.' Her gardening optimism knows no bounds: 'It has been, I know, a wonderful year for all things fruitful, and I feel 1934 is going to be as good!'

In *A Country Garden* (1936), written in diary form, Ethel Armitage shows more awareness of contemporary political and economic crises. They make her think twice about posting her seed order: 'It seems scarcely worth while sending off our modest order when in a week, at the latest, we shall be embroiled in a terrible cataclysm out of which no one can hope to come alive.' The threat of an attack from the air prevents her planting a group of maple trees: 'We felt we could not bear to see them blown to pieces by aerial bombardment, and their poor mutilated branches strewn over the countryside; and, of course, we should probably be strewn over the countryside with them.'

For Armitage, the Sino-Japanese war, which started in 1931, 'resulted in the long border being planted up with annuals, instead of being replanned and replanted with choice herbaceous things, for we were told the trouble was certain to involve all Europe'. Britain's abandonment of the gold standard, in the same year, and trouble in the Balkans also affected her gardening: 'When we take a tour round the garden now, we think rather sadly of how well the lilacs would have been budding up had it not been for the gold standard; that if the Balkans would only cultivate domestic virtues, our rock garden would be a dream of loveliness, and if the population of Japan would not increase at such a rate that it must have some more territory in which to live, we should show anyone who cared to come our long border, and be proud to do so.' She likens ground elder to 'a veritable Hun, overrunning anyplace it can get near', and states that it 'is no true Briton at all, having begun its career here as an undesirable alien'.

In a later book, *Garden and Hedgerow*, published in 1939, Ethel Armitage is less specific, but more ominous, writing of 'a world full of bewilderment, full of strange doctrines and still stranger and often terrible happenings, overloaded with disillusionment and despair'.

Vita Sackville-West also reflects political events in her gardening writing. Just before the Second World War she records in *Country Notes*: 'At 3 p.m. I was listening to the first report of Herr Hitler's speech to the Reichstag, but by 3.30 p.m. I had gotten myself with relief out into the very different atmosphere of the open fields, the quietly busy fields, busy with their April life.'

She spends the afternoon with Henry, the man who looks after the pigs, and concludes the article: 'Now why, I often ask myself, should these ordinary things give me so deep and lasting a satisfaction? Why should Henry's simple expressions move me more profoundly than any Dictator's rhetoric? which, after all, is likely to affect my life and the lives of my countrymen in far greater degree. Such things cannot be set into their right proportion; they must always return to the question of personal temperament. I sometimes think that the love of nature and the natural seasonal life may attain the proportions of a vice; may obsess one to the extent of desiring nothing else, nothing beyond: a drowning, a lethargy, an escape, an indolence and an evasion.'

At the time of the Munich crisis she contrasts strained nerves with the beauty of the countryside, on which it seemed inconceivable that devastation should fall. People were digging trenches in their gardens, joking as they dug: 'We dug a trench in the orchard here – a most inadequate trench which would certainly have fallen in at the first heavy rain, a most unscientifically constructed trench, which expressed the instinct to burrow into the friendly earth rather than any calculated attempt to provide a four or five years strong shelter against the attack of an efficient foe. Not that, out in the country as we are, danger seemed very likely; but one never knows, thinking of Spanish villages and the swoop of machine-guns. So one must make provision. This sudden hasty burrowing into the earth struck one as truly horribly uncivilised: man seeking refuge from man under the peacefully ripening apples and pears of September – man turning himself into a frightened furtive threatened creature like a rabbit or a mole.'

Helping the War Effort

As soon as war broke out, gardening writers were giving advice on how to help the war effort. In *Fruit Growing for Small Gardens* (1939) N.B. Bagenal foresees the difficulty in obtaining oranges to make marmalade: 'In war-time home-grown and home-bottled fruits from garden or allotment are needed to offset reduced imports, while home-made jams form an important addition to the butter ration, and may largely replace marmelade on the breakfast table.' The author was a technical assistant at the East Malling Research Station and he also advocates pruning old fruit trees to prolong their life: 'In many gardens there are old trees which might be recommissioned for service in war-time by being given a thorough overhaul. Dead and diseased branches can be cut out, and old fruit spurs thinned out.'

In 1940 *Food Production in the School Garden*, by Hardy and Foxman, was published. The front cover states: 'This book deals with the best methods of adapting the School Garden to meet war-time needs for intensive food production.' In the preface the authors write: 'The chief purpose of the School Garden in war-time is to produce food in the form of vegetables and fruit.'

In the same year *Gardening with Elizabeth Craig* appeared, subtitled 'A complete guide to all aspects of gardening in war-time'. The only mention of the war, however, is at the beginning when she addresses

her readers: 'To you townswomen who suddenly find yourselves established in a country home for the "duration", gardening will, more
likely than not, appear a highly intricate and mysterious operation. Let
me simplify it for you and help you to avoid those set-backs and that
waste of labour which so often damp the enthusiasm of beginners.'

The War Food-Growing Handbooks were also published in 1940.
This was a series edited by Walter Brett encouraging people to help the
war effort by keeping bees or rabbits, for example. In *Eggs from Your Garden*
the author quotes the Minister of Agriculture, warning of the billions
of eggs which can no longer be imported: 'I am looking to the ordinary
back-yarder – the man with something of a garden – to help here. I want
at least half a million people who don't now keep chickens to start doing
so straight away.'

In *Garden and Allotment Pig Keeping* Brett again quotes government
policy: 'The pig, the Government says, is the most valuable of all
domestic animals – the only part of him that cannot be used in war is
his grunt!' He refers back to the First World War and also urges his readers
to join pig clubs: 'Cottagers produced 5,000,000 extra pounds of pig
meat a year in the last war. They are asked by the Government to do
the same again, and more, this war.'

The following year, in *The Week-End Gardener*, C.S. Goodsman likewise
stresses the importance of keeping pigs: 'Since the fall by enemy action
of the Low Countries, Great Britain has ceased to import nearly
£30,000,000 of hams, bacon, pork and pig products. This deficiency has
to be made up by increasing home production. It is, therefore, imperative
that every house-holder with sufficient land, with home-grown vegetables
and kitchen waste, should keep at least one pig.' He devotes 25 out of
160 pages to the subject, as well as explaining how to look after goats
and poultry.

In *The War-Time Vegetable Garden* (1940), Eleanour Rohde reflects the
mood at the beginning of the war, claiming that 'there is the same general
enthusiasm as in the last war to put every available bit of ground under
cultivation'. She wants, however, to 'avoid the mistakes made in the
last war when in countless districts it was impossible to give away
cabbages'.

In 1941 H.V. Taylor's *Salad Crops* was published as a bulletin of the
Ministry of Agriculture and Fisheries. The author catalogues in detail
the massive reduction in salad imports: 'Before the outbreak of war large
quantities of lettuce were imported from the Continent. The imports
in 1938 were, from France, 57,229 cwt.; Belgium, 8,994 cwt.; Netherlands,
184,640 cwt.; Spain, 6,385 cwt. The supplies from Belgium, the
Netherlands and France are not possible at present, and supplies from
Spain will inevitably be reduced.' He points out that considerable

Advertising the 'War Food-Growing Handbooks',
edited by Walter Brett, published in 1940.

Advertisement encouraging people to grow vegetables for the war effort, from J.R. Wade's War-Time Gardening (1940).

quantities of radishes were 'imported from Guernsey, France and Germany before the war'. One suggested solution to the salad problem is an extension of the use of dandelions.

Also in 1941 the Royal Horticultural Society published *The Vegetable Garden Displayed*, three impressions being printed in the same year, with a total sale of 75,000 copies. By February 1942, a quarter of a million had been printed. It is introduced by R.S. Hudson, Minister of Agriculture and Fisheries, who notes the change in emphasis for the RHS. Previously it had concentrated on flowers, as at the Chelsea Flower Show: 'But with the war came a new need: the cry for food, and for food in increasing quantities, to defeat the menace to our shipping and to replace supplies from territories overrun by the enemy.'

There follows an exhortation by Lord Woolton, Minister of Food: 'This is a Food War. Every extra row of vegetables in allotments saves shipping. If we grow more Potatoes we need not import so much Wheat. Carrots and Swedes, which can be stored through the winter, help to replace imported fruit.' He goes on to encourage people to grow their own onions; before the war 90 per cent of onions were imported. There is an advertisement in the book for Sutton's Seeds which reads: 'Your garden is part of the national defences. Don't arm it with poor weapons.'

H.J. Massingham paints an even grimmer picture of the state of onion imports prior to the war: 'Of all the onions eaten by this nation before the war, only 2% were home-grown.' In *This Plot of Earth: A Gardener's Chronicle*, published in 1944, however, he states that by that time we were 'producing 65% of our own food'.

The food shortages during the war were of major concern to gardening writers. Geoffrey Henslow's *Allotment Gardens and Management* (1942) is clearly written with the war in mind and the author refers to the food shortages in Churchillian tones: 'Never before in the history of this country have salad crops been of such importance as they are to-day.' He urges his readers to grow their own food: 'By largely growing our own supplies in every district of the British Isles, we save transport and cut down not only national expenditure but reduce even the risk of starvation.'

Richard Sudell, in *Intensive Culture* (1942), wants his readers to produce 'four crops a year instead of one'. He acknowledges French skill in this area: 'We owe to French gardeners a debt of gratitude for their pioneer work in this direction.' In the same year, an advertisement on the back cover of his booklet entitled 'A National Food Production Guide for Garden & Allotment' encourages gardeners to grow more food to save seamen's lives.

In 1943 John Hampshire stresses the importance of growing fruit: 'In times of national necessity such as the present, it behoves every gardener

From Richard Sudell's Intensive Culture *(1942).*

to grow as much fruit as is possible. Although sugar for preserving
purposes is short, soft fruits can be kept for winter use by sterilisation,
using jam-jars with snap closures or sealed tops.' In *Specialisation in the
Garden* he recognises the difficulty of obtaining manure: 'Manuring,
especially in war-time, presents a problem to the gardener.' One source
is from pigs: 'With pig clubs springing up all over the country, a certain
amount of such manure may be procurable.'

Answering a question on the possibility of making home-made scents
the author writes: 'Not in war-time, because you will not be able to obtain
the necessary olive oil. In case peace breaks out before we think,
however, I will give the necessary directions.' He also comments on
growing herbs: 'Since the commencement of the present hostilities
herbs have rushed into the news with a vengeance, their latest incursion

Exhortation from A National Food Production Guide for Garden & Allotment *(1942) by Richard Sudell.*

into the headlines being the appeal by the Red Cross for herbs to add variety to the meals of prisoners of war.'

Justin Brooke, in *Peach Orchards in England* (1947), also writes about growing fruit during the war. Before the war the government afforded some protection against cheap foreign imports of blackcurrants: 'This pre-war protection proved of inestimable value to Great Britain, for it saved the bulk of our blackcurrant acreage from disappearing before the war, and so enabled the Government to provide blackcurrant syrup and purée to correct the deficiency of diet suffered by children then.' The author comments too on the amazing rise in the price of peaches, from 4 shillings a dozen before the war up to 7s.6d. each during the war.

The Vegetable Grower's Handbook by A.J. Simons gives the facts behind the government's war-time policy of urging more food to be grown at home: 'In 1939 this country imported 8,500,000 tons of food from overseas. In 1942 we imported only 1,300,000 tons.' In the 1945 Penguin edition of his book there is an advertisement for Chase Cloches inside the front cover which reads: 'Every Cloche user should get the "Cloches v. Hitler" Guidebook, post free 6d.'

In the second volume Simons records the government's ban on new potatoes during the war. Commercial firms were prohibited from lifting early potatoes before 21 July and amateur growers were encouraged to follow suit. The author recommends growing globe artichokes 'in the flower garden in war-time in order to save kitchen garden ground'. He also comments on the use of rhubarb during this period: 'The war at the outset awakened people to appreciate the real value of rhubarb and it fetched amazingly high prices. But the more recent surfeit of rhubarb, occasioned by the shortage of fresh fruit, has probably sickened many people of it for the rest of their lives.'

The Fate of Flowers

Flower gardening inevitably suffered during the war. In *War-Time Gardening* (1940), for example, J.R. Wade encourages gardeners to change over from growing flowers to producing vegetables and fruit. Considering the millions of gardens in the country, 'it will be understood how great and magnificent an effort for victory on the home front lies within the hands of those who own a garden'.

In the book's first chapter, famously entitled 'Digging for Victory', it is suggested that part of the lawn should be 'sacrificed in the interests of the country in this time of war for the growing of vegetables'. One of the advertisements in the book, however, for the weekly magazine *Home Gardening*, does propose that gardeners should not give up growing flowers altogether, because of the 'cheerfulness and colour that the cultivation of flowers can bring to your home, especially during the dark days of war'.

Stephen Cheveley refers to this argument in *A Garden Goes to War* (1940): 'Much has been said in the press since the war began about caution in destroying borders or lawns merely to grow vegetables, the chief argument apparently being that we must keep cheerful by having beautiful gardens even in war time.' He does not see this as a 'serious deterrent', however, and shows how digging up the lawn can eventually be beneficial to a garden. Reminding us how poor the vast majority of lawns are, he goes on to argue: 'By digging lawns now, growing vegetables, and re-seeding to grass after the war, it is certain that we have far better lawns in the long run.'

In *The Week-End Gardener* (1941) C.S. Goodsman explains how he responded to the 'Government's "Growmore" campaign' of the previous year: 'This meant sacrificing a long herbaceous border, and the

Advertisement from J.R. Wade's War-Time Gardening *(1940),
urging gardeners to dig for victory.*

From C.S. Goodsman's The Concise Week-End Gardener *(1941).*

transference of one or two shrubs and a few bulbs left in from the previous flowering.' Nevertheless he is not persuaded to dispense with flowers altogether: 'I did not, and still do not, see why we should deny ourselves the beauty of flowers, although they must, of necessity, be in smaller quantities.'

In *By Saint Phocas!* (1943) H.L.V. Fletcher starts by announcing: 'There is no mention of the war in this book.' His problem is whether to write about the war-time changes in gardens or to remember them as they used to be 'before there were carrots and beetroot flaunting it rudely among the flowers; before we dug out herbaceous plants to make room for onions, or filled the greenhouse with tomatoes instead of Begonias'.

He wants to do the latter, but adds: 'I also did not want to be an escapist, nor to be heartless and shut myself away from horrors behind the garden hedge.' In the end he concludes: 'But it became such a relief to get away from the war when I sat down to dream about the garden I began to think others might feel the same way. Others might like to forget the smell of cordite in recollecting the scent of a Rose; might like to remember bigger Dahlias rather then bigger bombs; rock gardens rather than gas masks, for an hour or two.'

Flowers inevitably seeded themselves during the war, but there were also deliberate attempts to carry on their cultivation. In *Flowers for the House and How to Arrange Them* (1951) C. Romanné-James writes that 'even a bombed site is glorified if the ugly debris be hidden with a mass of flowers', and claims that 'grim austerity has not been able to rob London of its flower-glory'. She mentions the war-time practice of planting flowers by the roadsides: 'What a joy during the war, that time of frustration, fear, and starvation of beauty, were the patches of calendula, nasturtiums, and other flowers planted by the roadside to welcome the service men and women home on leave from active service.'

Fred Streeter, an early radio gardener and one of the first television gardeners, was head gardener at Petworth Park Gardens in Sussex at the outbreak of the war. In Geoffrey Eley's biography of him, the effects of the war are outlined: 'Soon after the war started the first of the men from the gardens at Petworth joined up. It was hard for Streeter – years and years of hard work had just brought the gardens to their prime. And now all would be changed. Lord Leconfield told him: "You must get rid of all those plants and flowers. We must grow more vegetables – and, of course, your staff will be heavily reduced."'

The lawns were let go to grass, herbaceous borders turned into vegetable and salad plots, and five of the six boilers used for heating the greenhouses were closed down. Fuel rationing made it impossible to keep out the frost and many choice plants were frozen. Labour was short: 'One of the tragedies of the war was the number of these lovely old gardens, with their soils in the highest state of fertility, which were allowed to fall into decay through lack of facilities and labour. And yet, at the same time, the authorities ordered people to plough up their starved-out lawns and plant potatoes.'

Radio Broadcasters

Radio expanded quickly in the pre-war years, licences increasing from just over 2 million in 1927 to over 9 million by September 1939, when 73 per cent of households had a set. C.H. Middleton's radio gardening talks started in 1934 and continued after the outbreak of war, when three and a half million listeners tuned in to his Sunday afternoon broadcasts. He also spread his views in a gardening column in the *Daily Express* every Saturday.

Middleton, the son of a Northamptonshire head gardener, published his talks in *Your Garden in War-Time* (1941) where he objects to the restrictions on growing flowers: 'Hitler or no Hitler, war or no war, I'm going to grow a few bunches of sweet peas next summer, if at all possible.' But in general he urges his listeners to reorganise their gardens and 'turn them into munition factories; for potatoes and beans are munitions of war as surely as are bullets and shells; and the gardeners of England can do much to help the nation in its hour of need'.

Middleton refers to the blitz, to the cities and towns 'badly knocked about by Goering and Co'. He suggests that suitable stones from the bombed-out buildings could be used to make rock gardens in public parks, as a 'permanent memorial to those who suffered during the air raids'. He proposes soldiers' gardens in their camps and argues for communal allotments in villages: 'It may well be that the market growers and allotment holders will be able to drive the last nail into the Nazi coffin.'

Roy Hay considers that Middleton, by means of his radio broadcasts, 'must have made more converts to the gentle pursuit of gardening than any other single man'. Hay, the son of Thomas Hay, Superintendent of London's Royal Parks, succeeded Middleton as gardening broadcaster. In *Roy Hay Talks About Gardening* (1942), which covers the years 1939 to 1941, he explains that he has been mainly concerned with the 'rather sombre and utilitarian side of gardening'. Nevertheless he looks forward to the end of the war: 'Our thoughts turn towards the days when the clouds of war will have passed by and once more we can allow our thoughts to dwell on the more aesthetic side of gardening.' A favourite listeners' question was 'What can I plant to screen my air-raid shelter?' Hay suggests ivy, periwinkle, foxgloves, aubrieta, arabis, clematis, honeysuckle and climbing nasturtiums.

Roy Hay was one of the leading propagandists of the Dig for Victory campaign and he toured the country persuading people to take part in it. In *Gardener's Chance* (1946) he explains that the slogan originated in an *Evening Standard* leader in the autumn of 1939. The campaign was launched on 10 September 1940 with an appeal for half a million more allotments by the spring of 1941. Hay recounts stories from all parts of the country. In particular he praises the gardeners of Bethnal Green who grew cabbages and carrots, runner beans and tomatoes, not only in their gardens, but also on bomb-sites: 'Bethnal Green had made gardening history. Hitler could bomb their houses, smash their chicken-runs and rabbit-hutches, but he could never kill their enthusiasm for gardening.'

In Keep Fit in War-Time, *published in 1940, Harry Roberts recommends gardening: 'No other pursuit is so sure a remedy for "War Neurosis".'*

He sums up the achievement of the campaign: 'In 1944 the gardeners of Britain must have produced between 2 and a half and 3 million tons of food.'

A Socialist Gardening Writer

Despite the popular-front politics of this period and the alliance with communism to defeat Hitler, there are few explicitly socialist views expressed in war-time gardening books. An exception is Harry Roberts, one of the handful of committed socialists to write about gardens. In *Keep Fit in War-Time* (1940) he argues for food rationing: 'We must apply the old Communist formula: 'To each according to his need, from each according to his ability."'

Roberts was born at Bishops Lydeard in Somerset in 1871 and at the age of nine wrote a small pamphlet on ruled exercise-book paper entitled 'School Botanical Gardens, being a few hints on the formation of a small garden for the study of the principal natural orders of plants, written for the use of schoolmasters and others, by Harry Roberts 1880'. The first book he bought was Goldsmith's *Natural History* and his favourite English author was Cobbett.

He practised medicine at Hayle in Cornwall for a while, but spent most of his working life as a doctor in the East End of London where he was politically active and very popular. He had his nose broken at a suffragette meeting in Hyde Park by a man with whom he picked a fight for shouting obscene remarks at a suffragette speaker. He later moved to Oakshott, near Petersfield in Hampshire, where he had a garden of 34 acres.

Harry Roberts wrote fairly regularly for the *Gardener's Chronicle* and edited a series of Handbooks of Practical Gardening. These caused him a considerable amount of work in editing, for he commissioned volumes from practical men, regardless of their literary ability. Some of the manuscripts arrived hand-written in penny exercise-books.

Among his political works is *British Rebels and Reformers*, published in 1942 . In 1944 he wrote *English Gardens*, part of a series called Britain in Pictures. Roberts confesses his adherence to the style introduced by William Robinson, and quotes Ellacombe and Hole approvingly. At the end of the book, which is a brief history of gardening in Britain, he makes his political point, quoting the sociological survey method of the time: 'The findings of the recent Mass-observation enquiry on Housing into the real desires and aspirations of various groups of working people, establish the fact that although a number of the "observed" were unaccustomed to visualise a world in which they had any right of choice,

over eighty per cent of the total pictured their ideal home as a small
convenient house "with a garden". Should this bit of democracy mate-
rialise, the English cottage garden will have come into its own.'

*Portrait by Flora Twort of Harry Roberts, doctor and gardening writer, who had
his nose broken in a fight with a heckler at a suffragette meeting in Hyde Park.*

THE POST-WAR PERIOD

In 1946, a year after Labour's landslide victory, George Taylor makes a
brief reference to the contemporary ideology of democracy. In his little
book *British Garden Flowers* he concentrates much attention on the
artisan florists of the previous century: 'In our long history of British
Horticulture there is nothing more appealing than the devotion of the
old florists to their favourite flowers, and it is a chapter of peculiar interest
in these democratic days.'

He also seems less bitter than Mary Hampden in 1918 about the
German iris: 'The German Iris, *Iris germanica*, has been completely

stripped of its Teutonic character – if it ever had one. It has regularly come into favour, and is one of the very best plants for town gardens.'

Two years later he comments on the neglect of the big gardens during the war, most of them being 'now almost beyond restoration'. The economic conditions meant 'demolishing all, or nearly all, the glass-houses; cutting labour down from fifty, or more, employees to a couple of men and a boy'. Noting the demise of flower-breeding skills among artisans, he blames other leisure activities: 'To-day, many, very many I am afraid, of the artisans spend their Saturday afternoons at a football match or some other form of easy-going entertainment, and the time spent in their gardens is reduced to the minimum.'

The importance of growing food in the garden is still stressed by Stanley Whitehead, even after the end of the war. The Foreword to his book, *In Your Flower Garden* (1947), also emphasises the aesthetic side of gardening: 'These are days of moral and mental reconstruction, as well as of material, when we also need the inspiration and spiritual sustenance that come from the creation and enjoyment of beauty.'

In *The Woman Gardener* (1955) Frances Perry draws our attention to the renewed interest in growing fruit trees during the war and imme-diately after it, reminiscent of the period of the Commonwealth in the seventeenth century: 'It is probably true to say that at no period in history has the cultivation of fruit attracted so much serious attention from house-holder and scientist as at the present time. Possibly the two major wars of this century did much to force the issue by cutting off supplies from abroad. This had the effect, not only of giving a new lease of life to a rather neglected side of market gardening, but it also drove the ordinary gardener into growing on his own account. Nothing stimulates an industry like shortages and probably at no period in history were so many stocks and fruit trees sold as during the intermediate and post war years of 1940–50.'

For some time after the war bomb-sites continued to be a feature of the landscape. In *Mirror of Flowers* (1953) Dorothea Eastwood lists a number of plants which became common in these derelict areas: 'Coltsfoot, Shepherd's Purse, Squalid Senecio or Oxford Ragwort, Canadian Fleabane, Rosebay Willow-herb.' She emphasises the continual movement of plants from the wild to cultivation and back again to the wild: 'With the Oxford Ragwort, the Rosebay is the first flower to arrive on any blitzed area; but few people realize that the masses of magenta spires with their sunset-coloured buds may have originally escaped nearly four hundred years ago from Gerard's garden in Holborn.'

The harsh economic conditions of the post-war period are alluded to by Geoffrey Taylor in 1951: 'At the moment the outlook for gardening may not seem bright.' Nevertheless, in *Some Nineteenth Century Gardeners*, he puts forward this paradox: '*The Times* Horticultural Correspondent reports that Gardening enthusiasm tends to be in inverse ratio to Stock Exchange buoyancy.' This view is confirmed by William Beach Thomas in *Gardens* (1952): '"Whatever the depression," said to me one of our great commercial gardeners, "flowers are good business in war as in peace."'

In *Royal Gardens* (1953) Lanning Roper comments on the 'great wave of enthusiasm for horticulture which has swept Britain in the last few decades'. He sees more people turning to gardening than ever before: 'Perhaps it was the nightmare of war that made so many people seek refuge in nature and find solace and relaxation within their garden walls.'

GARDENING AND RETIREMENT

The link between gardening and politics illustrated in this chapter notwithstanding, there have been times when gardening interests have risen above war and politics. The idea of gardening as a retreat from politics was widespread around the time of the Civil War. Thomas Hanmer, a royalist, escaped to France in 1644. He later retired to his house and garden at Bettisfield in Flintshire, on the Welsh borders. He collected and exchanged plants, particularly tulips, one of which was named after him. Miles Hadfield notes in *A History of British Gardening*: 'In June 1655 he [Hanmer] had sent to General Lambert – a cavalier to a roundhead – "a very great mother root of Agate Hanmer".' Hanmer was also on friendly terms with another Parliamentarian, Samuel Hartlib, who called Hanmer one 'of three most exquisite gardiners'.

The two greatest gardening poets of the seventeenth century, Marvell and Cowley, both refer to the theme of gardening as a retreat from politics, though they were on different sides, as Sieveking (1908) notes: 'Marvell took the Puritan side in the great Civil Struggle. Cowley remained a keen if somewhat timid Royalist, and issued a Pindaric ode against Cromwell, whereas Marvell published an Horatian ode in his favour.'

During the Commonwealth many royalists retired to the country or the continent to cultivate their gardens. After the Restoration in 1660 gardening continued to be a compensation for those disappointed by the turn of political events. Keith Thomas notes in *Man and the Natural World* (1983): 'Many of the best-known rural idylls of the seventeenth century were compensatory myths, composed by or for the sake of such disconsolate figures: Thomas, Lord Fairfax, whose self-imposed exile from politics in the 1650s at Nun Appleton inspired Andrew Marvell; or Bulstrode Whitelocke, who, after escaping punishment at the Restoration, retired to Chilton Park in Wiltshire, where he wrote reflections on the superiority of rural life; or Sir William Temple, who retreated to Moor Park, Surrey, after being struck off the list of privy councillors in 1681 and wrote his essay "Upon the Gardens of Epicurus"; or the poetess Anne Finch, Countess of Winchilsea, who, having retired with her husband to the countryside because they were unable to reconcile themselves to the Revolution of 1688, composed poems celebrating the virtue of contented obscurity.'

One of the poems which Anne Finch wrote is called 'The Petition for an Absolute Retreat'. It is redolent of images of the garden of Eden:

> Fruits indeed (wou'd Heaven bestow)
> All, that did in Eden grow
> All, but the Forbidden Tree,
> Wou'd be coveted by me;
> Grapes, with Juice so crowded up,
> As breaking thro' the native Cup;
> Figs (yet growing) candy'd oe'r,
> By the Sun's attracting Pow'r;
> Cherries, with the downy Peach,
> All within my easie Reach;
> Whilst creeping near the humble Ground,
> Shou'd the Strawberry be found
> Springing whereso'er I stray'd,
> Thro' those Windings and that Shade.

No intruders are allowed into the garden and thoughts of worldly ambition and fame are banished.

The myth of the lack of Parliamentarian interest in gardening and the emphasis on retirement poetry in the seventeenth century, however, have tended to hide the important contribution of radical writers of the period. These authors not only expressed the pleasure and use to be had from gardens and gardening, but stressed that they were something to be enjoyed by all.

The Desire for Retreat and a Place of Refuge

The tension between the inevitable intrusion of worldly affairs and the desire for retreat and seclusion continues in the eighteenth century. Stephen Switzer, for example, celebrates retirement in *The Practical Kitchen Gardiner* (1727) with its dedication to Lord Bathurst: 'The retirement You are pleased to make into your fields and gardens, are evident demonstrations how greatly You prefer solitude before the noise and hurry of publick life.'

'*A Cottage Porch*', *from Lewis Castle's*
Flower Gardening for Amateurs *(1888).*

In 1738 Samuel Trowell claims there are very few who do not want a garden to divert their 'Leisure Hours from the Fatigue of Business'. He writes of the 'delight in Retirement', the 'pure Silence and Nature' in a garden, compared with the 'Noise, Hurry, and Uneasiness' of daily work.

Another contrast is made by Benjamin Whitmill in his *Kalendarium Universale: or The Gardeners Universal Kalendar* (1726), which by 1765 was in its seventh edition. Whitmill, a gardener from Hoxton, had been one of those who helped Miller with his dictionary, and he specialised in fruit culture. He makes a wry comparison between gardening and warfare: 'There are few Gentlemen of late, who are not themselves their chief Gardeners. And it certainly redounds more to the Honour and Satisfaction of a Gardener, that he is a Preserver and Pruner of all Sorts of Fruit Trees, than it does to the Happiness of the greatest General, that he has been successful in killing Mankind.'

In the nineteenth century Henry Phillips, in his *Flora Historica* (1824), continues the theme of gardening as a contrast to warfare, as well as being an occupation for retirement: 'We have lately seen a Kemble retire from the stage to amuse himself in a garden; and it also formed a great part of the occupation of the banished Napoleon.'

Lewis Castle was a professional gardener, beginning his career at Kew and eventually becoming manager of Woburn Experimental Fruit Farm. In *Flower Gardening for Amateurs* (1888), however, he recognises the use of gardening as a retreat from the worries of work: 'As a healthful recreation it is unequalled, and it is not surprising that millions have turned to gardening for pleasure as a relief from the cares of business, and have found in it a delight that never palled.'

In the twentieth century John Halsham, in *Every Man His Own Garden* (1904), expresses the view that the gardener's hobby is a constant consolation in a world of capitalist uncertainty: 'He may see his prints or china drop to the bottom of a market where blindest Fortune rules; he may find his cherished Hobbema or his Guarnerius a copy after all; but the massy bronzed pears on the south wall, the cauliflowers paling from cream to a purer white under the green tent of leaves, these are an investment that knows no fall.'

In the troubled year of 1936 Eleanour Rohde asks rhetorically: 'Do we not also need places of refuge where it is possible to look at this distracted world with clear eyes and minds undisturbed by clamour?' In *Herbs and Herb Gardening* she refers to the thousands who find in their gardens 'times of refreshing and quietude'.

Alicia Amherst similarly seeks refuge in a garden. Writing in 1938, she ends her *Historic Gardens of England*: 'In this world of wars and rumours of wars, and of rush and hurry, surely the peace of a garden is more needed than ever, and it is fervently to be hoped that nothing the future may bring will dim the glory of English gardens.'

The conflict between escapism and politics is very evident in Vita Sackville-West, who speaks of her 'incurably Tory soul'. She welcomes new growth in the spring, 'the new buds of the hornbeam pushing the old brown leaves off the hedges', as evidence of 'permanence in a changing world'. But she is constantly concerned in *Country Notes* (1939) that her gardening seems like a retreat from politics and the affairs of the world: 'Should I not believe that it is more important to concern oneself with the troubles and interests of the world, than to observe the first crocus in flower? More important to take an active part wherever one's small activity would be most welcome, than to grow that crocus?'

In *Week-End Garden*, first published in 1939, Phoebe Fenwick Gaye recounts making a cottage garden in Suffolk. Although she refers to the threat of bombing she tries to ignore the coming war: 'A ladybird risking everything on the path and sublimely unconscious of it becomes more vital than Hitler's bombing squadrons.' Commenting on a particular standard rose, she writes: 'I have an uneasy suspicion that it comes originally from Japan – but if politics can't be kept out of gardening notes what *can* they be kept out of?'

Writing after the Second World War, Frances Perry views gardening as a compensation for life's troubles. In *The Herbaceous Border* (1948) she sees solace in the reliability and attraction of the gardening world: 'Disillusionment and disappointment beset the traveller on life's road, but the philosophy of the gardener finds comfort in the knowledge that there will always be flowers, and in the changing beauty of the season.'

George Hall records the rebuilding of houses and gardens that was necessary after the devastation of the bombing. In *Garden Making for Amateurs* (1953) he refers to philosophers who have seen the garden as a 'healing retreat for the soul in the anxieties and hurly-burly of life'. His own view is similar: 'Never before this age has such a retreat been so necessary, owing to the difficulties and uncertainties that now surround us all.'

One of the difficulties after the war was finding work for all the men returning from the forces. Women who had worked during the war, for example in munitions and on the land, were encouraged back into the home and various theories, relating to child-care and women's 'natural' role, were put forward to justify this move. In gardening literature similar debates about the position of women have taken place. Women have sometimes been confined to particular activities in the garden and often been patronised or ridiculed. They have also been feared by men because of their herbal and horticultural knowledge, resulting in their persecution as witches over several centuries. As we shall see, this fear has also led to the invention of some quite extraordinary myths, which have taken a long time to dispel.

2

Good Housewives Delight: Women and Gardening

'And in the beginnyng of March or a lytell before: is tyme for a wyfe to make her garden and to get as many good sedes and herbes as she can gette: and specially suche as be good for the potte and for to eate. And as oft as nede shall require it must be wedde: for else ye wede woll over growe the herbes.'

John Fitzherbert, *The Boke of Husbandrie* (1523)

'Pruning appears, at first sight, a most laborious and unfeminine occupation; and yet perhaps there is no operation of gardening which a lady may more easily accomplish. With the aid of a small, and almost elegant pair of pruning shears, which I procured from Mr. Forrest, of Kensington Nursery, I have myself (though few women have less strength of wrist) divided branches that a strong man could scarcely cut through with a knife.'

Jane Loudon, *Instructions in Gardening for Ladies* (1840)

'I should like to record that I learnt all my practical knowledge of gardening as a child from my mother, who had always been devoted to gardening long years before it was considered a fashionable pastime for ladies.'

Alicia Amherst, *A History of Gardening in England* (1910)

'Years ago, too, women, – always defined as ladies – plied outdoor tools in semi-shame, afraid of being considered vulgar or unfeminine; now the spade is recognised as an honourable implement in female hands.'

Mary Hampden, *Every Woman's Flower Garden* (1915)

All the early gardening writers were men, which may partly explain the belief expressed in their books that women could injure plants just by looking at them. William Turner in his sixteenth-century *Herbal*, for example, quotes from Pliny concerning gourds: 'And let weomen nether touche the yonge gourdes nor loke upon them, for the only touchinge and sighte of weomen kille the yonge gourdes.'

Likewise Thomas Hyll in *The Gardener's Labyrinth* (1577) quotes Pliny's contemporary, Columella, who got it from the Greek Florentinus, that the same thing can happen to cucumbers. Special care has to be taken 'that no woman, at that instant, having the reds or monethly course, approacheth nigh to the fruits, especially handle them, for through the handling at the same time they feeble and wither'. In the fifth century BC Democritus was peddling the same view, extending the withering effect to all plants.

Watering from a pump, from the 1651 edition of Thomas Hyll's
The Gardener's Labyrinth, *first published in 1577.*

In 1717 it is melons that are in particular danger. In *Paradise Retriev'd* Samuel Collins, writing from Northamptonshire, does not need to rely on classical sources, for he has the evidence of his own eyes. He concludes his book with 'A Treatise on Mellons and Cucumbers', and, after advising that 'a Mellonry should be kept free from Weeds', ends with this dire warning: 'Ladies should not be invited to this Place, lest Nature should at that time prove in it's Venereal discharge, which has not only an Imaginary, but so real an Influence on Mellons newly set, that they will most of them drop off; I have found the consequences of this so fatal, that for many years last past (tho' they have been welcome to walk the rest of the Garden) I have been oblig'd at that time of fruiting, to deny their entrance into the Mellonry.'

John Evelyn, in *A Discourse of Sallets* (1699), is more complimentary. The book is written to advocate vegetarianism and the author attaches an appendix of recipes received from 'an Experienc'd Housewife'. He ends the section by writing: 'And thus have we presented you a Taste of our English Garden Housewifry in the matter of Sallets; And though some of them may be Vulgar, (as are most of the best things;) Yet she was willing to impart them to shew the Plenty, Riches and Variety of the Sallet-Garden: And to justifie what has been asserted of the Possibility of living (not unhapily) on Herbs and Plants, according to Original and Divine Institution, improved by Time and long Experience.'

WOMEN GARDENERS

Although women gardeners have often been hidden from history, it is certainly the case that they have always existed. Ever since medieval times, weeding the garden has been a lowly paid female job. Mollie Sands, in *The Gardens of Hampton Court* (1950), reminds us that 'those who did the "wedynge" often remain anonymous', but she provides a list of those who weeded the orchard of Hampton Court in 1516: 'It seems worth recording their names, as a tribute to this whole class of essential but little-regarded workers.' Most of them were women whose 'contribution to the beauty of the gardens in every age has been a vital one'.

Minnie Pallister (1933) records that 'from very early times, agriculture has been one of woman's traditional tasks', and points to her role in the Middle Ages: 'The woman of the house, in medieval times, relied on her garden for her flavourings and simples; so digging, delving, sowing and weeding do not come under the head of those new developments in women's work which give so much pain to so many eminent people.'

In 1577 Barnabe Googe translated and increased Heresbach's *Foure Bookes of Husbandry*. In this book the woman's place in the garden is taken for granted: 'Herein were the olde husbandes very careful, and used alwayes to judge, that where they founde the Garden out of order, the wyfe of the house (for unto her belonged the charge thereof) was no good huswyfe.' The margin note puts it more succinctly: 'An evyll Garden, token of an ill huswyfe.'

The same assumption is made by Thomas Tusser in *Five Hundreth Points of Good Husbandry* (1573):

> In March, May, and Aprill, from morning to night
> in sowing and setting, good huswives delight.
> To have in a garden, or other like plot:
> to trim up their house, and to furnish their pot.'

In the seventeenth century many women were gardening experts. In *Floraes Paradise* (1608), for example, Hugh Platt several times quotes the authority of Mistresse Hill. William Lawson also recognises this female sphere of activity in *The Country House-Wife's Garden, Containing Rules for Hearbs and Seeds of Common Use, with Their Times and Seasons when to set and sow them* (1617).

Women were particularly skilled in kitchen gardening. Gervase Markham, in *The English Hus-wife* (1615), expects the housewife 'to have knowledge of all sorts of hearbes belonging to the kitchin, whether they bee for the pot, for sallets; for sauces, for servings, or for any other seasoning or adorning, which skill of knowledge of the hearbes, shee must get by her owne labour and experience ... Shee shall also know the time of the yeere, moneth and moone, in which all hearbes are to be sowne; And when they are in their best flourishing, that gathering all hearbes in their height of goodnesse, shee may have the prime use of the same.' He shows indirectly that many women did not see their role as confined to the household when he argues that they should not usurp 'to themselves a power of preaching and interpreting the holy word' which 'many of our (vainly accounted pure) women do'.

Women were also skilled in the use of herbal medicine. In *The Shakespeare Garden* (1922) Esther Singleton notes that this was a continuing tradition: 'The Elizabethan lady was just as learned in the medicinal properties of flowers and herbs as her Medieval ancestor. She regarded her garden as a place of delight and at the same time as of the greatest importance in the economic management of the household.'

Midwives, too, relied on their knowledge of plants and flowers. The anonymous author of *A Book of Fruit and Flowers* (1653) describes one of his remedies as 'a Medicine to break and heale sore breasts of Women, used by Mid-wives, and other skillfull Women in London'. It consisted of oatmeal, sage and honey, along with 'Venice Terpentine'. *The Midwives Book* by Jane Sharp was published in 1671, going through several editions and competing with Culpeper.

In 1673 Bathsua Makin wrote *An Essay to Revive the Antient Education of Gentlewomen*, in which she recommends that young women should have a scientific education to prepare them for future occupations, for example: 'To buy Wooll and Flax, to die Scarlet and Purple, requires skill in Natural Philosophy. To consider a Field, the quantity and quality, requires knowledge in Geometry. To plant a Vineyard, requires understanding in Husbandry.' She started a school of her own where 'Gentlewomen may learn the Names, Natures, Values and Use of Herbs, Shrubs, Trees, Mineral-Juices, Metals and Stones'.

Eighteenth-century Lady Gardeners

Another sphere of women's gardening was the flower garden. At the beginning of the eighteenth century Charles Evelyn writes in *The Lady's Recreation* that the 'Management of the Flower-Garden in particular, is oftentimes the Diversion of the Ladies'. Evelyn especially praises the Duchess of Beaufort whose gardens at Badminton provide the 'greatest Example of Female Horticulture, perhaps, that any Nation can produce'. She thought it 'no Diminution to concern herself in the directing Part of her Gardens', and 'arriv'd to so great a Perfection, that she could challenge any foreign Gardens to produce greater Curiosities than her own'.

Stephen Switzer (1715) also thought highly of the Duchess of Beaufort. According to her servants, excluding her devotions: 'Gard'ning took up two Thirds of her time.' Similarly the Countess of Lindsey supervised her gardening 'without any regard to the rigid Inclemency of the Winter Season'. She took part herself in 'measuring and laying out the Distances of her Rows of Trees'. Switzer concludes that 'these illustrious Heroins shine with unusual Splendour'.

Again in the eighteenth century, Charles Bryant writes of ladies whose 'fondness for plants seems to be blended in their very natures'. He goes on to ask: 'Yet, where are the Ladies who have made any great progress in the scientific knowledge of plants? They certainly are as capable as the opposite Sex. But where are the books proper for teaching them?' He criticises Linnaeus for being 'too concise and technical', as well as for writing in Latin. Bryant is also one of the few authors to comment adversely on Philip Miller's style, daring to call it long-winded: 'Nor can the laboured Dictionary of Miller answer this end, it being too prolix and general.'

What is needed is a book of simplified botanical science, for then, Bryant affirms: 'I doubt not, but that the Ladies will be able to keep pace, as far as such a guide may lead them, with the Gentlemen.' The solution lies in the author's work of 1790, *A Dictionary of the Ornamental Trees, Shrubs, and Plants, Most Commonly Cultivated in the Plantations, Gardens, and Stoves, of Great-Britain*. It is 'Chiefly intended for the Use of the LADIES, but proper for all who wish to amuse themselves with the Study of PLANTS, and to pronounce their Names with Propriety'.

Priscilla Wakefield's *An Introduction to Botany*, aimed at young people, was first published in 1796, and by 1841 it had reached its eleventh edition. The author was a Quaker philanthropist who founded a 'frugality bank' for the poor, the origin of the English savings bank. She was a firm believer in the fixity of the class system and supported Joseph Lancaster's educational ideas. In 1792 she helped to establish a school for the daughters of poor parishioners, teaching there herself on a voluntary basis.

In *Reflections on the Present Condition of the Female Sex* (1798), Priscilla Wakefield advocates educating young women to fit into their respective four classes: nobility, merchants, tradesmen or mechanics. She warns that education above one's station could lead to prostitution, and argues that women need some kind of useful education in case they have to earn a living due to the loss of a father or husband. For the top two classes of women, she suggests the job of gardening, by which of course she means supervising gardening work: 'That species of agriculture which depends upon skill in the management of the nursery ground, in rearing the various kinds of shrubs and flowers, for the supply of gentlemen's gardens and pleasure grounds, would supply an elegant means of support to those women who are able to raise a capital for carrying on a work of that magnitude. Ornamental gardening, and the laying out of pleasure grounds and parks, with the improvement of natural landscape, one of the refinements of modern times, may likewise afford an eligible maintenance to some of those females, who in the days of their prosperity, displayed their taste in the embellishment of their own domains.'

In the eighteenth century, working-class women carried out many physically exhausting jobs in the garden. While male labourers mowed the grass of the landscape gardens with scythes, women would follow them and sweep up the cuttings. In Lancashire it was usually women who dug up the potatoes, for which the county was famous. In *An Account of the Manner in which Potatoes are Cultivated and Preserved* (1796) H. Kirkpatrick writes that potatoes are 'the chief maintenance of the lower classes of people here, and are almost the sole food of children'. The women were paid one shilling a day, though 'some years since their wages was only eight-pence'.

Women were also employed to pick insects from plants. In *Every Man His Own Gardener* (1767) Abercrombie gives the task of killing slugs to women and boys. They are to fill a watering-pot with 'soap-suds and urine, mixed with tobacco-water' and pour it over the pests. The significant factor here, of course, is class, for these were no 'ladies'.

The Nineteenth-century Struggle for Equality

In the nineteenth century many of the famous gardens belonged to women. In 1851 Edward Kemp refers to several in and around London, including the Duchess of Bedford's gardens at Campden Hill in Kensington; Dropmore, the seat of Lady Grenville, about six miles from Windsor; Mrs Lawrence's gardens at Ealing Park in West London; Pain's Hill, the seat of Mrs Cooper, at Cobham in Surrey; and Mrs Marryat's Wimbledon House gardens.

Opposition to middle-class women gardening, however, was common in the nineteenth century, though they were often encouraged to study botany and take an interest in flowers. The anonymous male author of *The Young Lady's Book of Botany* (1838), for example, states: 'That the mental constitution of the fair sex is such as to render them peculiarly susceptible of whatever is delicate, lovely, and beautiful in nature and in art cannot, we think, be controversial; we are not therefore surprised that Botany receives more of their attention and study than any other science.'

Similarly, in *The Elements of Botany for Families and Schools*, the tenth edition of which came out in 1865, Thomas Moore writes: 'Botany possesses this peculiar advantage, that its investigations may be carried on, and carried out to the fullest extent, without involving anything which can cause distress to a feeling mind. For this reason it is a pursuit especially adapted for ladies and young persons.' He adds that it also reminds the learner of the 'power, wisdom, and goodness' of God.

In 1856 the Liverpool Ladies' College held its first session and the following year the inaugural lectures were published. The principal was a woman, but all 17 professors were men, including T.C. Archer who, in his lecture 'On the Study of Botany', claims: 'As a study, Botany is peculiarly well adapted for training the female mind in those mental exercises which elevate the intellect and increase its energies.' Despite the existence of intrepid female travellers at this time, he asserts that 'ladies cannot roam the world, gun in hand, to shoot zoological specimens, or scale the mountains, with hammer and satchel, to collect fossils and minerals; but in the study of flowers there is no real obstacle.'

Mrs Ewing, in *Letters from a Little Garden* (1886), refers to the early part of the century when most lady gardeners were botanists and painted a little: 'The education of women was, as a rule, poor enough in those days; but a study of "the Linnean system" was among the elegant accomplishments held to "become a young woman".'

In the same period Edmund Bartell (1804) provides examples of women gardening. He considers gardening 'a pleasure equally enjoyed by the females of a family; who, generally, are not only fond of gardening to excess, but cultivate a small spot with equal care. Indeed, some of the neatest that I have seen, and those by no means unproductive, have been cultivated by women far advanced in life.'

George Johnson, writing about the state of horticulture in 1829, confirms women's place in the flower garden: 'Flowers are equally highly prized and sought after, among the most generous of their fosterers stand pre-eminent our fair countrywomen.' Jane Loudon also asserts that the 'management of the flower-garden ... is pre-eminently a woman's department'.

The inculcation of this gendered division of labour began at an early age. In 1824 one of the first children's gardening books was published, entitled *The Juvenile Gardener*, by an anonymous lady, written for the use of her own children. Frank, aged six, is given a garden for growing vegetables, fruit and flowers and his father tells him: 'I give you notice, that I expect you will be industrious, and attend to William's [the gardener] directions, and keep your ground free from weeds, and put away all your tools in their proper places, when you have done working.'

Four-year-old Agnes, however, is told by her mother 'that when she was a little older, she would give her some ground for a flower-garden to herself'. She also explains to her daughter: 'When you are older, Agnes, you shall learn to draw; and then you may copy flowers from nature, which is a charming amusement.' The book is written with a clear religious and moral purpose and the children are presented as incredibly virtuous: 'They were very good children, obedient to their parents, attentive to their lessons, civil to the servants, and kind to animals.'

The Rev. Henry Burgess also limits female activity to the traditional sphere of herbs and flowers. In *The Amateur Gardener's Year-Book* (1954) he encourages the 'fair sex' to garden when the weather is not too bad: 'Let them see that their favourite tender Roses are defended from the coming winter; that plants of Thyme and Sage are provided with some temporary shelter against the blasts of the east.' An interest in gardening, like domesticity, comes 'naturally' to women: 'The retiring habits of ladies make them turn to flowers with an almost instinctive love, and dispose them to fill up their spare moments in tending and training these ornaments of their homes.'

The anonymous author of *The Garden that Paid the Rent* (1860) gives women a wider scope: 'Most ladies have a natural taste for gardening, and with a gardener once a week, there is nothing which they could not do. Indeed, I know one lady who alone keeps in order a garden of a quarter of an acre, and two greenhouses. She also attends entirely to her poultry.' He lists the benefits accruing to women who take up gardening: 'Did young ladies of the present day devote themselves more to the pursuit of gardening, they would gain in every way, health, beauty, and temper. Headaches would not so often be known, and nervous affections be almost a thing of the past.'

In *Domestic Floriculture* (1874) F.W. Burbidge quotes Harriet Beecher Stowe, author of *Uncle Tom's Cabin*, on the subject: 'There is nothing better for wives and daughters, physically, than to have the care of a garden – a flower-pot, if nothing more ... The advantages which woman personally derives from stirring the soil and sniffing the morning air, are freshness and beauty of cheek and brightness of eye, cheerfulness of temper, vigour of mind, and purity of heart.' He also adds his own patronising comment: 'In tasteful homes, where there are ladies, the window-gardening may safely be left in their hands; and it is really astonishing what quick progress the dear, nimble-fingered creatures make in this delightful art.'

A similar tone is adopted by Samuel Wood in *The Ladies' Multum-in-Parvo Garden* (1881). He does not explain the Latin in the title (which means getting a great deal in a small space) and, although the book is addressed to female readers, the author is hardly complimentary to them. He thinks that a lady is more willing to spend money on a dress than on plants for the garden: 'I earnestly wish that the beautiful art of gardening even now has as much influence with the lady as the silk mercer has.'

Wood also considers women incompetent. When discussing the *Mesembryanthemum crystallinum*, he writes: 'There are many ladies who would be very glad to possess a few specimens of this remarkable and useful plant, but it often happens that they cannot be had for money, and there are not many lady amateur gardeners who can raise it from seed. Not that this is difficult, but they fail nevertheless from one cause and another.' He goes on to explain that this is mainly because the seeds are 'not sown carefully enough'.

Around the same period, on the other hand, Mrs Ewing thinks it is 'very common for the ladies of the family to be the practical gardeners'. This is certainly true of Frances Hope of Wardie Lodge, near Edinburgh, who wrote *Notes and Thoughts on Gardens and Woodlands*, published in 1881, the year after her death. Testimony is given in the Preface to her work in the garden: 'She was up early, and at work late in it – working as hard as her men, and doing everything much better than they.' Her compatriot Herbert Maxwell, in *Flowers: A Garden Note Book* (1923), remembers her in a 'lilac sun-bonnet that crowned her working dress of short skirts, soiled gauntlet and heavy shoes'.

In Germany, Elizabeth von Arnim (formerly Mary Beauchamp), an Australian cousin of Katherine Mansfield, writes of how socially restricted she felt as a woman when it came to gardening: 'I wish with all my heart I were a man, for of course the first thing I should do would be to buy a spade and go and garden, and then I should have the delight of doing everything for my flowers with my own hands, and need not waste time explaining what I want done to somebody else.'

Her book *Elizabeth and her German Garden* (1898) was very popular at the turn of the century, going through 20 editions within ten years. It is written in the style of a diary, containing conversations with her visitors and making several comparisons between England and Germany, including mention of the beautiful English lawns, 'not to be had in the Fatherland'. She sees her garden as a place of 'refuge and shelter', but objects to the idea of female delicacy: 'Give me a garden full of strong, healthy creatures, able to stand roughness and cold without dismally

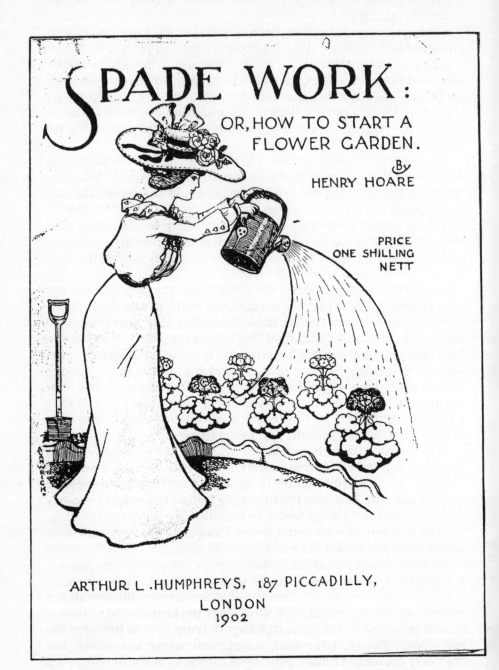

SPADE WORK:

OR, HOW TO START A FLOWER GARDEN.

By
HENRY HOARE

PRICE
ONE SHILLING
NETT

ARTHUR L. HUMPHREYS, 187 PICCADILLY,
LONDON
1902

Front cover of a book aimed at ladies who know nothing about gardening.

giving in and dying. I never could see that delicacy of constitution is pretty, either in plants or women.'

Working-class women gardeners were far from delicate. Those working in London's market gardens had to endure extremely long hours of work, as C.W. Shaw (1879) reveals: 'Everywhere, during the fruit season, may be seen gangs of women and boys busily engaged in gathering Raspberries, Gooseberries, and Currants. Collectively, they earn large sums of money, good hands making as much as 11s. per day at Gooseberry picking, but the average rate is only about 6s. per day, and that only by means of hard work from light till dark.'

Twentieth-century Prejudice

Henry Hoare's *Spade Work: or, How to Start a Flower Garden* (1902) is aimed at ladies who know nothing about gardening: 'It is hoped that the following few pages will enable any one who knows nothing about gardening to make a start in that direction, in a simple and effective way, with the assistance of a gardener who merely understands the art of vegetable and fruit growing, and the practical part of sowing seed, pricking out, &c.' The illustration on the front cover assumes that flower cultivation is the lady's sphere, and the text makes it clear that she also needs to control her gardener, whose job is to look after the vegetable garden: 'Do not allow your gardener to treat your flowers with contempt, and as if anything were good enough for them. Make him treat them just as generously as he does his vegetables and fruit-trees.

Ménie Muriel Dowie reveals the land-owner's attitude to the traditional weeding women in *Things About Our Neighbourhood*, published in 1903. Her book is similar to Jane Loudon's *The Lady's Country Companion*, as the author hopes it will be 'of use to settlers or dwellers in the country' and it is written 'in a manner which is at once practical and light in tone'. She refers to the old Squire 'of whom it was reported that if, while riding, he sighted a dock or thistle on his land, he would "send a woman two mile and better to pull it up"'. But now there remains only Maria Digweed, 'the only creature who weeds in the old way up in the Squire's gardens'.

In the USA at this time Helena Rutherford Ely was advising wealthy women to garden in order to preserve their health. In *A Woman's Hardy Garden* (1903) she recommends: 'if the rich and fashionable women of this country took more interest and spent more time in their gardens and less in frivolity, fewer would suffer from nervous prostration, and the necessity for the multitude of sanitariums would be avoided.' Her emphasis is on flower gardening which she considers to be 'preeminently

A woman is used in an advertisement to illustrate how easy it is to operate the new lawn-mower. From Suburban Gardens *by T. Geoffrey W. Henslow (1934).*

emphasis is on flower gardening which she considers to be 'preeminently a woman's occupation and diversion'.

She also recognises how much physical labour a woman is capable of, when she describes the little garden of a tenant farmer's wife: 'She has six children, and must cook and bake and clean for four men in addition; yet, some time every day, she finds a few minutes to tend her flowers.'

In 1904 John Halsham's *Every Man His Own Garden* was published. Despite its title, it was written, according to its author, 'with the needs of lady gardeners kept continually in mind'. He maintains that 'there is really no garden work, on a reasonable scale, which she may not do, with notable advantage to health and strength, even up to veritable digging'. Later this statement is qualified with reference to the difficulty of digging in clay soil and with an attempt, presumably, to protect ladies from the indelicate smell of manure: 'Equipped with proper armour of gloves and stout boots, and clad in "old things", a lady need not turn back from any of the heavier jobs hereafter described; except perhaps in the case of the more wholesale manures, and in dealing with that gardener's affliction, a really stubborn clay soil.'

Halsham still leaves a way out for ladies who prefer not to garden. They need to read the book however, in order confidently to control their gardeners: 'Though you cannot dig or hoe yourself, you will be able to judge the quality of your jobbing man's work and if necessary to put him right with a satisfactory conclusiveness, and to issue your orders with a confidence which will abash the most uppish of underlings and will probably produce unwontedly prosperous results.'

Similarly, Rider Haggard is concerned lest women strain themselves doing manual work in the garden. In *A Gardener's Year* (1905) he remarks on the fact that women were taking to gardening in increasing numbers and receiving an 'education in that art at various colleges'. He has heard one complaint, however, that 'sometimes the strength of growing girls is overstrained by setting them to dig and other heavy tasks. This is quite unnecessary, as a man at half-a-crown a day will do more sod-lifting than any three of them ought to attempt. It is better that they should confine themselves to the higher walks of the profession, in which there is ample room for skill and intelligence.'

In 1908 Emmeline Crocker, a widely-travelled Londoner, published *Thirty-Nine Articles on Gardening*. Based on the gardening calendar, the articles originally appeared in *The World*. For November the author advises the 'thinning, pruning, and cutting of trees', but considers it basically a man's job: 'This needs a practised hand. When watching the men at work it all looks so simple and easy; but try it yourself, and you feel quite overpowered with even the small branches that the experienced

Keep your garden tidy

Advertisement from the Popular Gardening Annual *(1928)*
edited by H.H. Thomas.

man manages without the slightest effort. Time is saved in the end by employing skilled woodmen.'

In 1912 Mrs Earle and Ethel Case still have grounds for complaint at the prejudice against women gardening: 'It is extraordinary, the objection there still seems to be, especially in the suburbs, against women doing the work in the garden.' They could well have been thinking of someone like Reynolds Hole who, in the preface to *A Book About the Garden*, recommends a division of labour between men and women: 'If politicians would send teachers of horticulture into our villages, and would show the men how to grow fruit and vegetables, and the women how to preserve and cook them, I should have some faith in their "Reforms".'

In *The Evolution of a Garden* (1927) E.H.M. Cox assumes that gardening is for men, while women merely potter and children only play: 'There is no hobby so healthy as gardening. After a long day's work indoors, a man goes into his garden and throws off the worries of everyday life; he uses his muscles, and his mind is at rest, and he returns to his home with the pleasant feeling of being bodily tired. A garden pleases the woman of the household, not only for the fresh produce and flowers, but also because she can potter in it, while children love it, because they can play without supervision.'

Beverley Nichols continues the tradition of male opposition to women gardeners. Writing from Huntingdonshire, in *Down the Garden Path* (1932), he begins by admitting that 'all my early days bear memories of the finest woman gardener I ever knew or ever shall know – my mother'. Thereafter, however, he sprinkles his book with sexist comments, such as that 'two women gardeners can seldom be friends', or that 'they are such appalling liars about their gardens'. His main contention is that women are not tough enough as gardeners: 'Most women – and I do indeed apologize for this – are really too *gentle* to be good gardeners. If the word had not be made so hideous by abuse I should have written "dainty". For daintiness is their besetting sin. You cannot be dainty, for example, when you are planting daffodils. It is fatal if you mince about on tip-toe, pushing one bulb behind a laurel bush, popping another into the stump of an old tree, and whisking a third, with a whimsical gesture, into the middle of the lawn.' His conclusion is: 'It needs a man to plant daffodils.'

Minnie Pallister, on the other hand in *Gardener's Frenzy* (1933), praises the energy of women gardeners. They are very thorough and have not learnt the man's art of leaning on his spade: 'Women are notorious "whole hoggers"; they do not known the meaning of "moderation".' She also claims that digging is 'just as good for the figure and complexion as it is for the flowers': 'Why women who have access to a bit of ground should buy expensive contraptions of steel and elastic, wherewith to do wild and woolly exercises in the bathroom, is a mystery. Why pay heavy fees for an exclusive gymnasium wherein to endure a slimming treatment? Why roll and contort themselves to get their hips down, or worse still swallow patent poisons? Why pay for Turkish baths in order to induce perspiration, when they can seize a spade and perspire all they want to, for nothing? Digging exercises the neck, the back, the arms, the legs, and there is a glorious sense of accomplishment every time a spadeful of earth is tossed over.'

During the Second World War many women joined the Dig for Victory campaign. Roy Hay writes in *Gardener's Chance* (1946): 'Women have taken to vegetable-growing with enthusiasm.' At Yiewsley and West Drayton an old orchard was ploughed up for use as women's allotments: 'This field, now entirely cultivated by women and known affectionately

April.   *Mae.*

"Grand planting weather."

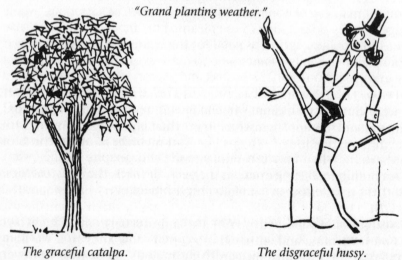

The graceful catalpa.   *The disgraceful hussy.*

Illustrations by the author, from Peter Ender's Up the Garden Path *(1944).*

as "Eve's Paradise", looked as prosperous and well cared for as any allotment field I have seen anywhere.' Hay goes on to record that many of the cups for the best allotment were awarded to women. None of this is reflected in the images of women contained in Peter Ender's *Up the Garden Path* (1944) which is called: 'Pure, unadulterated fun for gardeners and gardeners' friends and relations – in fact everyone. The illustrations are a sheer delight.'

After the war, in *Garden Plans and Designs* (1947), George Hall still assumes that a male gardener will be in charge, though he patronisingly encourages the participation of the rest of the family: 'Do not let the garden become a one-man affair. Take the other members of your family into the business of garden making, for they will all want to join in the fun sooner or later, and you may find that they have ideas you have overlooked.'

WOMEN GARDENING WRITERS

There are many women gardening writers today and several newspapers have female gardening correspondents. In the eighteenth century, however, there were only a few gardening books written by women. These include Elizabeth Blackwell's *A Curious Herbal* (1737) – a collection of 500 engravings based on her drawings, with the text taken from Joseph Miller's *Botanicum Officinale* – and Mary Lawrance's *A Collection of Roses from Nature* (1799), which she also illustrated.

Blanche Henrey, in her *British Botanical and Horticultural Literature Before 1800* (1975), mentions four other female authors: Margaret Meen, Charlotte Murray, Priscilla Wakefield and Maria Elizabetha Jacson. They mainly produced books on botany or works consisting largely of illustrations.

The tradition of women botanical artists continued into the nineteenth century. In 1831, for example, Hugh Ronalds, a nurseryman in Brentford, wrote a book on apples, 'assisted by my daughter Elizabeth, who has drawn them on stone from specimens of my own growth'. The book contains over 40 plates of her drawings.

According to U.P. Hedrick, in *A History of Horticulture in America to 1860*, the first American gardening book was written by a woman. This was *The Gardener's Kalendar* by Martha Logan, written when she was 72 years old and published in 1779. The author came from Charles Town in South Carolina and, although no copy is now known, it was long quoted as an authority on gardening matters. After this, however, Hedrick lists nearly a hundred American gardening books up till 1860, not one of them written by a woman.

THEOPHRASTUS   DIOSCORIDES

Dat. Comitiis Censoriis ex Ædibus Collegii nostri
Die primo Julii. 1737.

Imagines hasce Plantarum Officinalium per Dominam
ELISABETHAM BLACKWELL *delineatas, æri*
incisas & depictas, iis qui Medicinæ Operam
dant, perutiles fore judicamus. ——

THOMAS PELLET, *Præs.*

HENRICUS PLUMPTRE,
RICHARDUS TYSON,   *Censores.*
PEIRCIUS DOD,
GULIELMUS WASEY,

Engraving, commending the author's work,
from Elizabeth Blackwell's A Curious Herbal (1737).

In *On the Portraits of English Authors on Gardening*, first published in 1828, Felton surveys 54 English gardening writers, none of them women. In the second edition of 1830 he brings the total up to 69, and then adds a further 50 which he has taken from Johnson's *A History of English Gardening* (1829), but the list still contains no women writers.

There is a similar dearth of female authors in Sieveking's anthology of gardening writing, published in 1899. He quotes well over a hundred male writers between 1300 BC and the end of the nineteenth century, but refers to only a handful of women, half of whom are French. There is no mention, for instance, of Jane Loudon who was the pioneer of women's gardening writing in the nineteenth century.

In a more recent anthology, *Leaves of Grass* (1987), which covers the last two hundred years, the editors Clare Best and Caroline Boisset include a higher proportion of female writers. Out of over fifty contributors, eleven are women, including Jane Loudon, Frances Jane Hope, Gertrude Jekyll, Frances Wolseley, Vita Sackville-West, Margery Fish and Beth Chatto.

In 1816 Maria Elizabetha Jacson (not Jackson, as spelt by her publisher), the daughter of a clergyman, wrote *The Florist's Manual*, addressed particularly to a female readership. She had already written three other books on botany, all anonymously, beginning with *Botanical Dialogues* in 1797. Her purpose seems to have been to support her brother who was in financial difficulties.

Jacson was born in 1755 at Bebington in Cheshire, where she spent the first 22 years of her life, and where she 'derived the most interesting amusement of her youth' from flowers and their cultivation. After the death of her father in 1808, she finally settled in Somershal Hall, Uttoxeter, in Staffordshire.

In 1822 an enlarged edition of *The Florist's Manual* came out. In this book the author expresses the hope 'that the hints contained in these few pages may enable my sister gardeners to cultivate their flowers to a degree of perfection suited to their wishes'. Her aim is to familiarise her readers with the system of Linnaeus and she says that, combined with cultivating their favourite flowers, this will 'exercise the mental along with the corporeal faculty'. She puts forward gardening as a 'panacea to the daily chagrins of human life'.

During this period, however, the general cultivation of the garden does not seem to have been part of the household responsibilities of the middle-class woman. *Practical Hints to Young Females, on the Duties of a Wife, a Mother, and a Mistress of a Family* (1815), for example, written by Ann Taylor of Ongar, is addressed to 'females in the middle ranks of society', but contains no hints on gardening.

Likewise *Domestic Duties*, written by Mrs Parkes in 1825, and subtitled 'Instructions to Young Married Ladies on the Management of Their Households', contains no advice on gardening. The author has a brief section on preserving fruit and vegetables, with the implication that they have been bought. She then refers the reader to John Loudon's recently published *Encyclopaedia of Gardening* for further information. Nevertheless she does include the gardener in her list of servants, giving his average annual wage in London as between £15 15s. and £42. This compares with the coachman at £21 to £31, the cook £26 5s. to £31 10s. and the butler £42 to £50.

Jane Loudon and Middle-class Women

In the 1840s Jane Loudon started at last to encourage middle-class women to cultivate the garden. She had to do it gently, but in *The Lady's Country Companion* (1845) she firmly expresses the view that women should dig the garden: 'The operation of digging requires considerable strength, as it requires first to be able to force the spade into the ground, and then to raise as much earth as will lie upon the spade and turn it over. It is, however, a fine healthy occupation, not only from its calling the muscles into vigorous action, but from the smell of the new earth being particularly invigorating; and you might have a lady's spade, with smooth willow handle, that will enable you to dig a small bed without much difficulty.'

Her advice is noted by T. James, writing during the same period. He begins by quoting Evelyn: 'My lady skilled in the flowery part; my lord in the diligence of planting', calling this 'a division of country labour which almost universal consent and practice have sanctioned'. Then he refers to Jane Loudon's revolutionary views: 'In her *Gardening for Ladies*, Mrs Loudon, indeed, initiates them far beyond the mere culture of flowers, and those lighter labours which have usually been assigned to the amateur. She enters into practical details in real good earnest, gives directions to her lady-gardeners to dig and manure their own parterres – on this latter subject there is no mincing of the matter – she calls a spade a spade.'

This was a time when, according to E.P. Thompson (1991), 'women's presence retreated into a serial world of private households'. Dorothy Thompson (1976) identifies when this occurred for working-class women. She first points to the contrast between the classes: 'One of the many hypocrisies of Victorian conservative thought was its typification of woman as a frail, delicate and decorative creature, and its simultaneous tolerance of, and indeed dependence on, the exploitation of vast numbers of women in every kind of arduous and degrading work, from coal-mining to prostitution.' Then she shows how women's involvement in Chartist politics suddenly came to an end and the middle-class ideology of the family triumphed: 'Working-class women seem to have retreated into the home at some time around, or a little before the middle of the century.'

This is precisely the period in which Jane Loudon was writing. In one sense she confirms this general retreat, in that the garden is an extension of the home; but in another way she embodies the spirit of women trying to break the bounds of what was thought acceptable, at a time when feminism was at a low ebb. It is after this decade, for instance, that the main movement began for women's higher education and entry into the professions, led by Emily Davies. Not until the 1868 Royal Commission on School Education (Taunton Commission) was official concern expressed about the lack of physical education for middle-class girls.

It is remarkable that Jane Loudon's work has been so neglected. Janet Dunbar's book *The Early Victorian Woman: Some Aspects of Her Life (1837–57)*, published in 1953, covers the two decades when Jane Loudon was most active, but there is no mention of her, nor of gardening. An earlier book by Edwin Pratt, *Pioneer Women in Victoria's Reign* (1897), does refer to the growing involvement of women in gardening, but dates it at the end of the century, and again there is no mention of Jane Loudon. A more recent book, *The Scientific Lady: A Social History of Women's Scientific Interests 1520–1918* (1990) by Patricia Phillips, has two references to horticulture: one to Priscilla Wakefield and the other to Jane Loudon, who merits less than half a page.

During the same period in which Jane Loudon was active, Louisa Johnson wrote *Every Lady Her Own Flower Gardener* (1839). She also encourages ladies to garden, though, unlike Jane Loudon, she confines them to flowers and is not sure that they will be able to make the necessary effort: 'Many females are unequal to the fatigue of bending down to flowers, and particularly object to the stooping posture. In this case, ingenuity alone is required to raise the flowers to a convenient height; and, by so doing, to increase the beauty and picturesque appearance of the garden.'

Like Jane Loudon, she recommends special tools and equipment for ladies, but if the work is too hard, they can simply supervise it: 'I shall speak now of the ornamental shrubs which decorate a flower garden, and which a lady may *superintend* herself, if her own physical powers are not equal to the fatigue of planting. A labourer, or a stout active girl, may act under her orders, and do all that is necessary to be done, in removing or planting flowering shrubs and evergreens.' It is noticeable that the only gardening writers to whom she refers are both women, Mrs Gore and Mrs Loudon, and she maintains that 'the amusement of floriculture has become the dominant passion of the ladies of Great Britain'.

Another writer to acknowledge Jane Loudon is the anonymous Dublin author of *Handbook of Town Gardening* (1847). She states that Mrs Loudon is 'deservedly held in such high estimation', although she disagrees with her advice given in *Gardening for Ladies* on how to grow hyacinths. The writer goes on to describe her own gardening, but is not so confident in a woman's strength as Jane is: 'The results have been attained without the assistance of a professed gardener, and any lady can manage a small town garden with the aid of a common labouring man, such as a helper in a stable. This help would be required in digging large holes, sifting and mixing earth, clipping grass and hedges, raking and rolling gravel, and similar fatiguing operations, for which a lady has not sufficient strength, but every thing besides may be, and has been, easily done alone; and there is great pleasure in feeling, when we have been successful, that it is the work of our own hands.'

A little later in the nineteenth century, Elizabeth Watts stresses the domestic nature of gardening, linking it to the moral virtues of home-making: 'A well cared for garden displays – and displays to good advantage too – the love of home, domestic taste, a wish to please, industry, neatness, taste, and all the sweet household virtues that create home wherever good women rule, and that make Englishmen, when blessed with such as wives or relatives, so fond of it and of them.' In *Flowers and the Flower Garden* (1866) she goes on to encourage men and children to garden too: 'To the little ones of the family also, the value of the garden may have no limit: give a little boy or little girl a bit of ground to call his own or her own, and encourage the young owner to cultivate it well, and it may be the nursery of all the good qualities that I have named, and many more.'

Ladies' Gardeners

Middle-class women often expressed contempt for their working-class gardeners. In 1863 Miss Maling's *The Indoor Gardener* was published, having first appeared as a series of articles in the *Gardeners' Chronicle*. 'I am not writing for people who have large hothouses and great gardeners, but for those who have perhaps a fairly good working gardener, or, possibly, a man-servant who devotes his spare time to flori-culture. Of course, such men are not to be expected to have an intuitive knowledge of "scientific subjects", even in this small way. For air-giving and air-currents, for the doctrine of saturation, as well as for radiation, the mistresses must manage to do all the science themselves. Still, some simple books on such subjects may teach people a great deal; and it is remarkable how interested they get in anything that explains the things they see daily happening.'

Another writer of this period illustrates the class conflict between ladies and their gardeners, and the clash between the two different spheres of house and garden. The anonymous author of *Every Lady's Guide to Her Own Greenhouse* (1851) is determined not to 'submit to the whim and caprice of a professed gardener'. She recommends that her readers should 'obtain a man who does not know too much; not a gardener, but a man who can turn his hand to ordinary things, a man who has a good imitative genius and memory, but one who has not been spoiled in a garden establishment; one who will fetch and carry, wash, sweep, and clean, attend to what he is told, and not act on his own opinion; for it is unpleasant to be subject to the invisible sneers of a man who considers you wrong, as also to be contradicted, and we very often know that this is done without being able to prove it.'

She has a separate kitchen gardener who is not allowed to set foot in the greenhouse, which is her domain. Her warning on the servant problem is dire: 'I declare I know ladies who submit to blank looks, impertinent remarks, rude sneers, and other uncouth behaviour, in a manner that I would not submit to even from my husband – that is, if I could help it.'

Maud Maryon is even more insulting about her gardener in *How the Garden Grew* (1900). It is a story about a clergyman's daughter called Mary who becomes interested in gardening. The first thing she tries to do is sack Griggs, the old gardener, because she claims the bulbs he planted never came up. She talks to her father: 'I believe he planted them topsy-turvy. I suppose there is a right side up to bulbs, and if so, Griggs would certainly choose the wrong. It's his nature. Can't we get rid of him, sir? Isn't there any post besides that of gardener which he might fill?' She later calls him an 'unutterable idiot', who 'gave one the idea of working with all parts of his person except his brains'.

Emmeline Crocker (1908), on the other hand, comes to the defence of the gardener against a capricious employer: 'I have known a mistress of a garden go out, and on finding her staff employed planting cabbage, stop the work, saying she wished none planted, and then, in a few months, demand and expect a supply for a large household. Now, is this reasonable?'

By the end of the nineteenth century women's gardening writing was firmly established. Perhaps the most famous book of this period was Mrs Earle's *Pot-Pourri from a Surrey Garden* (1897). Certainly the most influential woman gardening author at this time was Gertrude Jekyll, whose *Wood and Garden* appeared in 1899.

Mary and old Griggs, the gardener. Frontispiece by Gordon Browne, from Maud Maryon's How the Garden Grew *(1900).*

WOMEN'S EDUCATION

The burgeoning of female gardening writers coincided with the development of women's education. The movement for women's education really got under way in the second half of the nineteenth century, though there had been earlier proponents such as Mary Astell and Bathsua Makin in the seventeenth century, and Mary Wollstonecraft and Priscilla Wakefield at the end of the eighteenth century.

Women first attended horticultural college in 1891, when female students were admitted to Swanley College in Kent. In the same year the national census revealed that there were 900,000 more females

Illustration by Gordon Browne, from Maud Maryon's
How the Garden Grew *(1900).*

than males in the country. During the previous three decades there had been growing pressure for women's education and employment opportunities, and there was a dramatic increase in female professional employment between 1861 and 1891. It was initiated by the 'Society for Promoting the Employment of Women', set up in 1859 by Jessie Boucherett, who argued that women needed technical training. The Society was the first, for example, to start typewriting classes for women.

According to the *Englishwoman's Review* of October 1894, there were 19 county councils providing classes on the cultivation of fruit and flowers, and it was clear that women had started to move into the male preserve of professional gardening. In 1901 Mrs Leslie Williams asserts in *A Garden in the Suburbs*: 'Many women make money out of their gardens.'

In 1897 Edwin Pratt writes in *Pioneer Women in Victoria's Reign*: 'A Women's London Gardening Association takes charge of London gardens, conservatories, window-boxes, and room plants, gives advice on the management of country gardens, arranges table decorations, and so on. One lady, who devotes herself to this last-mentioned branch, visiting the houses of the wealthy according to her list of "engagements", is reputed to be in receipt of an income which would make many a struggling professional man's mouth water. Other ladies have made a speciality of garden produce, plants, bulbs, agricultural seeds, cut flowers, and poultry, and one in Devonshire "receives young ladies as pupils in practical gardening".'

In *The Gentlewoman's Book of Gardening* (1892) Edith Chamberlain and Fanny Douglas express their support for the innovation of women attending horticultural college, though they do not necessarily agree with the curriculum: 'For the sum of £70 to £80 per annum the female students are boarded in a bright and comfortable home, close to the college, in the grounds of which they pursue their studies. The course includes botany, chemistry, zoology, physics, building, construction, and book-keeping.' In a chapter entitled 'Gardening as a Profession', the authors argue for women being trained as gardeners because of the 'surplus number of unwedded women', but they warn prospective students that gardening is hard work: 'The actual rough work, such as digging, etc., will always be done by men, but there is much toilsome stooping and bending to be endured.' They think that women should be capable of stooping to use a hand fork because 'in these days of athletic training, when women take part in so many out-door sports, there are surely few who do not possess a muscular back'.

Chamberlain and Douglas are no feminists. They want women to take up gardening rather than campaign for higher education and the vote: 'It is only of late years that women have assumed their right place as the presiding genii of the garden ... They could not well find a more agreeable pursuit, for surely all true women will agree that the fragrant air of the garden is sweeter than the dim and dusty atmosphere of the lecture-room, that the cult of flowers is more befitting and more enjoyable than the frenzied pursuit of a vote.'

Gardening is seen by them as the antithesis of politics: 'Gardening soothes and calms the mind whilst public strife unsettles the temper and destroys tranquillity.' They view the contemporary woman as 'all cosmetics, all whale-bone, all nerves'. Nevertheless they do make a few scathing remarks about the 'undiscriminating male gardener'. When encouraging women to do floral decoration and window gardening for a living, they comment that many 'would prefer to have a softly footed and shod lady coming in and out of their houses to tend their window-boxes. The average man has a singular talent for displacing things, and no idea of replacing them.'

Frances Buss, one of the most famous campaigners for women's education, was a member of the governing council of the Women's Branch of Swanley Horticultural College. By 1896 there were 39 female students, and in 1903, the year Emmeline Pankhurst founded the Women's Social and Political Union, the college went over completely to women students, numbering 63.

In 1897 Mrs Earle visited the college and realised the new possibilities for women's employment in gardening. She considers, however, that the 'lady pupils at Swanley were too young to profit by the instruction', and thinks that they should go to the college at 18 or 20, rather than 16. In *A Third Pot-Pourri* (1903) she concludes: 'The employment of women as gardeners is still very much in embryo, although two of the Swanley pupils have been accepted at Kew.'

Mrs Earle later became a patron of the School for Lady Gardeners at Glynde, the first horticultural college established specifically for women. Other patrons were Gertrude Jekyll, William Robinson and Ellen Willmott. It was founded in 1901 by Frances Wolseley (1872–1930).

Frances Wolseley

Frances Wolseley wrote a number of books on gardening, including *Gardening for Women* in 1908. In this book she insists on equal pay for women, but is keen to allay the fears of male gardeners. The ambition of lady gardeners, she maintains, is not to supplant men, nor compete with them, but to assist in securing the 'better cultivation of our great country' by lending intelligence, good taste and refinement: 'What they lack in physical strength they endeavour to compensate by other equally important, yet softer, womanly qualities.'

There is a fascinating section which gives a detailed list of clothes suitable for a woman gardener and the meals which she should eat. Breakfast is to consist of porridge and milk, a boiled or poached egg, and perhaps a rasher of bacon. There should be a midday meal and, work having been finished at 6 p.m., supper should be taken at 7.30. Women have to be fit for physical activities for, as the author argues, unlike in Jane Austen's day, hunting, shooting, golf, cricket, swimming, hockey, climbing and walking are all now acknowledged as safe for women.

The woman gardener also has to exercise authority over men. The way to do this is to dismiss the first drunken under-gardener she encounters; thereafter the others will respect her and not try to take advantage of her because she is a woman.

The book ends with a list of available horticultural syllabuses for women at places like Swanley, Studley in Warwickshire, and the Department of Agriculture and Horticulture at University College in Reading, which was founded in 1893.

Working costume at the School for Lady Gardeners, Glynde, Sussex, from Frances Wolseley's Gardening for Women *(1908).*

By the time she wrote *In a College Garden* (1916), Frances Wolseley was not so involved with running her college, but she still insists on the suitability of gardening for women: 'There is so much connected with it that requires the dainty touch of a woman, much that her inborn gentleness can help.' She grants that heavy operations are more suited to men, 'with their superior muscular strength', but the care of plants, the 'lighter side of gardening, which needs so much patience, is best understood by women'. To attain the 'soft, gentle, feminine qualities' which are required, only certain candidates are appropriate. The 'somewhat rough-mannered, undisciplined middle-class woman' should not be tolerated as a gardener, and 'maidservants who have grown tired of household duties and would welcome a change to outdoor life' are also totally unsuited. Viscountess Wolseley wants in her college 'educated women, the daughters of professional men', while 'for the maidservant or secondary-school girl it would seem that farm and not garden life holds out far more suitable prospects', as 'ultimately success depends upon higher education and qualities of directorship which do not come easily to maidservants'.

There was no shortage of jobs for the students, particularly during the First World War. Wolseley describes a lady arriving to hire one of the students, after observing them at work. She eventually picks the one she wants: 'It was all settled very much in the way that a good hunter is selected, after he has been successfully put through his paces.'

The college uniform consists of a khaki coat and short tight skirt, brown boots and leggings, so that the students can walk in and out of the cabbages without getting a long skirt wet. They wear white shirts and brown soft-rimmed hats. The only colour allowed (the college colours of red, white and blue) is to be seen in the twisted cord round the hat and the silk sailor tie. The uniform is 'neat yet essentially becoming and feminine'. When it rains they wear 'thick oilskin coats, buttoned up high round the neck' and sou'-westers.

The pressure for women's education in this field and the demand for equal opportunities in horticultural employment are linked to the growing movement for women's suffrage. Helena Rutherford Ely, in *A Woman's Hardy Garden* (1903), relates women's thirst for education to Eve's eating the fruit of the tree of knowledge in the garden of Eden: 'Oh! Eve, had you not desired wisdom, your happy children might still be tilling the soil of that blessed Eden. The first woman longed for knowledge, as do her daughters to-day.'

In *Every Woman's Flower Garden* (1915) Mary Hampden writes of the 'democratic spirit' of the time and insists on equality with men: 'All gardening, however, is well within the capacity of a woman of average health and strength, and some of the best home Edens of England are those managed wholly by their Eves.' The book is offered as a 'simple encouragement to women who wish to maintain their own gardens' and there is continual reference to the woman gardener: 'The woman who thinks that digging manure into a plot of land is undignified had better – not refrain from the healthy exercise, but – learn to blush for her opinions.'

Mary Hampden recommends sensible waterproof clothes for gardening and refers to some of the horticultural training colleges where 'the costume consists of very short skirts over very visible knickers, all of blue serge or holland'. Nevertheless she still emphasises the woman's fundamental domestic role: 'Woman's province is daily expanding further, but who will deny that it begins with home? By undertaking charge of the garden the wife or daughter can reduce expenditure, gain continual scope for the use of many talents, and accomplish the triumph of giving a lovely frame to domesticity.'

WOMEN'S EMPLOYMENT

With male gardeners fighting in the trenches, there were plenty of opportunities for women, as Mrs Stebbing notes in 1917: 'The openings for women as gardeners have lately become so numerous that it has really proved one of the most promising careers that women can enter for nowadays.' In *The Flower Garden and How to Work In It*, written mainly for women, she expresses the view that women excel in the cultivation of flowers because of 'the natural qualities of a woman, such as taste, sense of colour, and proportion'. Nevertheless she does not rule out any gardening activity for women: 'Speaking purely from a woman's point of view, I can say from personal experience that for those of us who have muscles hardened by exercise and games, there is no department of gardening that one cannot undertake.'

In Manchester, during the war, women were trained to work in the parks. W.W. Pettigrew, the superintendent of the parks department, records how at Heaton Park they trained 'young women to take the places of professional gardeners who had joined the army'. In his *Handbook of the City Parks and Recreation Grounds* (1929) he goes on to chart their progress, which lasted till the end of the war: 'Under this service no less than fifty young women were trained for a period of six weeks. Many of them afterwards filled responsible positions throughout the length and breadth of the country – positions which they held until the return of the men after the War was over.'

Not all the women left their gardening jobs at the end of the war, however, and several career openings remained. Alice Martineau mentions the success of these women gardeners: 'I have heard of girls who were most successful in the carnation houses and vineries, where their work rivalled that of any men.' In *The Secrets of Many Gardens* (1924) she has a chapter entitled 'Gardening as a Career for Women', in which she particularly recommends them to 'learn landscape gardening and town planning' where 'there are large new openings'.

One of the dangers, however, was that women were expected to do too much, combining the job with more traditional female tasks. M.G.

Kennedy Bell refers to 'that rather modern innovation, the woman in the garden'. In *A Garden Timepiece* (1925) she writes: 'In short, she must combine the work and skill of the elderly man gardener with some of the duties of a companion or lady's help. And surely that is over-much work, and rather much versatility to expect from one person.'

In 1943 W.J.C. Lawrence acknowledges the progress that women have made: 'In view of the increasing number of women entering horticulture, brief particulars of the positions open to them are given below.' These brief particulars, however, do not fill up even half a page. On the previous page, while discussing superintendents of public gardens, he states bluntly: 'There are some four hundred superintendencies in Britain. Openings for women apparently do not exist.'

In his gardening broadcasts during the Second World War, C.H. Middleton (1941) mentions 'some good colleges where girls are trained in horticulture', referring to Swanley and Studley. He is grudging, however, about women's gardening abilities: 'Ladies frequently write to me about their daughters who want to take up horticulture as a career. There are a great many girls in the gardening profession now, and some of them don't do so bad.' As a result he received correspondence complaining about his views, and in the following programme had to apologise. He says he is sorry for discouraging girls and then states: 'There are plenty of girls to-day who can tackle any job and do it as well as a man.'

Women's Independence

Marion Cran stresses the importance of girls learning to earn their own money and she looks forward to 'the day when women are in the heart of the state instead of in the lap of it as they are now'. After the First World War, in *The Garden of Experience* (1921), she realises how the 'forcing-house of War' has affected the position of women: 'Women on every hand recognise the necessity and appreciate the advantages of being independent. What I, as an advanced woman, was bold enough to proclaim as an idea for parents to aim at, is now the accomplished fact of thousands of young girl lives. And a very good thing it is too.'

In 1934 she looks back on the changes: 'But what a fight it was for a woman to earn her own living not so *very* long ago! When horticultural colleges for women started, about forty years since, there was a tremendous amount of prejudice and misconception about the business of training women to be practical gardeners. It was "unwomanly" – it was too "rough" – it was indeed another step on the slippery downward path to that pit of disaster, woman's independence, and so on and so forth. Then the war came ... I know, we all know, that many women overdid their physical strength those days; they put in years of heavy digging, of barrowing, and lifting which broke their health later. But they proved that they could make good gardeners, and blazed the trail for girls who followed.'

During the Second World War women were again encouraged to garden and work on the land. By 1944, 80,000 had joined the Women's Land Army. Vita Sackville-West, in her book of that title, published under the auspices of the Ministry of Agriculture and Fisheries, lists the tasks of the Land-girl: 'She milks; she does general farm-work which includes ploughing, weeding, hoeing, dung-spreading, lifting and clamping potatoes and other root crops, brishing and laying hedges, cleaning ditches, haymaking, harvesting, threshing; in more specialised ways, she prunes and sprays fruit-trees, picks and packs the fruit, makes and lays thatch, makes silage, pulls flax, destroys rats, works an excavator, reclaims bad land, works in commercial gardens and private gardens, works in the forests felling timber, measuring timber, planting young trees.'

Prior to 1943, over 10,000 girls had chosen to go into horticultural employment. Two-thirds of their time was devoted to food-production and the other third could be given over to the flower-garden. Over 600 girls took the Correspondence Course in Horticulture and a number of these entered the examinations set by the Royal Horticultural Society. Many girls were thankful, writes Vita Sackville-West, 'for this occasion to take up a profession they might otherwise never have thought of. For gardening is surely an ideal profession for the woman who likes it. The work is not so heavy as to put too great a strain on her physical capacity; and in the more expert branches the possibilities and range of interest is really unlimited. We might even live to see a woman appointed as Director of Kew or of the Royal Horticultural Society's gardens at Wisley!'

After the war women were expected to give up their jobs to the returning men. They were encourage to go back into the home and see their roles as wives and mothers. This is the period when Elizabeth Craig, who is better known for her cookery books, wrote *Practical Gardening*. She stresses that 'a garden is one of the housewife's best friends'. In her chapter on the fruit garden she writes: 'I emphasise the importance of growing fruit in small gardens, not only from the point of view of the gardener, but from the point of view of the housewife.'

The Woman Gardener by Frances Perry, published in 1955, is also addressed to the housewife. Frances Perry was trained at Swanley, now Wye College, and then became head gardener on a private estate near Taunton. An expert on water gardening, she helped Hellyer revise

THE
WOMEN'S
LAND
ARMY

by

V.
SACKVILLE-
WEST

★

64
Illustrations

★

Published under the
auspices of
THE MINISTRY OF
AGRICULTURE
AND FISHERIES

Front cover of The Women's Land Army *(1944) by Vita Sackville-West.*

Sanders' Encyclopaedia of Gardening and published her own book *Water Gardening* in 1938. In 1978 she became a vice-president of the Royal Horticultural Society and in 1991 was still the only woman out of twelve vice-presidents. She died in 1993, aged 86.

Illustration from Frances Perry's Water Gardening *(1938).*

Frances Perry follows the tradition of Louisa Johnson rather than Jane Loudon, believing that 'the majority of women have neither the strength nor the inclination for the heavier types of cultivation'. The Woman Gardener does not deal with the cultivation of all types of vegetables: 'Generally speaking most women are not interested in the bread and butter type of vegetables, that is the main root crops, the potatoes and the cabbage family generally.' She finds that most women are more interested in soft fruit than in apple and pear trees, which they leave to their husbands. Her views seem to be based on the idea of innate differences between the characters of men and women, with particular emphasis on the female role of nurturing: 'The principles of plant propagation seem to have particular interest for women, and they show a natural aptitude in tending the young plants. It may be an inherent instinct which impels them to care for the weak and helpless, but, the fact remains – they *are* attracted to the task and have proved uncommonly good at it.'

The idea of separate spheres of activity for men and women in the garden has been with us a long time, its ebb and flow related to wider political and economic events. One strand of the movement for women's education at the end of the nineteenth century represented a similar ideology. It was based on the views of people like Dorothy Beale and Anne Clough, who advocated a kind of education for women which was completely different from that provided for men.

This is also the position put forward by Edith Chamberlain and Fanny Douglas (1892), advocating education for a woman's domestic role: 'The object of the enlightened woman of to-day should be not to discard household and domestic duties, but to apply to them the results of recent researches in hygiene, economics, science, and art, so as to elevate what was once mere domestic drudgery to an honoured and honourable occupation.'

This contrasts with the ideas of Frances Buss and Emily Davies who wanted women to have exactly the same academic education as middle-class men. Neither position, however, really took account of the class dimension, which is more associated with people like Sylvia Pankhurst. Just as women's gardening activities have often been hidden from history, so the subject of the next chapter, the labour of workers in the garden, has often been ignored.

3

When Adam Delved:
The Division of Labour

'The Gardner had not need be an idle, or lazie Lubber, for so your Orchard being a matter of such moment, will not prosper. There will ever be some thing to doe. Weedes are alwaies growing.'

William Lawson, *A New Orchard and Garden* (1618)

'I Humbly affirm, that all Lands, and the advantages thereof are the Common-wealths in generall.'

Walter Blith, *The English Improver Improved* (1652)

'The Gard'ners year is a circle as their labour, never at an end.'

John Reid, *The Scots Gard'ner* (1683)

'If paid labourers do some of the actual toil the honour will still belong to the selecting mind in command.'

Mary Hampden, *Every Woman's Flower Garden* (1915)

'There are a few magnificent old gardening books written by learned scholars, but I think the majority of us love most those written by homely folk, who not only owned gardens, but worked therein themselves, for their books are redolent of the soil and of lifelong intimate friendship with plants.'

Eleanour Rohde, *The Old English Gardening Books* (1924)

Historically, much gardening work has been done by people obeying orders. The division of labour, along with the assumption that certain people have manual labour at their command, goes back a long way. As an ancient Egyptian notes: 'The scribe is released from manual tasks: it is he who commands.'

Similarly, the Chinese literati despised physical work, as Joe McDermott explains in a review of a book on Chinese gardens: 'Many Chinese literati enjoyed having a hand in designing their own garden, just as Buddhist monks had often done for their own temple. But we can be confident that in a land where men who worked with their heads were thought to rule naturally over those who worked with their hands, literati traditionally seldom did the manual work in building a garden and were not expected to do this work for others. Particularly when done for remuneration, such manual work stank of labour by the artisan class. The opprobrium on making garden designs appears to have been less absolute, with a pair of renowned painters mentioned by Keswick practising this art/craft for other eminent families. But, the makers of gardens usually go unidentified in the historical record.'

The Garden of Eden

In the Introduction to his *Paradisus* (1629), Parkinson takes us back to Adam in the garden of Eden, 'wherein even in his innocency he was to labour and spend his time'. This was the enjoyable labour before the expulsion, after which it became harsh and burdensome.

Later in the seventeenth century John Evelyn, like Milton in *Paradise Lost*, still tries to see gardening in that original light, as a satisfying task. In his *Kalendarium Hortense* (1664) he stresses that a gardener's work is never at an end, but it has compensations: 'There is not amongst Men a more laborious life than is that of a good Gard'ners; but a labour full of tranquillity, and satisfaction.' Working in a garden produces great benefits, as it 'contributes to Piety and Contemplation, Experience, Health and Longaevity'.

Similarly, Eleanour Rohde admires the 'happy' woodcuts in *The Gardeners Labyrinth* (1577) by Thomas Hyll. In *The Old English Gardening Books* (1924) she describes them as 'illustrations depicting Tudor gardens, with people in the costumes of the period, all working so cheerfully and busily'.

The whole subject of Adam's work in the garden of Eden is dealt with in William Harper's 'Sermon Preach'd at the Parish-Church of Malpas, in the County of Chester, At a Meeting of Gardeners and Florists. April, 18, 1732.' Harper was chaplain to George Lord Viscount Malpas whose 'Excellent Gardens at Cholmondeley' are acknowledged. The sermon as published is entitled *The Antiquity, Innocence, and Pleasure of Gardening* and the text is taken from Genesis: 'And the Lord God took the man, and put him into the garden of Eden to dress it and to keep it.'

Harper begins by asking what this verse means, seeing that the garden must have been created in a state of perfection. He argues that, as there were no weeds, what was meant was simply that 'the Man shou'd divert himself by taking off the luxuriant Branches, or improving the Trees and Flowers by Art and Culture'. The eighteenth century was a great time for 'improvement' and Harper applies this policy even to the garden of Eden: 'God probably had left it yet capable of Improvement, and of being carried to greater Perfection.'

Raking and digging, from Thomas Hyll's The Gardeners Labyrinth *(1577).*

What Adam could do, for example, might involve 'transplanting the Trees and Flowers; shaping them into such Forms, as were most agreeable to him; and making, where he cou'd, such additional Decoration, as shou'd make Paradise it self still more Paradisiacal'. This line of reasoning leads him to argue that improving flowers is a laudable occupation, which was a suitable conclusion, given that he was addressing a meeting of auricula growers.

Harper goes on to discuss the expulsion from Eden, after which Adam had to dig, manure and weed: 'He was now to learn what it was truly to labour.' He also comments on the ensuing division of labour. There are those who have to labour and those who are exempt. Nevertheless he quotes from the classics to show that it is acceptable for 'persons of any Rank to divert themselves in employing some of their leisure Hours in Horticulture'. Those who do not have to labour may labour for recreation: 'The Men indeed of Fortune and Eminence, who Providence has plac'd above the Danger of Want, take it as their Privilege to be exempt from manual Labour ... but still the Example of our First Parents is a Demonstration, that the Greatest of their Progeny (when they have nothing more important to engage them) may take a pleasing Recreation in the Nurture and Improvement of Flowers and Fruit-trees, or in devising some new Plan, which may at once commend their Judgement, and entertain their Fancy.'

Digging and planting with a dibber, from the 1651 edition of The Gardener's Labyrinth *by Thomas Hyll, first published in 1577.*

Invisible Labour

In 1644 John Evelyn visited the Luxembourg Palace in Paris and he describes in his *Diary* (1 April) the 'beautiful and magnificent' gardens, full of 'persons of quality, citizens and strangers, who frequent it, and to whom all access is freely permitted, so that you shall see some walks and retirements full of gallants and ladies; in others, melancholy friars; in others, studious scholars; in others, jolly citizens, some sitting or lying on the grass, others running and jumping; some playing bowls, others dancing and singing'. He ends with this significant note: 'What is most admirable, you see no gardeners, or men at work, and yet all is kept in such exquisite order, as if they did nothing else but work; it is so early in the morning, that all is despatched and done without the least confusion.'

The invisibility of workers was to be a particular ambition of owners of eighteenth-century landscape gardens. But already in the seventeenth century, as James Turner shows in *The Politics of Landscape* (1979), poets generally leave out any reference to the violent labours of the countryside: 'It takes some effort to appreciate what has been censored from the ideal landscape. There is virtually no mention of land-clearance, tree-felling, pruning, chopping, digging, hoeing, weeding, branding, gelding, slaughtering, salting, tanning, brewing, boiling, smelting, forging, milling, thatching, fencing and hurdle-making, hedging, road-mending and haulage. Almost everything which anybody *does* in the countryside is taboo.'

In *A Dialogue, (or Familiar Discourse) between the Husbandman, and Fruit-Trees* (1676) Ralph Austen objects to the gentleman's disdain of manual work, putting his view in the words of the Fruit Trees: 'The worke, and labour about us seems to be but a meane work, Young, proud Gentlemen thinke it a worke, and imployment much below them, to digg in the ground to set Trees; they account it too mechanical, and therefore have a kind of disdaine of such an imployment.' The Husbandman agrees with the Fruit Trees, but cites some exceptions such as Adam, 'Dioclesian Emperour of Roome', and 'Cyrus King of Persia' who 'was diligent, and most exact in this worke of Planting Fruit-trees; with his owne hand'.

The same case is made by John Evelyn in *A Discourse of Sallets* (1699), in which he states that many great men were interested in gardening. After performing 'the Noblest Exploits for the Publick, they sometimes chang'd their Sceptres for the Spade, and their Purple for the Gardiner's Apron'. They were concerned not only with grand ideas, such as 'the Philosophy of the Garden and Parterre', but also with more mundane subjects, such as 'Herbs, and wholesome Sallets'. He refers, for example, to the gardens belonging to Cicero, who used to 'prune, and water them with his own Hands'. According to Evelyn, less than one acre, 'skilfully Planted and Cultivated', is 'sufficient to furnish and entertain his Time and Thought all his Life long, with a most Innocent, Agreeable, and Useful Employment'.

In his *Directions for the Gardiner at Says-Court*, which he wrote over a period of years at the end of the seventeenth century, Evelyn outlines the first task of the gardener: 'The Gardiner should walke about the whole Gardens every Monday-morning duely, not omitting the least corner, and so observe what Flowers or Trees & plants want staking, binding and redressing, watering, or are in danger; especialy after great stormes, & high winds and then immediately to reforme, establish, shade, water &c what he finds amisse, before he go about any other work.' He describes the work of mowing and rolling in detail, advocating a two-week cycle of mowing to cover his 100-acre garden in Deptford. He also refers to the traditional role of the woman weeder: 'Note that whilst the Gardener rolls or Mowes, the Weder is to sweepe & clense in the same method, and never to be taken from that work 'til she have finished: first the gravell walkes & flower-bordures; then the kitchin-gardens; to go over all this she is allowed One moneth every three-moneths, with the Gardiners assistance of the haw, & rough digging, where curious hand-weeding is lesse necessary.'

John Rea, a nurseryman from Shropshire, wrote his *Flora, Ceres and Pomona* of 1665 in such a way that 'every person of any capacity may be enabled thereby to be his own gardener'. At the same time he assumes that his readers will be assisted by 'ordinary Labourers'.

It is these labourers who are referred to by implication in Andrew Mollet's *The Garden of Pleasure* (1670), when he writes that the lawn must be rolled every day and 'mowed at the least twice a week'. The garden walks also 'must be neatly kept by Weeding and Rouling of them daily with a stone Rouler'. In the Preface Mollet praises Louis XIII and his brother the Duke of Orleans, who 'disdained not to change the Scepter, sometimes for the Pruning knife'. But it is unlikely that they ever changed the pruning knife for the scythe or roller.

THE DIVISION OF LABOUR IN THE EIGHTEENTH CENTURY

At the beginning of the eighteenth century Stephen Switzer describes the gardener's job as 'one continued circle of labour and toil'. In *The Practical Kitchen Gardiner* (1727) he writes: 'Nor is it hard labour alone that will do', but also 'a continual preparation and foresight for what may befall him.' In other words, he also stresses 'the labour of the brain', and because of the complex nature of the work he wants the status and conditions of the gardener to be improved: 'I can't help considering a good Gardiner both as a philosopher and a politician, and one whose employ ought to place him very near the eye and favour of his master, and above that ill usage with which they commonly meet.'

In general in the eighteenth century the division of labour is explicit. Thomas Hale's *Eden: or, A Compleat Body of Gardening* (1757), later attributed to John Hill, contains the following distinction: 'We shall endeavour to inform the Gentleman and Mechanic together; to establish the one as the Head to plan and to conduct, and accomplish the other as the Hand to execute.' The book cost £1.16s., originally appearing in sixpenny weekly numbers, and claims to be the first book to use Linnaeus's system of plant classification.

The separate spheres of gentleman and gardener are further elaborated. Instructions for cultivating the useful products of the garden are given in simple language for the gardener, while the aesthetic concerns of the gentleman are expressed in a different style: 'Gardening is to be considered in a double Light; as it regards Products of Use, and those of Pleasure: these should be always perfectly distinguished; and they will be here treated in a separate Style. The Directions concerning the first, being such as the Gardener must understand, will be delivered in the most familiar Manner, and in the plainest Words: every Article respecting the Management of the Kitchen and Fruit Ground shall be thus explained. On the other hand, as the Names of Flowers and curious Plants are the proper knowledge of the Gentleman, they will be treated in the Manner of Science; and he will be taught to speak of them in proper Terms.'

The work that went into creating and maintaining eighteenth-century landscape gardens was prodigious. John Hill in *The Gardener's New Kalendar* (1758) recognises this when discussing their style: 'It is an air of irregularity we advise, not irregularity itself: there requires more art by far in this distribution, than in any other: and there requires afterwards the great additional labour of concealing it.'

William Cowper calls 'Capability' Brown, who was the main architect of these landscape upheavals, an 'omnipotent magician' and in *The Task* (1785) ironically catalogues his tricks:

> He speaks. The lake in front becomes a lawn,
> Woods vanish, hills subside, and vallies rise,
> And streams as if created for his use,
> Pursue the track of his directing wand
> Sinuous or strait, now rapid and now slow,
> Now murm'ring soft, now roaring in cascades,
> Ev'n as he bids.

The workers who carried out these transformations are only occasionally remembered. In her diary for 1776, Caroline Powys records her visit to Henry Hoare's Stourhead estate in Wiltshire: 'Fifty men are constantly employ'd in keeping the pleasure-grounds, rides, etc., in order, in all about 1000 acres.'

Ten years later Thomas Jefferson visited England and toured some of the famous landscape gardens in order to 'estimate the expense of making and maintaining a garden in that style'. At Stowe he found 'fifteen men and eighteen boys employed in keeping the pleasure grounds'; and he writes of Blenheim's 2,500 acres: 'Two hundred people employed to keep it in order, and to make alterations and additions. About fifty of these employed in pleasure grounds. The turf is mowed once in ten days.'

Batty Langley, who was an architect and garden designer, unintentionally reveals the exploitation of these gardeners when writing about tree planting in *A Sure Method of Improving Estates* (1728). He is trying to persuade land-owners of the profit they can make from timber, and is very precise about the expense. To clear land for sowing acorns, they will have to pay 4d. per rod within ten miles of London, and in more remote regions only 2d. or 3d. He also gives the exact cost of ploughing land, which is cheaper than many authors make out. His conclusion is that much profit is to be had from growing timber on estates near London, but 'where poor Mens Labour is much cheaper than there, the Expence will be much lesser, and consequently the Advantages greater'.

The wide-ranging nature of gardening work is evident in an aside by William Speechly, who was the son of a Northamptonshire farmer. In *A Treatise of the Culture of the Vine* (1790), he discusses the Syrian vine, which produces 'most astonishingly large bunches', and adds this footnote: 'In the year 1781, a bunch was produced at Welbeck that weighed 19 pounds and an half. It was presented by his Grace the Duke of Portland to the late Marquis of Rockingham, and was conveyed to Wentworth House (a distance of more than 20 miles) by four labourers, who carried it, suspended on a staff, in pairs, by turns. Its greatest diameter, when hanging in its natural position, was 19 inches and an half; its circumference four feet and an half; and its length 21 inches three quarters.'

NINETEENTH-CENTURY CATEGORIES OF GARDENER AND HARD LABOUR

Class was very explicit in the nineteenth century and within each class gradations of work and status were often clearly demarcated. The range of different kinds of gardening labour is well illustrated by John Loudon in his *Encyclopaedia of Gardening*. He distinguishes four groups engaged in the practice and pursuit of gardening, including tradesmen, designers and patrons. The remaining group he calls 'operators or serving gardeners' of which there are ten categories, from garden labourer to royal gardener: 'The garden labourer is the lowest grade in the scale of serving gardeners. He is occasionally employed to perform the common labours of gardening, as trenching, digging, hoeing, weeding, &c.: men for the more heavy, and women for the lighter employments. Garden labourers are not supposed to have received any professional instruction, farther than what they may have obtained by voluntary or casual observation. In all gardens where three or four professional hands are constantly employed, some labourers are required at extraordinary seasons.'

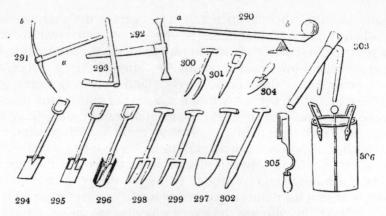

Implements of gardening, from John Loudon's
Encyclopaedia of Gardening, *first published in 1822.*

James MacPhail managed to move from the bottom to near the top of Loudon's list. He certainly knew about hard labour, for at the age of 17 he was a farm labourer in Aberdeenshire. Later he became 'Gardener and Steward' to the Earl of Liverpool and in 1803 wrote a book called *The Gardener's Remembrancer*. It is written for professionals and also for those who 'cannot afford to keep a gardener'. If the author's instructions are followed, readers may 'perform the work of their own gardens themselves, or direct a common labourer to do it for them'.

Frederick Mott, a wine merchant from Loughborough, also seems to have recognised at an early age the hard work involved in gardening. In 1843, when he was 18, he wrote *Flora Odorata*, a book about 'sweet-scented flowers and shrubs cultivated in the gardens of Great Britain'. He emphasises the importance of a tidy garden: 'The flower-garden must be kept in high order; those who will not take the trouble to attend to this, had much better have no garden at all, as nothing can look more slovenly than flower-beds covered with weeds, gravel walks carpeted with moss and grass, unmown lawns full of daisies and dandelions, or box edgings dead in some parts and six or eight inches high in others.'

In *The Indian Amateur Gardener* (c. 1880) Landolicus gives detailed labour requirements for gardening in India: 'For an ornamental irrigated area one man is sufficient to look after three acres, and for a non-irrigated area one man is sufficient to look after ten acres. For nursery ground half an acre per man.'

The author gives instructions on how to construct irrigation channels alongside the vegetable plots, but clearly does not expect English gardeners themselves to carry out his manuring advice: 'The use of liquid manure will be found of great benefit to the majority of crops and a

Illustration from William Barron's The British Winter Garden *(1852).*
This 100-year-old yew tree, 14 feet square and 18 feet high,
had been brought to Elvaston Castle from 25 miles away.

good way of supplying this is to get a man to rub up cow-dung between
his hands into the running water at the head of the channel.'

In *The British Winter Garden* (1852), William Barron, head gardener
at Elvaston Castle, describes the work involved in moving large trees,
on which he was an authority. His aim is to show how quickly and easily
it can be done: 'Eight men and five or six horses have been sent several
miles, starting early in the morning, and have brought a large tree
home in the evening of the same day, without any previous preparation having been given to the tree.'

Lawn-mowing

Well after the invention of the lawn-mower in 1830, the hard work of
scything lawns continued, as Robert Thompson confirms in 1859. In
The Gardener's Assistant he still recommends using the scythe 'where
there are many trees, flower-beds, or grass terraces; but in extensive lawns,
it is much more cheaply done by a mowing machine drawn by a horse.

Illustration from William Barron's The British Winter Garden *(1852), of a yew 'luxuriating and feeding upon its own decayed trunk'. The tree, many centuries old and 33 feet high, had been replanted at Elvaston Castle in Derbyshire.*

Small machines worked by two or three men are not on the whole considered much more economical than the scythe in good hands.'

Scything was a skilled job: 'Nothing but a considerable amount of practice will make a man a good mower.' Skill was needed to 'make the edge of the scythe throughout its whole length sweep at a uniform height above the surface, instead of paring it in places, and thus leaving the face of the lawn marked for days with numerous unsightly scars.' Gathering up the cuttings also had to be carried out meticulously:

'Sweeping should be done so as not to leave any portions of cut grass to wither, for such become tough, and will obstruct the edge of the scythe at the next mowing.'

Scything. Wood engraving by Clare Leighton from her book
Four Hedges: A Gardener's Chronicle *(1935) by permission of David Leighton.*

In the same decade, however, others were singing the praises of the mowing machine. In *The National Garden Almanack* by John Edwards (1854), Alexander Shanks & Son, from Arbroath in Forfarshire, advertise an improved machine for mowing grass, which mowed, rolled and collected the cuttings at the same time. The advertisement includes glowing testimonials concerning previous machines, particularly from the royal gardens and from chief gardeners, one of whom claims a 'saving of labour of seventy per cent'. Charles McIntosh, the gardening writer and chief gardener to the Duke of Buccleuch, says that 'the expense of the Machine will be saved in one year'.

Also in this book Lord Kinnaird, from Rossie Priory in Inchture, writes with great exactitude of the cost of labour which he is saving: 'I shall have much pleasure at all times in recommending your Mowing Machine, as answering most perfectly in every respect, as I have had some months' trial of it, and find that a man and horse, and one woman, can cut and clean up upwards of two acres and a half in seven hours, while it formerly took four men and three women nearly three days to put the same ground in order.' The chief gardener to the Duke of Athol shows that he can make an even greater saving, putting more people out of work: 'On our level ground and grass walks we can cut with the Machine in one day, nearly as much as eighteen men can cut with scythes.'

Later in the century Charles Kingsley makes a similar point: 'There is that boy, fresh from the National School, cutting more grass in a day than six strong mowers could have cut, and cutting it better, too; for the mowing-machine goes so much nearer to the ground than the scythe, that we gain by it two hundredweight of hay on every acre.' In *Madam How and Lady Why* (1870), a book for boys, he goes on to ask: 'But if the machine cuts all the grass, the poor mowers will have nothing to do.' The sanguine reply comes back: 'Not so. They are all busy enough elsewhere. There is plenty of other work to be done, thank God; and wholesomer and easier work than mowing with a burning sun on their backs, drinking gallons of beer, and getting first hot then cold across the loins, till they lay in a store of lumbago and sciatica, to cripple them in their old age.'

UNEMPLOYMENT

Despite this optimistic view of employment prospects for redundant mowers, it is at least a realistic account of work in the countryside. With the move to the towns, following the Industrial Revolution, many criticisms were made of the harsh working conditions in the factories. Sometimes, however, they were contrasted with a romantic view of rural labour.

Anne Pratt, for example, in 1838 compares the 'pale artisan', shut up in a room all day, with the 'cheerful employment' of the peasant: 'Labour such as his seems to be a blessing to him who is engaged in it; placing him in scenes where all that is fair is around him, and affording him that exercise so conducive to health and cheerfulness.' In *Flowers and their Associations* (1840), she describes the work of the peasant child: 'His labours are fitted to inspire him with cheerful feelings, and he drives the birds from the field, or wanders with the cattle down the green lane, or otherwise joins in rustic employ, with as light a heart as the morning bird or the evening grashopper.'

George Glenny is more accurate in his assessment of rural employment and unemployment. Much gardening work is seasonal. He reminds landowners that 'the winter of 1848 and 1849 will be a season of awful suffering among the labouring classes, unless they are employed, and therefore, that it behoves every gentleman who can improve his estate by labour, to engage it by all means'. In his *Garden Almanac* of 1849, he goes on to explain that 'a whole village may be saved from incalculable suffering, by the engagement of a few labourers through the winter'. He repeats this appeal to noblemen and gentlemen in *Gardening for the Million* (1849). Earlier, in 1838, Glenny had set up the Benevolent Society for the Relief of Aged Gardeners.

George Johnson (1852) is also more realistic in his comments on the conditions of work of gardeners. He wants to protect them from working in all weathers and so help to safeguard their health: 'The under gardeners, though necessarily hardy, and the open air is their appropriate whereabouts, should have work assigned to them appropriate to the clemency or inclemency of the season; for no men are more liable to suffer early in life from rheumatism.'

Likewise the myth of the cottage garden is undermined by Robert Adamson. In *The Cottage Garden* (1856) he is more concerned with practicalities than romance: 'A portion of the garden ought to be allotted for, and occupied with the following conveniences, a small tool-house, washing-house, pig-sty, privy, and dung-pit – it being impossible that any cottager and his family can be comfortable where any of the above requisites are unprovided.' The cottager needs information which is 'useful, practical and economical'. The author stresses neatness and hard work: 'Wage a constant war against all weeds.' Even in December there is work for the cottager to do, 'putting in proper order all the various tools used in the cultivation of the cottage garden'. Also this is the time for him to study the seed catalogues and other gardening literature: 'He can be much edified and instructed by the perusal of such cheap publications as those which treat on the subject.'

Despite the prevalence of casual work for gardeners, one area where there was usually permanent work was in market gardening, especially in propagating plants. Nevertheless the work was very hard, as C.W. Shaw explains in *The London Market Gardens* (1879): 'Propagating is carried on with wonderful skill and rapidity, and a man well versed in such work is seldom out of employment. Everything done in such establishments is done at high pressure, everybody is in a hurry, and the work performed in one day in such places would surprise many a young gardener in a private establishment who thinks himself overworked.'

The market gardens during this period were gradually spreading out further from the centre of London, due to high rents and because the land was needed for building and for the extension of the railways. But there were still some family businesses in London which could provide a 'fair livelihood'. Shaw describes one market garden in Tottenham of less than an acre which benefited from the personal involvement of its workers: 'All the labour connected with the place is performed by members of the family, and to this fact may be attributed to some extent the satisfactory results that are obtained, each having a personal interest in the business.'

PAY AND CONDITIONS OF WORK

The conditions of work of gardeners have normally been harsh: long hours and low pay, often with the added insecurity of casual work.

Samuel Gilbert (1682), for instance, refers to the precariousness of the gardener's employment in the seventeenth century, stating that gentlemen who do not understand gardening 'either hire ill Gardiners, or if they light of a good one, but for a year, who not sure of his stay hath no encouragement, does not, or if he endeavour'd, could not in that time bring his designs to perfection'. He argues that these gentlemen ought to take advice from those who understand gardening. When they employ a good gardener, they should 'give him assurance of his stay for five or six years' and also provide him with the proper resources for the job.

Living conditions for gardeners could be atrocious. On big estates they usually had to live next to the gardens. In *Modern Eden: or, The Gardener's Universal Guide* (1767), Rutter and Carter explain why this was necessary: 'It is always best for the gardener to have his lodging on the spot, if that can be done with any convenience; for small accidents, if not seen and remedied in time, often bring on great mischief.' The implication is that the gardener has to be on duty more or less 24 hours a day.

They go on to discuss the gardener's apartment which seems to be of less importance than the area in the same building which is set aside for tools and seeds: 'A very slight structure will do for this; or any old building that is upon the spot may be used for the purpose. If the gardener's bed-room be upon the upper floor, all the rest may be managed below with little expence or trouble.'

In the nineteenth century, with the phenomenal growth in the population of London, market gardens grew very rapidly around the edges of the city. According to Henry Phillips, in *Pomarium Britannicum* (1820), there were 6,000 acres of them within twelve miles of the centre. These gardens provided jobs, but some of them were seasonal, particularly the women's: 'It is gratifying to see the number of hands this ground employs. Even during the six winter months, it is computed that it affords work to five persons an acre, and at least double that number for the summer months, who are principally females.'

Gardeners' pay has often been a bone of contention. The implication from Stephen Switzer (1715) is that sometimes they were not paid at all. He advises noblemen and gentlemen, when designing their estates, to set aside enough money to pay their gardeners. Otherwise they may be in for trouble and their rural relaxation disturbed: 'Labourers unpaid are of course the most impertinent, troublesome Persons that can be, and by their Clamour, Noise, and Thievery occasion a very large Allay in, and Discount from the Pleasures of a Country Life.'

Gardener's wages have always been low. In 1838, for example, according to Loudon, they were 4s. to 4s. 6d. a day, half those of a bricklayer. John Edwards, in *The National Garden Almanack* of 1854, warns of the danger of strikes if florists and gardeners are not properly rewarded for their work. As a member of the National Floricultural Society, he encourages his readers to subscribe to the Gardeners' Benevolent Institute: 'There daily and hourly exists sorry and heart rending wants beyond the power of this Society to relieve.' He goes on to deplore 'that with so many claimants so few can be comforted in the winter of their long life'.

In *The Plain Path to Good Gardening* (1871) Samuel Wood describes the kitchen gardens attached to villas and cottages, where the work is 'generally committed to a jobbing man, who may be a very indifferent hand, or if a good hand, is so badly paid that justice cannot be done'. The job was peripatetic, for the gardener 'must attend six or seven such places within the week to make anything like a living'.

Likewise in *Town and Home Gardening* (1893) Edith Chamberlain explains how residents in small squares keep up the garden by paying a subscription. The results are unsatisfactory because they 'make a contract with a gardener on terms which are often so low as to preclude any possibility (if only they knew it) of justice being done, or the place being kept in a sightly condition'.

Henrietta Batson, in *A Book of the Country and the Garden* (1903), describes how her regular gardener leaves after several years, 'tempted by a large wage', and goes to Northumberland, though he later returns. In the meantime she expresses the usual complaints at the difficulty in hiring a good gardener: 'We tried five in our unhappy year. One drank; a second neglected his work; others proved impossible in various respects. The last was an admirable gardener, but he never succeeded in living on speaking terms with more than one person at a time, his temper being execrable.'

Nevertheless she does put in a good word for the garden boy: 'It has often struck me as odd that no one has ever written about the garden boy.' One reason is that he was often invisible: 'He is of so little importance in many establishments that I believe there are countless employers who do not even know that they have a garden boy.'

Henrietta Batson's house and garden in Hoe Benham, Berkshire, from A Book of the Country and the Garden *(1903).*

Even skilled head gardeners were badly paid. In *The Herbaceous Garden* (1913) Alice Martineau protests at their average pay of a guinea a week: 'Gardeners' wages are on the whole very inadequate. Much is expected of them; not only hard and constant work in all weathers, but knowledge and artistic feeling, and taste.'

For a head gardener with eight or nine men under him, 30 to 35 shillings was considered a good wage. She summarises the qualities needed: 'He needs to be a good business man, as often there is fruit to be marketed; and yet he has to have an insight into things artistic and beautiful. He must be a good disciplinarian, and manage his men well, to say nothing of finding them. He has a long and arduous training from boyhood in many branches, and yet he gets considerably lower wages than a chauffeur who has perhaps learned his business by driving for six months.' She thinks it a 'wonderful thing that these

Henrietta Batson's gardener, garden boy and carrier,
from A Book of the Country and the Garden *(1903).*

able, intelligent men can be found for a payment so out of all proportion
to their ability', and concludes: 'Little wonder that they die poor men,
often leaving wife and family totally unprovided for.' In *The Secrets of
Many Gardens* (1924) she makes a similar point: 'In many cases gardeners
are none too well paid for the class of men they are – able, active, and
experienced.'

Charles Thonger, in *The Book of the Cottage Garden* (1909), recognises
the tiring work that has to be carried out in the large gardens of the
rich: 'The taint of money is everywhere – tons of soil removed from one
spot to another; terraces and balustrades glittering with newness;

artificial lakes on elevated ground; fountains playing; exotics, which in winter must be sheltered in heated structures, dotting the lawns and stairways. There is no peace or rest in such gardens. An army of men is constantly at work, sweeping, trimming, clipping, tidying – an endless round of wearisome and profitless labour. We forget the garden in the stupendous prospect of the wages bill.'

During the Second World War W.J.C. Lawrence warns his young readers of the long hours and hard work for which they should be prepared. In *The Young Gardener* (1943) he writers: 'It is not likely that your working day will be much shorter than 7 a.m. to 5 p.m. and sometimes you may have to work through week-ends. You will have to do rough and dirty jobs and you must face up to hard study for a number of years.'

Servants

Traditionally gardeners have been treated as servants and the arrogance of their employers has sometimes been very evident. At the end of the seventeenth century Timothy Nourse sees them as part of 'our Common People', many of whom are 'very rough and savage in their Disposition, being of levelling Principles, and refractory to Government, insolent and tumultuous'. In *Campania Foelix, or A Discourse of the Benefits and Improvements of Husbandry* (1700), published a year after his death, he offers this advice to his gentlemen readers: 'The best way therefore will be to bridle them, and to make them feel the Spur too, when they begin to play their Tricks, and kick.'

Nourse was a well-known preacher, who became a Roman Catholic in 1672. Writing from his estate in Newent, Gloucestershire, he gives his considered view of servants: 'What I shall write concerning them, is not out of Prejudice or Passion, but from a disinterested Spirit, and upon manifest Experience; for I dare boldly affirm, that there is not a more insolent and proud, a more untractable, perfidious, and a more churlish sort of People breathing than the Generality of our Servants.'

We tend to forget how many maids, servants and gardeners were employed in the nineteenth century, when even lower-middle-class people kept a servant. In 1871, according to Eric Hobsbawm in *Industry and Empire*, there were 1.4 million domestic servants in the United Kingdom out of a population of 35.3 million. In York 29 per cent of the population had servants. Harold Perkin, in *The Rise of Professional Society*, claims that the figure rose even higher. In 1891 one in six of the labour force was a servant and in 1911 the total peaked at two million.

The number of gardeners employed as domestic servants increased from about 75,000 in 1881 to nearly 120,000 by 1911.

In 1851 the anonymous author of *Every Lady's Guide to Her Own Greenhouse* explains how she used two servants just to help her look after her indoor plants: 'I have always found that, with the aid of a man-servant, who, although perfectly ignorant of gardening and plants, was always ready to work where I was directing, and the still more frequent assistance of a female domestic, I could get through all the labour of managing my indoor plants.'

Alicia Amherst's (1902) family must have had many servants, though she herself learnt about hard work when making her childhood garden: 'My wild garden was mostly such poor, sandy soil that not only had I to dig hard, but I was given a wheelbarrow, and I used to carry away loads of stone and sand and get leaf-mould, from the gardeners' leaf-heap, to mix with the sand that was left.' Nevertheless she counts on there being several gardeners around to help: 'If you look at the gardeners in the hot-houses, if there are any at your home, you will find them now taking cuttings from the dahlias. The roots, which have been dried and stored all the winter, are put with a little earth and sand in heat, and cuttings made of the young shoots that spring up. If you have room in your garden, and are really taking care of it, I feel sure you could persuade the gardener to put in a few more cuttings than he wants and let you have them.' John Sedding (1891) likewise assumes 'a bevy of workmen, horses and carts' to transform a given 'acre or two of land' to make a garden.

In a chapter on the herb garden, written in 1908, E.T. Cook takes it for granted that there will be maids in the household. He recalls the olden days when 'the culture and culling of simples was as much a part of female education as the preserving and tying down of "rasps and apricocks"'. Then he writes: 'To those who cannot give up room for a whole herb garden, my advice is, have a border of herbs; let it be near the kitchen, and teach the maids to use it.'

Writing during the First World War, H.H. Thomas assumes his readers will want to hire labour for the hard initial work of creating a garden. *In Gardening: A Complete Guide* (1917) he realises that the cost of labour has increased in the previous two years, but it should still be available at 6d. an hour: 'A piece of ground 20 yards long and 10 yards wide would cost 8s. to dig; such an area requires two loads of manure, thus increasing the cost by 12s., including the labour of getting it on the ground, making a total expense of £1.'

The twentieth century, however, saw a rapid decline in servants, particularly after the First World War, when Marion Cran (1921) writes: 'Nowadays we look back on the many servants of pre-war days without regret, but at first the shortage of domestic labour pressed heavily not in mine alone, but also in countless other British homes; we had always had cheap and plentiful labour in these isles; the leisured women were quite untrained and unprepared for housework, unlike Canada, Australia and the United States, where the problem has been faced from the first with sound common sense.' Her last domestic servant had gone to work in a munitions factory, though she still had a gardener who was too old to enlist. She had to learn how to boil a potato, while the gardener's wife gradually taught her the principles of housework.

Between the wars many people employed a gardener on a casual basis, as Minnie Pallister explains in *Gardener's Frenzy* (1933): 'Most of us cannot afford a real gardener, with college training and diplomas, who lords it over underlings and employer alike. We have to be satisfied with one of the jobbing variety who comes once a week, or fortnight, according to the state of the exchequer.'

As late as 1940, however, Stephen Cheveley still assumes his readers will have a maid. In *A Garden Goes to War* he poses the key question: 'What vegetables are required for a family consisting of man and wife, two children, and a maid?'

After the Second World War labour was short, as were food supplies. In *Gardener's Medley*, published in 1951, Major C.S. Jarvis describes the situation: 'Owing to the uncertainty of every form of supplies, it is essential to grow everything that one needs and today in England I have the added difficulty of shortage of labour, which did not worry me in the East.' He is referring to his own desert gardening experiences, proudly announcing that he made one garden in Libya and two in the Sinai, where he was governor of a province and where there was an unlimited supply of labour from the local prison: 'In El Arish a ring on the telephone was all that was necessary to obtain the services within some ten minutes of forty hefty labourers, most of them with knowledge of gardening, so that the digging over of an acre of virgin land, or the construction of a new drive, was a matter of no consequence, and completed almost as soon as projected.' The unpaid prisoners were rewarded with cigarettes.

In 1947 Montagu Allwood comments on the country's labour force: 'English work-people are good, but they can, and do become lazy if there is not strict supervision.' He puts it down to 'too much "spoon-feeding" by trade unions'. Some gardeners he praises, though he utters a damning indictment of others: 'But all gardeners are not good; many are a disgrace to their calling, being lazy, avaricious, often thieves, and not infrequently liars.'

GARDENING FOR ONESELF

Gardening writers often celebrate the pleasure in gardening for oneself. At the height of the eighteenth-century landscape garden, for example, the poet William Cowper in *The Task*, expresses his delight in doing his own gardening:

> Friends, books, a garden, and perhaps his pen,
> Delightful industry enjoy'd at home,
> And Nature, in her cultivated trim
> Dress'd to his taste, inviting him abroad –
> Can he want occupation who has these?

In the previous century, in *A New Orchard and Garden* (1618), William Lawson contrasts employing gardeners, so losing some of the profits, and gardening for oneself, with the consequent hard work: 'If you bee not able, nor willing to hyre a gardner, keepe your profites to your selfe, but then you must take all the paines.' Next to the frontispiece of three gardeners, who are planting and pruning fruit trees, he has inscribed: 'Skill and paines bring fruitfull gaines.'

Making an orchard, from William Lawson's
A New Orchard and Garden, *first published in 1618.*

Ralph Austen also wants to encourage people to grow their own fruit trees, but he recognises the difficulties involved for tenants with no security of tenure. In *A Treatise of Fruit-Trees* (1657) he writes that landlords should encourage their tenants to plant fruit trees 'by assuring them, that so doing they should enjoy the same so long (or have such other recompence) as might be a sufficient encouragement to them to labour there about; but when Tenants feare, and suspect, that the more they labour herein, and improve their Livings by such meanes, the sooner they shall remove out of it, they have little reason to stirre a foote towards such a worke'.

Similar problems relating to cottagers gardening for themselves are raised by Edward Hobday in *Cottage Gardening* (1877). Like Austen, Hobday encourages them to grow fruit trees: 'I fail to see why every man who has ground enough to plant half-a-dozen Apple trees should not do so; in fact, I should like to see every cottage gardener turn his attention more than is now done to fruit culture, not only to supply the wants of his family, but also where favourably situated for the purpose of adding to his income.' The difficulty is, however, that they do not usually own the property: 'But there is one great drawback to men of slender means planting fruit trees. The moment a tree is planted the planter, if an ordinary tenant, loses all right of property in it.' Because of insecurity of tenure 'some other person may step in and reap the benefit'.

Hobday recognises that some owners of cottage property supply their tenants with fruit trees, but 'much, very much more might be done in this direction'. He suggests that landlords should take the responsibility for planting suitable fruit trees in their cottage gardens.

Middle-class tenure was more secure and in *How to Lay Out a Small Garden* (1850) Edward Kemp writes of 'how few there are among the middle classes who do not possess a small garden'. But it was Jane Loudon who actually encouraged middle-class women to garden for themselves. It was a significant move of hers to stress in *Instructions in Gardening for Ladies* (1840) the importance of working with one's hands: 'The great point is to exercise our own skill and ingenuity; for we all feel so much more interested in what we do ourselves than in what is done for us, that no lady is likely to become fond of gardening who does not do a great deal with her own hands.'

Edwin Cooling, a nurseryman in Derby, writes to encourage cottagers to garden for themselves, in particular to profit from keeping bees. In *The Domestic Gardener's Assistant* (1837) he points out, however, that 'the wages of labourers are too low to enable them to purchase a swarm, especially where they have families'. His solution is to persuade the nobility and gentry to provide them for each cottager, 'or bestow them as a reward for superior industry', since bee-keeping is 'a healthful and profitable amusement to this useful and laborious class of men'.

For Elizabeth Watts, gardening is a job for the whole family, though with a suggested division of labour. In *Vegetables and How to Grow Them*

(1866) she also argues that this saves money: 'No gentleman who loves his fruit-trees as we do should leave the pruning of them to a gardener; no gardener's fingers can prick out young plants of cabbages, celery, lettuces, and such like, with the same chance of their doing well that they will have if young ladies' delicate soft little dexterous hands undertake the job; and careful active industrious children are first rate weeders. In any family where the expense of a gardener is an item worth considering, all the sowing, planting, hoeing, raking, pruning, and weeding may be done by the family; and where is there so pleasant a sight as the members of one family all working together, united in the pursuit of health, enjoyment, and more enjoyable garden produce than money can get? Then it will only be necessary to hire for digging, mowing, and such jobs as ladies and gentlemen would not like to undertake.'

Mrs Earle and Ethel Case (1912) stress the importance of doing the work oneself: 'Gardening to a certain extent must be done by oneself, or one never gets a real interest in it. I remember some years ago taking some seedlings to a neighbour, and I said, "They must be put in at once"; she replied, "Oh! I am sorry, my man is just gone." I answered, "Give me a trowel, and I will put them in." This gave her the idea, as she told me afterwards, that she could do things for herself, and she is now an excellent gardener.'

Eleanour Rohde expresses her agreement with this view in the Preface to *A Vegetable Grower's Handbook* (1922), which she wrote with Fanny Bennett: 'One cannot help feeling that those who do not work in their own garden know very little of the joys of gardening. It must be very poor fun to own a ten-acre garden, for instance, and not be allowed to work in it!'

Marion Cran (1925) emphasises using one's own hands in gardening: 'I do not think I care much for the delicate white hands which are so much admired in novels: "lily-white with rosy nails". I like the hands which are browned with sun and hard with all the giving of themselves to any sort of work – they are rich hands, hard, knotted, beautiful, generous hands. Rich with work done ...'

Just as middle-class women often complained about the behaviour of working-class gardeners, so did middle-class men. In *Cordon Training of Fruit Trees* (1860) the Rev. T. Collings Bréhaut wants to help everyone to be his '"own gardener", and be thus liberated from a degrading dependence on the caprice of unskilled men'.

Henry Bright concludes *The English Flower Garden* (1881) by encouraging his readers to become involved in gardening, though mainly on the management side: 'The garden will soon grow dull, and the flowers lose their attraction, unless we take the management, partly at least,

into our own hands, and be masters not in name but in reality.' Part
of his concern, however, is to make sure that the gardener carries out
the owner's orders: 'We are too often the absolute slaves of our gardeners,
and they in turn (of course I am not speaking of exceptions) are too
often the slaves of an unintelligent routine.'

This is also the argument of the Rev. Paterson in *The Manse Garden*
(1836). He criticises hired gardeners for their stereotyped work and for
not carrying out instructions. His solution is to learn about gardening
oneself, thus having no need to rely on expensive gardeners. Then one
can manage with only an unskilled labourer: 'Know a little of the thing
yourself, and with the help of a common labourer, you have time and
tide in your hands.'

Samuel Graveson is wary of unskilled gardeners, however, expressing
the following complaint in *My Villa Garden* (1915): 'I discovered that
the simple-minded man who is employed to cut the lawn had exceeded
his instruction – not for the first time either – and four choice plants
from one of the adjoining beds had been consigned to the dustheap.
He thought they were weeds!' Although his garden only measures
'approximately twenty-five feet wide by one hundred feet long', he still
employs gardeners. He exhibits a master's contempt for his servant,
meditating 'gloomily on the crass stupidity of some of the men we employ
to tidy up our gardens'.

Mrs Boyle's solution is to have a regular gardener and give him a
measure of freedom in the garden. In 1895 she pays tribute to her
gardener 'Jesse Foulk, by whose rare skill this plot grew into a Garden
of Pleasure, whose ceaseless care has maintained its charm for three-
and-twenty summers, and who completes the Thirtieth year of his
devoted service on the 22nd of May'. She offers the following advice
to other employers: 'Give him a free hand over all affairs which come
specially under his control. Give him a living interest in the garden by
letting him exercise his taste (subject always to yours), in planting and
in arrangement of colours, etc., and by showing your own constant
interest in it.'

Maude Haworth-Booth, on the other hand, did all her planting
herself. Her book *My Garden Diary* (1934) is written expressly for
gardeners like herself, not for those with large gardens, nor for those
who employ many gardeners. Her only help has come from God and
she is proud to proclaim: 'In this garden of mine no plant is there that
I have not planted with my own hands, except the seedlings which God
blew here and there.'

Many gardening writers have overcome physical disabilites in their
gardening. The most famous are John Loudon, who had his arm
amputated, and Gertrude Jekyll, who had very poor eyesight, her natural

focus being only two inches. Another is H.J. Massingham, who lost the use of an arm and a leg in an accident. In *This Plot of Earth: A Gardener's Chronicle* (1944) he reveals the resulting pain and pleasure: 'Do I enjoy cutting grass edges with but one natural leg and one useful arm? No, but I love to see the straight line when it is done and that straight line is the measure of a well-tended garden.'

SIZE OF GARDEN

The recommended size of a garden depends on the historical period and it varies, of course, according to class. Pliny records that, in the earliest days of Rome, 'just over an acre was enough land for the Roman people and no one had more'. But in the first century, when he was writing, he notes the change, with one of his typical attacks on avarice: 'Now they want fish-ponds larger than that, and we are lucky if they do not want kitchens covering a larger area.'

According to H.J. Massingham (1944), it was 'Elizabethan law that every labourer's cottage should have four acres of land'. Sir William Temple, in 'Of Gardening in the Year 1685', thinks that a garden of between four and eight acres is sufficient also for any gentleman, and 'will furnish as much of all that is expected from it, as any nobleman will have occasion to use in his family'. He argues in 'The Garden of the Ancients' that gardens appeal to all classes of people: 'As it has been the inclination of kings, and the choice of philosophers, so it has been the common favourite of public and private men; a pleasure of the greatest, and the care of the meanest; and indeed an employment and a possession, for which no man is too high nor too low.' His words, however, almost hide the fact that ownership and consumption ('possession' and 'pleasure') often belong to one class of people, and the labour ('care' and 'employment') is usually done by another class.

Samuel Fullmer gives an indication of how the kitchen garden varied in size in the eighteenth century according to class. In *The Young Gardener's Best Companion* (1781) he advises that, 'for a family of fashion, much less than an acre will be insufficient'. A half or a quarter of an acre would be 'sufficient for some middling or small families', but 'some families of rank, have kitchen gardens from two or three, to six or eight acres'. He adds that 'a garden of about an acre will nearly employ one man almost the year round'.

At the beginning of the nineteenth century John Loudon also grades gardens according to the class structure of English society. He is particularly keen to ensure that labourers have gardens of an adequate size attached to their cottages. He recommends in his *Encyclopaedia of*

Gardening that the space needed for the house and garden of a man and wife with no children is no less than an eighth of an acre. His idea of a 'smaller suburban garden' was between an eighth and half an acre, corresponding with the size of his own garden in Bayswater.

Many people in the nineteenth century suffered a complete loss of land due to increasing urbanisation. This is described by Alexander Dean in *Vegetable Culture* (1896): 'With the enormous increase in population that has been evidenced during the latter half of the present century, it has been found needful to erect cottages in immense numbers that have no gardens, indeed vast numbers of our working population have thus, as it were, been absolutely severed from the land.'

Dean was a seed grower and lectured on vegetable culture for Surrey County Council. He founded the National Vegetable Society and wrote a weekly gardening column for *Reynolds News*. His solution to 'the land hunger of the mass of the people' is to support 'that great movement in favour of the creation of allotment gardens which has become one of the chief social features of the age'. He thinks that garden plots of '20 to 40 rods in area' (one-eighth to one-quarter of an acre) are usually sufficient, and 'rarely is it the case that these plots are not admirably cultivated and cropped. It seems to matter little what may be a worker's vocation, gardening appears to come to him almost instinctively.'

In *Allotment Farming for the Many* (1856) Robert Errington vividly contrasts the moral effects of possessing and not possessing a garden: 'Whilst the cottager, who occupies a mere hovel without a garden, is all torpidity and indifference, the allotment holder, who takes a pride in his plot, is all animation. The latter feels he has a stake in the country, whilst the monotony of the day-dreams of the former is scarcely disturbed by anything but the thoughts of the poor-law union or the almshouse.'

Errington was a gardener at Oulton Park in Cheshire and was aware of the great 'distress among the labouring classes'. He objected to people warning of over-population, however, because there was plenty of land to develop, for instance 'the roadside garden of the sluggard, choked with weeds, half-dug, half-manured, a prey to devouring insects, stray animals, and neglect'.

He writes of the allotment holder with a nice garden 'of from a quarter to half an acre' and continues the contrast between him and those without gardens: 'His children will have been taught and made to work many an hour, when the children of the former class have been lounging about lanes, pillaging sticks out of every hedge, robbing orchards, or, if nigh a village, dawdling about the village green, or congregating in nooks and corners, to the moral corruption of each other.'

While many working-class people were being forced to move off the land in the nineteenth century, Edward Kemp records the simultaneous acquisition of land by the middle classes with their increasing ownership of gardens. He argues in *How to Lay Out a Small Garden* (1850) that, although he does not want to 'shut out a smaller but higher or more wealthy class', his book is 'clearly required by the multitude, for how few there are among the middle classes who do not possess a small garden'. His idea of a small garden, however, is 'From a Quarter of an Acre to Thirty Acres in extent', and he thinks that a quarter of an acre is 'the very extreme of smallness'.

The aim of *The Garden that Paid the Rent* (1860), by an anonymous author, is to show how an acre of garden devoted mainly to fruit and vegetables can produce a profit. In the same year a similarly anonymous country parson from Fordington vicarage writes of how he managed with half an acre. In fact his garden was only a tenth of an acre, but he also had use of the churchyard. This was an acre in size, but as it contained many tombstones, being the burial place of 3,000 people, it left him just half an acre of pasture for his cows. In his book, *My Kitchen Garden; My Cows, and Half an Acre of Pasture*, he states that 'from these three sources combined, I and my family have for some years derived a good supply of vegetables, fruit, and milk'. His garden also benefited from the churchyard as he used the cow manure to fertilise it.

Alfred Smee had a garden of eight acres. In *My Garden: Its Plan and Culture* (1872) he gives a thorough account of it, including the history and geology of the area in which it was situated. It contained nearly 300 varieties of apple trees and he announces: 'Every garden ought to have at least thirty kinds of dessert apples, so as to command a variety of flavour and a constant succession.' Needless to say he had a gardener to do most of the work.

William Paul also expects his middle-class readers will 'require a gardener, either occasionally or constantly'. In *Villa Gardening* (1876) he assumes 'the possession of two-and-a-half acres of land'. This is made up of an acre of flower garden, half an acre of kitchen garden, and a meadow of one acre which may be an orchard or a park.

On the other hand, Andrew Meikle, originally from Edinburgh, writes 'chiefly for the industrial classes'. When he was a gardener at Read Hall, Whalley, in Lancashire, he addressed his 'fellow-working men' in *Window Gardening for Town and Country* (1870). Later, when working at Clifton Nursery, Maida Hill, in west London, he wrote *The Cottage Garden* (1874), in which he discusses the size of garden: 'From 400 to 600 yards of ground is sufficient to make a very nice sized cottage garden, and will be found quite large enough for anyone who has other daily work on hand to manage properly without calling in the jobbing gardener. In

fact, a little garden ten yards square would far more likely be attended
with greater pleasure than one of larger dimension, where the owner
could not give the time nor spare the expense for its cultivation.'

'Lawn Mower', from William Paul's Villa Gardening *(1876).*

Changes in the Twentieth Century

At the beginning of the twentieth century large gardens employing many
gardeners were still quite common. W.H. Divers, in *Spring Flowers at Belvoir
Castle* (1909), for example, is clearly writing about one of Fullmer's
'families of rank'. The author was head gardener to the Duke of Rutland
and he describes his employer's kitchen garden of seven acres, with 120
varieties of pear and 160 varieties of apple. Two and three-quarter acres
were allotted to vegetable culture, providing for 'the family and a large
number of servants and other persons throughout the year; the total
number when the family is in residence often amounts to 130 persons'.

This aristocratic ownership of land is discussed by Thomas Smith in
The Profitable Culture of Vegetables (1911), which was written for 'Market
Gardeners, Small Holders, and Others'. Smith was born in 1857 and left
school at the age of nine to become an apprentice to a Manchester printer.
His radical views are immediately evident in the dedication: 'This book
is dedicated by the author to his friend, Joseph Fels, in admiration of
the gallant fight he is making throughout the world to break down the
monopoly in land.' Fels was an American businessman who worked with
George Lansbury to found the first farm colony for the unemployed in

the East End of London, after 1,000 women had marched from Mile End to Westminster in support of the scheme. He helped Margaret McMillan establish her school clinic in Deptford and wanted to extend nature study in schools to include the theory and practice of gardening.

Thomas Smith (1911) quotes Goldsmith at the beginning of his book:

> Ill fares the land, to hast'ning ills a prey,
> Where wealth accumulates and men decay.

He also refers to Kropotkin's *Fields, Factories and Workshops* in which the Russian anarchist claims that, if the land in the United Kingdom were properly cultivated, it could provide food for 80 million people. Smith attacks the nineteenth-century depopulation of rural districts and strongly advocates the adoption of French gardening with its intensive culture, whereby a gardener could harvest 'six or seven crops in the season from the same soil'.

At the beginning of this century English horticulturists had visited gardens in Paris and, as a result, gardens in the French style were laid out in 1905 at Evesham in Worcestershire and in 1906 at Mayland in Essex, as well as in various other places. Smith concludes: 'Working men who have small gardens might, with great advantage, imitate many of the methods of the French gardener.' All that was needed was a quarter of an acre, representing 'the maximum area which one average man can manage on this system'.

John Weathers also argues for each house to have sufficient land attached to it. In *A Practical Guide to School, Cottage, and Allotment Gardening* (1908) he remarks on the decline in the size of the cottage garden: 'Sometimes cottage gardens may be from twenty to forty yards in length in old-fashioned places, by rarely more than four or five yards in width. The modern cottage garden cannot boast of anything like these dimensions, and many of them do not exceed six or seven yards long by four or five in width.'

Allotments only partially solve the problem, since 'when they are a mile or two away from a man's dwelling, it is only on rare occasions that he feels inclined to tramp that distance after ten or twelve hours' hard work, and carry his implements into the bargain'. The real solution, according to Weathers, is to build houses with sizeable gardens, so 'every householder would then have his allotment at his back door'.

William Robinson's garden in Sussex was 200 acres. In *Gravetye Manor* (1911), a gardening diary, the scale of planting is evident. In 1890 he records: 'Over 5,000 wild roses (sweet-brier) planted so far.' In 1898: 'Planted in January nearly 100,000 Narcissus.'

In *Little Gardens* (1908), by contrast, Harry Thomas writes about gardens of about an acre in size. Later, in *Gardening in Towns* (1936), however, he still takes it for granted that there will be a lawn in the garden for games such as tennis, clock golf, croquet or bowling.

In 1920 George Dillistone's *The Planning and Planting of Little Gardens* was published, though it was actually completed in 1914. It is an account of a competition, which took place just before the outbreak of war, to design gardens 'ranging from a narrow suburban plot, 40 feet wide, to a triangular site of about half an acre'. The 400 entries were judged on 17 October 1914. Out of the four categories, one first prize went to a woman and the other three to men.

The author introduces the book by quoting a speech of King George V on 11 April 1919: 'Can we not aim at securing to the working classes in their homes the comfort, leisure, brightness, and peace which we

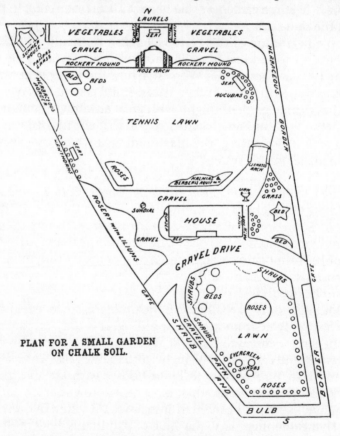

PLAN FOR A SMALL GARDEN
ON CHALK SOIL.

From Little Gardens and How to Make the Most of Them
by H.H. Thomas, published in 1908.

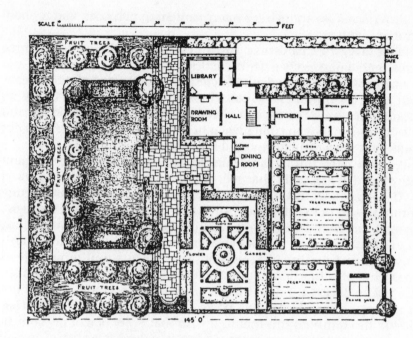

First-prize Design by Miss I. Grant Brown, from George Dillistone's
The Planning and Planting of Little Gardens *(1920).*

usually associate with the word "HOME"? The sites of the houses must be carefully chosen and laid out, the houses themselves properly planned and equipped.' Dillistone adds his own comment: 'If there is one thing more than another necessary to make an Englishman's house his home, it is a garden.'

Although the competition is described as 'designed essentially for the benefit of those who garden for themselves', it does not seem to be aimed at the working class. In the smallest garden or 'average small suburban plot', measuring 40 feet by 120, a servant is still assumed to be employed; and designs for the third-of-an-acre garden and the half-acre garden contain tennis courts.

Most of the famous gardening writers of this period had assistance in their gardens, which is why their idea of a small garden seems so large. Gertrude Jekyll employed eleven gardeners. In *Colour in the Flower Garden* (1908) she wishes she had a larger wood: 'As it is, I have to be content with my little wood of ten acres; yet I am truly glad to have even that small space to treat with reverent thankfulness and watchful care.' Henry Bright (1881) writes of his 'garden of moderate pretensions' in Lancashire: 'Exclusive of meadowland there are only some four acres, but four acres are enough for many gardening purposes, and for very great enjoyment.'

Rider Haggard's garden in Ditchingham, Norfolk, was over three acres, including a kitchen garden of three-quarters of an acre, lawns and flower-garden of one and a half acres, and an orchard of one acre, as well as six greenhouses. He considers the labour employed as 'by no means excessive'. It comprised a head gardener, two sub-gardeners and a 'labouring man who comes when he is wanted, or when he does not think that the weather is too bad for outdoor work'.

With the move towards gardening for oneself, however, the optimum size of garden gradually changed. In *The Book of Old-Fashioned Flowers* (1901) Harry Roberts thinks that it is 'as easy to create a lovely picture within an area of twenty square yards as in the space of a palace garden'. A small garden is a greater test of gardening skill and can provide just as much enjoyment: 'Fully as great pleasure may be extracted from a tiny plot as from broad acres, and a few plants well grown are as productive of satisfaction as is the largest collection.' He likens the garden to a poem: 'It is at a sonnet that we small gardeners must aim and not at an epic, or great narrative poem.' Later, in *Keep Fit in War-Time* (1940), he continues this theme: 'I wish that every one of my compatriots possessed in his own right as a British citizen an eighth of an acre of British soil.'

In *Every Man His Own Garden* (1904) John Halsham recommends anything up to an acre: 'For a real gardener, who does not allow society or politics or books seriously to interfere with his work, an acre of diggable ground may not be too much; for one who has to make the most of summer evenings and half-holidays, twenty yards of lawn and a couple of borders along the fence may be quite sufficient employ.' E. R. Anson, in *The Owner Gardener* (1934), agrees on the same limit. His book is written for the reader who has retired from business and moved into the country with an acre of land.

In *Wild Gardening* (1929) E.H.M. Cox refers to the wholesale reconstruction of gardens which sometimes took place, comparing this to his own modest achievement: 'You may, of course, dig and delve and raise hills and excavate pools in what was a flat field; but that is another matter. The types of wild garden about which I am writing are meant for the gardener with a moderate income, not for the man with so much money to burn that he can change a countryside for a whim.' Even so, his own wild garden in east Perthshire consisted of four and a half acres.

Cox worked out how much labour was needed to maintain this garden. It comes to about 1,000 hours a year, not including inspecting and superintending, and he suggests it could do with another 500 hours: 'The thousand hours include the thorough clearing of about 150 square yards of fresh ground every year, weeding, watering, mulching, planting, removing dead wood, and routine work in the nursery, but it does not take into account seedlings raising in the house and the work attached to young plants in the frames.'

During the Second World War Eleanour Rohde ran a sizeable nursery garden at Cranham Lodge in Reigate, Surrey, from where she sold seeds and plants. She dedicates her book *Uncommon Vegetables* (1943) to 'my loyal, cheerful staff, to whom I owe so much of the pleasure of this "unusual" nursery'. Vita Sackville-West expounds in the *Observer* (12 March 1950) on designing a small garden: 'By a small garden I mean anything from half an acre to two acres.'

By 1984, however, Susan Campbell, in her introduction to a new edition of *Pot-Pourri from a Surrey Garden*, can describe Mrs Earle's garden as 'a largish, 2-acre garden'. The reason is clear, for the average size of a British garden is now one-twentieth of an acre.

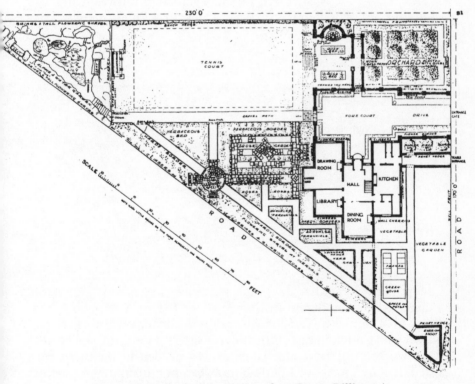

First-prize Design by John Hatton, from George Dillistone's
The Planning and Planting of Little Gardens *(1920).*

Garden size is obviously related to the labour available to manage it. With the development of gardening for oneself, there was an expansion in the number of smaller gardens and a corresponding growth in gardening literature to meet the needs of the amateur gardener.

Whatever the size of the garden, however, whether small cottage garden or vast landscape park, the idea is often expressed that there is something special about it being English. It is to this recurring theme of race and nationalism in gardening books that we now turn.

4

England's Green and Pleasant Land: Race and Nationalism in Gardening Literature

'Boast not proud English, of thy birth & blood,
Thy brother Indian is by birth as Good.'

Roger Williams, *A Key into the Language of America* (1643)

'And see! where, elevated far above,
A Column overlooks yon nodding Grove;
On which, the Scene of Glory to compleat,
Deck'd with the Ensigns of Imperial State,
Stands the great Father, George, whose equal Sway,
With Joy Britannia's happy Realms obey.'

Gilbert West, *Stowe, The Gardens of the Right Honourable
Richard Viscount Cobham* (1732)

'So favourable to vegetation is the climate of this happy island,
that we can, with care, raise every shrub, plant, and tree, that
flourishes in any part of the world. In fact, we can make the World
of Vegetation our own!'

Gilbert Brookes, *The Complete British Gardener* (1779)

'The Rose is, in addition to other merits, an English flower, almost
an English institution, and I am glad you have made it the subject
of special study and commemoration.'

William Ewart Gladstone, letter to Dean Hole (28 March, 1877)

There is much chauvinism in English writing on gardening. It is often assumed that the English love gardens more than any other people; that the creation of the English landscape garden is unique and has been copied all round the world; that English plant hunters were the bravest collectors; that more people in England have a garden than in any other country; and that English horticulture is the most advanced in the world. It is often difficult to separate the myth from the reality.

This chapter looks at the rise of English nationalism and our ignorance and often wilful misrepresentation of gardening in other cultures, for example that of native Americans. It deals with the growing concern with race in the nineteenth century and the racism linking colonialism and gardening, particularly in India and Africa. It then examines the renewed competition with France from the end of the eighteenth century and the growing interest in Japanese gardens at the end of the nineteenth century. Finally, the marginalisation of Scotland and Wales is discussed, as well as the role of the plant hunters.

Seventeenth-century Nationalism

One reason for stressing Englishness in the sixteenth and seventeenth centuries was in order to escape from foreign influence on English gardening books. In 1569 Leonard Mascall states that we compare poorly in planting and grafting to Greece, Barbary, Italy and France. He starts *A Booke of the Arte and manner how to Plant and Graffe all sorts of Trees* rather apologetically: 'Gentle Reader thou shalt understand, I have taken out of divers Authours this simple work, into our English tongue.'

Three stages of grafting, from Leonard Mascall's A Booke of the Arte and manner how to Plant and Graffe all sorts of Trees *(1569).*

As the Elizabethan era developed, however, it witnessed the flowering of English literature, and in the seventeenth century English became a major European language. Science and commerce grew and national confidence increased. In 1608 *The Husbandmans Fruitfull Orchard* by N. F. was published. In the Epistle to the Reader the author looks back over recent history, noting the earlier reliance on continental horticulture: 'Afore I proceede to the Treatise it selfe, I thinke meete to acquaint thee, from whence our great plentie of fruite, in England, came ... One Richard Harris of London, borne in Ireland, Fruiterer to King Henry the eight, fetched out of Fraunce great store of graftes, especially pippins: before which time there was no right pippins in England. He fetched also, out of the Lowe Countries, Cherrie grafts, & Peare grafts, of divers sorts.'

He goes on to describe how Harris made an orchard of 140 acres in Kent, from land belonging to the King. He confidently concludes: 'And by reason of the great increase that now is growing in divers parts of this Land, of such fine & serviceable fruit, there is no need of any foraigne fruite, but we are able to serve other places.'

In 1613 Gervase Markham, from Nottinghamshire, is even more assertive. He states as his justification for writing *The English Husbandman* that all other similar works are just translations from Latin or French writers, who are 'all forrainers and utterly unacquainted with our Climbes'. So he decides to 'set downe the true manner and nature of our right English Husbandry, our soyle being as delicate, apt, and fit for increase as any forraine soyle whatsoever'. Later in the book he repeats his aim, to 'rebell against forraine imitiation'. Markham had been a soldier in the Low Countries and he compares England with France, Italy and Germany: 'In all the forraine places I have seene, there is none more worthy then our owne.' He concludes with what was to become a characteristic nationalist motto: 'I will neither begge ayde nor authoritie from strangers.'

English nationalism grew in the seventeenth century, extending beyond the country's borders. In 1624 Richard Eburne, from Somerset, wrote *A Plaine Path-Way to Plantations* to encourage the planting of 'our English people in other countries'. He refers to the first chapter of Genesis where God commands Adam to 'fill the earth and subdue it', and so justifies colonialism: 'Wee Englishmen have as good ground and warrant to enter upon New-found-Land, or any other Countrey hitherto not inhabited or possessed by any Nation else, Heathen or Christian, and any other that we can lawfully, (I say lawfully) get of those that doe inhabite them, as to hold our owne native the English soyle.'

In *The English Bible and the Seventeenth-Century Revolution* (1993) Christopher Hill comments on the symbolic meaning of the garden during this period: 'The garden represents privacy, property, the family, civilization, growing luxury, all cut off from the vulgar by the hedge. It can stand for the chosen nation in a heathen world, the colonial errand into the wilderness. It also asserts the godly's control over their congregations, the encloser's status; the superiority of the colonizer over the "natives".'

The progressive aspect of the English Revolution, in stimulating democracy and encouraging the spread of knowledge, had its negative side, particularly in the wholesale categorising of other peoples as the enemy. In *The Hireling Ministry* (1652), for example, Roger Williams, who was generally supportive of North American Indian culture, discusses the conversion of the Indians and writes ominously: 'We have Indians at home, Indians in Cornwall, Indians in Wales, Indians in Ireland ...'

The anonymous author of *Soyle for an Orchard*, around 1650, is more generous in acknowledging the contribution of other cultures to our gardens: 'For outlandish flowers giving beauty & bravery of their colours so early before many of our own bred flowers, that they seeme to make a garden of delight even in the winter time, do so give their flowers one after another, that all their bravery is not fully spent, untill that Gilloflowers, the pride of our English gardens do shew themselves.' He also writes of 'those that are called usually English flowers', explaining that 'the most of them were never naturall of this land, but brought in from other Countries in former times'.

At the end of the seventeeth century English horticultural confidence continued to grow, despite the French influence on gardening style. John Evelyn deprecates this influence when writing the Preface to *The English Vineyard Vindicated* (1666) by John Rose, who was 'Gardn'r to His Majesty, at his Royal Garden in St. James's'. He particularly compliments Rose because his observations on growing vines are 'the native production of his own Experience'. Evelyn goes on to criticise the 'many mistakes and errours' which come from men following 'such Directions as they meet withall in Print, or from some Monsieurs new come over, who thinke we are as much oblig'd to follow their mode of Gard'ning, as we do that of their Garments, 'til we become in both ridiculous'.

Culpeper had a similar view of foreign plants. In *The School of Physick* (1659) he argues that native plants are quite good enough to cure English people's illnesses: 'What can be more pleasant to thee, then the enjoying of Medicines for cure of thine Infirmities, out of thy Native Soyl, and Countrey, thy Field, thy Orchard, thy Garden?'

In 1670 Andrew Mollet, who was 'Master of His Majesty of Englands Gardens in His Park of St. James's', dedicated his *The Garden of Pleasure* to the King. The author describes English lawns as better than 'any other Country of the World, by reason that the Gardeners are more expert and skilful in laying and keeping of Turff then any other Country Gardiners'. He also praises 'the Garden-Alleys', which are 'the chiefest Ornaments of a Garden, and wherein England excelleth other Countreys, as well as by its art in Turffing'.

Charles Cotton, who had a famous garden at Beresford in Staffordshire, is concerned at the number of orange and lemon trees which were being imported from France and other countries, when English growers could be producing them. In *The Planters Manual* (1675) he attacks the style of the French, wanting to avoid being 'debauch'd by their effeminate manners, luxurious kickshaws, and fantastick fashions, by which we are already sufficiently Frenchified, and more than in the opinion of the wiser sort of men, is consistent either with the constitution, or indeed the honour of the English Nation'.

The Eighteenth-century Landscape Garden

In 1718 John Laurence complains about the continuing French influence. In *The Fruit-Garden Kalendar* he writes: 'Indeed it seems to me no small Reproach to the English Nation, that we suffer so many French Books of Gardening to be obtruded upon us, containing Rules calculated for another Climate, and which tend to lead us into many Errors.'

As late as 1728, in *New Principles of Gardening*, Batty Langley still compares English gardens unfavourably with the continent: 'If the Gentlemen of England had formerly been better advised in the laying out their gardens, we might by this Time been at least equal (if not far superior) to any Abroad.'

Earlier, in 1700, however, Timothy Nourse is to be found claiming England's pre-eminence in its variety of plants: 'As for Curiosities of Plants, Fruit-Trees, Flowers, and other Rarities of the Gardens, brought over from Foreign Countries, we have certainly as great a Collection as any Nation under Heaven, there being none to be found which is so universally stor'd with all Provisions of this kind as in England, and possibly some parts of the Low Countries; which benefit we have from the great Trade we drive in all Parts of the World.'

In 1722 the apothecary Joseph Miller also claims herbal superiority over the rest of the world. In his herbal, *Botanicum Officinale*, he writes about London: 'There is no City in the Universe better supplied with simples and compound Medicines than ours, nor where more Care is taken in the making them.'

In the eighteenth century the English announced their own unique gardening style. According to Richard Pulteney in 1790: 'English gardeners have shewn themselves equal, if not superior, to most others.'

William Robinson, who was of course an Irishman, stresses the significance of the eighteenth-century English landscape garden. In *Gravetye Manor* (1911) he writes: 'Before the English invented and carried out landscape gardening the foreigner, like ourselves, was content with the mason's idea of a garden.'

'Ananas, or West-Indian Pine-Apple', from Richard Bradley's A General Treatise of Husbandry and Gardening *(1726). Engraving by John Pine.*

The elegance and moderation of this English landscape gardening style is expressed by Jane Austen in *Emma* (1816): 'It was a sweet view – sweet to the eye and the mind. English verdure, English culture, English comfort, seen under a sun bright, without being oppressive.' But as Edward Said points out in *Culture and Imperialism* (1993): 'In Jane Austen's *Mansfield Park* Thomas Bertram's slave plantation in Antigua is mysteriously necessary to the poise and the beauty of Mansfield Park.' The mystery is uncovered when we realise how money from the plantations was used to transform the English landscape.

The eighteenth century also saw the improved cultivation of fruit and vegetables in hot-beds. Stephen Switzer (1727) writes of cucumbers ripening in March and melons in April. He claims that the gentry of Great Britain 'now equal, if not much excel the French and Dutch in their curious collections of seed', and he puts the progress down to 'the industry and skill of our kitchen Gardiners only, who are now behind no country in their performances'.

John Gibson thinks Britain has 'the happiest government on earth' and 'a superiority to other people in taste'. In *The Fruit-Gardener* (1768) he proudly claims: 'We can with justice boast of flowers and fruit of our own raising, equal, if not superior, in beauty and goodness to those of any other nation whose situation is similar to our own.'

Luxury tropical fruits, such as the pineapple, were increasingly cultivated in the eighteenth century. In 1769 Adam Taylor, a gardener from near Devizes, published *A Treatise on the Ananas or Pine-Apple*, in which he writes that the pineapple 'undoubtedly surpasses all the Fruits with which the World is at present acquainted'. He is in some doubt, however, as to whether the Africans know how to eat it properly: 'The ANANAS or PINE APPLE is a Native of the hotter inland Parts of Africa, where it is said to be very destructive to the Health of the Inhabitants, who devour it too eagerly.'

Nineteenth-century Chauvinism

Nineteenth-century British pride knew no bounds. Edmund Rack writes in 1803: 'But without any improper partiality to our own country, we are fully justified in asserting, that England alone exceeds all modern nations in husbandry. To the natural genius of the people, have been added the theory and practice of all nations in ancient and modern times.'

In 1823 Henry Phillips claims that the shrubbery 'originated in England, and is as peculiar to the British nation as landscape-planting'. He adds that it 'has indisputably sprung from the genius of our soil'. Patrick Neill, a Scot, thinks that nowhere has gardening 'made greater progress than amongst ourselves'. He writes in 1838: 'All circumstances being favourable, a British garden is perhaps unrivalled in fertility by any cultivated spot in the world.'

Charles McIntosh in 1855 maintains that London market-gardeners are 'the best culinary gardeners in the world'. Writing during the same period, James Cuthill, in *Market Gardening*, agrees: 'All admit that London furnishes the finest flowers, fruits, and vegetables in the world; and the reason is, London contains the world's wealth, being the great resort of the aristocracy, and the very centre of commerce.'

The Rev. T. Collings Bréhaut (1860) writes of 'the inferiority of continental gardening, taken as a whole, compared with that of England'. William Robinson, in *Hardy Flowers* (1871), put it down to geography: 'We live in a country which is, on the whole, better calculated for the successful culture of the most beautiful vegetation of northern and temperate climes than any on the face of the earth.'

In 1872 James Anderson links the landscape garden with English liberty. He argues against fences being erected around individual trees in a landscape park because it would attract 'notice by the appearance of restriction and formality, instead of the ease and English-like freedom we look for'. In 1877 Mollison boasts: 'Of all countries in the world Britain stands first for her gardens. With us it may be said that we have reached the height of perfection in the taste and beauty of design displayed in our gardens.'

In 1883 John Simpson claims that 'the Grapes produced under our sunless skies by English gardeners are hardly excelled in any part of the world'. In the same year Grant Allen, in *Flowers and their Pedigrees*, declares that our own native British flora 'can fearlessly challenge the rest of the whole world in general mingled effect of gaiety and luxuriousness'. After a long debate as to whether Belgian horticulture is better than British horticulture, John Wright states in 1893: 'I believe the best British gardeners are equal to any in the world, and superior to most.'

Twentieth-century Pride

The story continues in this century. William Robinson, in *The Garden Beautiful* (1906), sets out his aim to teach his readers 'that our own country's trees are the most beautiful we shall ever have, and our native flowers as fair as any'. Mrs Richmond writes (1908): 'Roam the world where we may, there will never be found a sweeter spot of cultivated soil than a British garden.'

In *Alpine Flowers and Gardens* (1910) George Jackson Flemwell describes the British race as 'strenuous, athletic, and sports-loving'. He quotes E.T. Cook's *Gardens of England* approvingly: 'There is a love of flowers fast knit into the very fibre of our British nature.' E.H.M. Cox writes in *The Evolution of a Garden* (1927): 'It has been said, and with a great deal of truth that we are the premier gardening nation ... Surely it is due to our inherent love of flowers.'

Anson maintains in 1934: 'No other country has such wonderful examples of horticultural skill as those which may be seen when travelling in England.' Ralph Hancock, in *When I make a Garden* (1936), asserts that the skill did not travel to the New World: 'Few Americans possess the deeply rooted love of gardens and gardening which is an inherited instinct of all classes of English men and women.'

The following year W.E. Johns claims that the English garden is 'the loveliest in the world'. In 1938 Alicia Amherst writes in *Historic Gardens of England*: 'One may well ask what is the cause of this far-spreading love of gardening. There seems to be no direct answer, except that it is just a British characteristic!'

Roy Hay states in 1942 that 'in the actual technique of seed production this country leads the world'. In 1944 H.J. Massingham assumes national superiority: 'It is often said that we are a nation of gardeners and as such easily overtop all other nations. But it is seldom asked why this is so.' Following Cobbett, in style and politics, he argues that it is due to the 'legacy from our pre-industrial past', when 'we were a self-supporting nation based on peasants, yeomen and squires with our roots deep in our native soil'.

Albert Gurie, the garden editor of the *News Chronicle*, puts it down to 'a suitable climate and an average soil'. In the *News Chronicle Gardening Book* (1952) he calls on foreign witnesses: 'It has been said that we are a race of gardeners. Some may not agree, but perhaps the best judges are travellers who visit these shores from time to time. Do they not leave for their own lands with the impression that they have seen some of the most beautiful gardens and garden flowers in the whole world.'

Similarly Robert Jackson (1953) claims that 'no country in the world has such beautiful gardens as Great Britain'. In *Beautiful Gardens of the World* he writes patronisingly of other countries' traditions: 'The British, wherever they have gone, have carried with them an inherited love of flowers and gardens, but that must not blind us to the fact that other nations have had and still have their garden lovers who have made gardens after their fashion.'

OTHER CULTURES

Most of us are ignorant of gardening traditions in other countries. Historical studies usually refer to the influence of Italian, French and Dutch gardens, and perhaps mention Persia, Japan and China. But

John Loudon calls Chinese attempts to imitate uncultivated nature 'truly ridiculous' in his Encyclopaedia of Gardening, *first published in 1822.*

what do we know about gardening in the Americas before Columbus, for example, or in Africa?

One of the first surveys of international gardening appeared in John Loudon's *Encyclopaedia of Gardening* in 1822, expanded in the revised edition of 1834 from 110 to 420 pages. The author writes of pre-Columbian gardening: 'The Mexicans were extremely well skilled in the cultivation of kitchen and other gardens, in which they planted, with great regularity and taste, fruit trees, and medicinal plants and flowers.' He also describes their celebrated royal gardens and the chinampas, or floating gardens. For the rest of North America, however, he sees only European gardening.

Loudon is also surprisingly scathing about the Chinese, finding 'nothing interesting in their style of gardening' and 'no rational design'. He thinks their attempts to imitate 'uncultivated nature' are on 'such a diminutive scale, that the attempts are truly ridiculous'. He admits, however, that his views are ethnocentric: 'Their decorative scenes are carried to such an extreme, so encumbered with deceptions, and what we would not hesitate to consider puerilities, and there appears throughout so little reference to utility, that the most mature and chastened taste of Europeans cannot sympathise with them. Chinese taste is, indeed, altogether peculiar; but it is perfectly natural to that people, and therefore not to be subjected to European criticism.'

As for Africa, Loudon mentions Egypt as well as the 'Mahometan States of the North of Africa' and the colonists' gardens in the south, concluding: 'As an art of design and taste, there are but few specimens of gardening in Africa.' About the west coast of Africa he writes: 'Gardening can hardly be said to exist in a country which can scarcely be considered within the pale of civilisation.' Yet according to the American anthropologist G.P. Murdock, writing in 1959: 'Agriculture was independently developed (circa 5000 B.C.) by the Negroes of West Africa. This was, moreover, a genuine invention, not a borrowing from another people. Furthermore, the assemblage of cultivated plants ennobled from wild forms in Negro Africa ranks as one of the four major agricultural complexes evolved in the entire course of human history.' Similarly Ivan van Sertima, in *They Came Before Columbus* (1976), argues that Africans introduced cultivated cotton, bananas and plantains into the New World before Columbus set sail.

Although, not surprisingly, African gardens rarely feature in English gardening books, there are references in the accounts of travellers and explorers. In *Travels and Discoveries in North and Central Africa* (1857), for example, Henry Barth describes visiting Barakat, just beyond Ghat in Libya, and writes that 'most of the gardens were well kept'. In Niger he is shown Ashu's garden in Agades to compare plants. He has to admit to the owner that in Europe there is 'neither senna, nor bamia, nor indigo, nor cotton, nor Guinea corn, nor, in short, the most beautiful of all trees of the creation, as he thought – the talha, or Mimosa ferruginea'.

When he arrives in Kano, in Nigeria, he finds that a typical house has a 'yard neatly fenced with mats of reed'. In it there would be 'a fine spreading alleluba-tree, affording a pleasant shade during the hottest hours of the day, or a beautiful gonda or papaya unfolding its large feather-like leaves above a slender, smooth, and undivided stem, or the tall date-tree, waving over the whole scene'. Later, on his way to Timbuctu, he sees a 'large extent of kitchen-gardens' in Masena.

J.B. Falade draws on such travellers' accounts, as well as archaeological excavation and actual remains, to challenge the 'current disbelief in the existence of Nigerian garden styles and ideas'. In an article entitled 'Yoruba Palace Gardens' he writes: 'Certainly, the Yoruba people of southern Nigeria attached great importance to garden design as an art. It could be said that they were preoccupied with building elaborate gardens for their deities, kings and chiefs.'

AMERICAN INDIANS

In *The Garden: An Illustrated History from Ancient Egypt to the Present Day* (1966) Julia Berrall has chapters on Egypt, Mesopotamia, Persia and the Gardens of Islam. Her chapter on the 'American Garden Heritage', however, begins with the settlers in the early seventeenth century. The Indians, or native Americans, are mentioned in only one sentence and then simply to describe them as a constant worry. In nearly 400 pages there is not a single reference to the great Aztec gardening tradition of Central America which utterly amazed the Spanish conquistadores.

Such ignorance and prejudice is nothing new. Robert Hogg, who edited several gardening magazines, wrote books on fruit trees, helped found the British Pomological Society and became General Secretary for the International Horticultural Congress of 1866, is the author of *The Dahlia: Its History and Cultivation* (1853). In typical colonial fashion he remarks on 'the hitherto unknown treasures of the New World'. He writes of Hernandez, physician to Philip II of Spain, who was sent to study the natural resources of Mexico: 'In such a country, where no botanist had ever trodden, the success which attended his labours was of course very great.' On the contrary, Aztec botany was probably more advanced than any to be found in Europe at the time.

It is worth quoting in full Hogg's account of the discovery of the dahlia, for it stands as an archetype of colonial presumption: 'For ages before even the New World itself was discovered, there existed on the mountain plains of Mexico, a wild, neglected weed, called by the natives Acocotli. There, in its native prairies, it performed its part in the great chain of creation, year by year blooming, and fading, and dying, but it attracted no interest, unless perhaps its large fleshy tubercules furnished, at some period, a rude meal to the wild and barbarous Toltecans. In course of time the Spaniards occupied Mexico; a new field was opened up for conquest and for science, and, accordingly, we find that every facility was afforded for investigating the natural productions of the newly-acquired territory: of these the vegetable kingdom furnished numerous and interesting examples.'

In fact, as well as appreciating the flower's aesthetic qualities, the Aztecs made water pipes out of dahlia stems, and from the root a sweet extract was used for medicinal purposes.

A similar assumption about the dahlia is made by George Gordon, president of the National Dahlia Society and editor of the *Gardeners' Magazine*. In *Dahlias* (1913) he recognises that the *Dahlia Yuarezii*, from which the race of cactus varieties has descended, was a cultivated plant in Mexican gardens previous to its introduction into Europe, and it had undergone considerable modification before it left its native country'.

But he assumes that the earliest record of the flower is that of the Spanish conquerors: 'There is no evidence to justify the belief that there is an earlier record of the Dahlia than the one given by Francisco Hernandez, physician to Philip II of Spain, in his work on the plants and animals of New Spain, or Mexico, which was published in 1615.' The author refers to its 'Mexican name of Acocotli', but fails to mention the extensive botanical science developed by the Aztecs, most of which was destroyed by the invaders.

American Gardening Writers

This neglect of the indigenous horticultural tradition of the New World is just as prounounced in American gardening writers. Between 1900 and 1902 the four volumes of L.H. Bailey's *Cyclopedia of American Horticulture* appeared, written by a host of American experts. According to these experts the history of the dahlia begins in 1789, when it was first cultivated in Europe. They concede that the 'Indians cultivated corn, beans, pumpkins and other plants when America was discovered', and linguistic derivations are also acknowledged: 'The white settlers early learned from the American Indians the use of Maize as an article of food. Several Indian names for certain preparations which they adopted or adapted, have passed into the language of the American people, as, for example, samp, hominy, succotash.' But there is no reference to native American gardens. The entry under Indian Territory, an area in the Midwest around Muskogee, describes native horticulture as very primitive: 'The people are not sufficiently educated in agricultural industries to be successful in fruit culture.' They need white know-how: 'The soil and climate of Indian Territory are both very favorable to the production of fruit, and with permanent white settlement, horticulture has a bright future within the borders of the Territory.'

Likewise H.E. Vandeman, the author of the chapter on America in Bunyard and Thomas's *The Fruit Garden* (1904), only grudgingly admits that the Aztecs 'probably cultivated a few fruits along with the cereals and vegetables which they grew'. As for the 'aboriginal inhabitants of North America', they 'paid only slight attention to the culture of fruits'. When the Spaniards established colonies on the coast of Florida and brought with them oranges and lemons, 'the natives, seeing that the trees produced good fruit and were of easy culture, planted them in their rude way'.

In *The Story of Gardening* (1934) Richardson Wright records the first reference to Indian gardens on the Atlantic seaboard, in the report made by Francis Drake of an attack on an Indian village in Florida in

1583, when he 'burned their buildings and destroyed their gardens'. Wright is dismissive of these gardens, describing them as 'probably merely corn and bean patches and peach-tree groves'. The northern Indians grew a small black plum, from which they made prunes, and in the south the 'Creeks, Cherokees and Choctaws grew the peach and distributed the kernels of it as far north as Rhode Island'. Women and children did most of the work, described by Wright as 'crude and slovenly and yet quite productive'.

Indians planting corn and beans. From Theodore de Bry's India Occidentalis *(1590–91), reprinted in U.P. Hedrick's* A History of Horticulture in America to 1860, *published in 1950.*

Wright judges the native Americans simply by how much they can benefit the invading Europeans: 'The Iroquois in New York kept a Corn Festival, a thanksgiving period that lasted four days, during which the Red Men gorged themselves on succotash. If they had taught the new settlers nothing more, they would amply have justified their existence by handing on this succulent mixture of corn and beans. They also traded in their crops, both with other tribes and with settlers, and on more than one occasion they kept the latter from starvation. Certain Indian methods of agriculture were adopted by these settlers. The Indian made still another valuable contribution – his manual labour. The first "hired man" in America was an Indian.'

Another American writer, Martha Flint, regrets that the Indian names of native plants have been neglected. In *A Garden of Simples* (1900) she mentions a few of the established names, including maize, pecan and yucca, and says 'surely the few remaining native names should be conscientiously kept in use'. Nevertheless, in her chapter entitled 'Indian Plant Names', she refers to the 'Indian's crude craftsmanship' and the 'primitive economy of the vanishing Indian'. She calls them 'barbarians' and states that 'the red man's aesthetic sense was quite undeveloped'.

Hildegarde Hawthorne, also writing from the USA, is even more dismissive of the native Americans. In *The Lure of the Garden* (1911) she puts it bluntly: 'The red man was in no other way so truly savage as in the fact that he knew nothing of gardens.'

In *Historic Gardens of Virginia* (1923), Edith Sale assumes that real gardening began only with the settlers and that they taught the Indians how to garden: 'Gardens began early in Virginia. At Varina, in 1614, lived that wedded pair, John Rolfe and Pocahontas, daughter of Powhatan. Rolfe experimented with tobacco, and who shall say that in turn he did not show the young, wonderful Indian woman how they set flowering bushes, how they made beds of flowers, in Norfolk, in England?'

Likewise Rosetta Clarkson, in *Magic Gardens* (1939), asks: 'But what about our own American tradition to guide us in making our gardens?' Completely ignoring native American gardening, she goes on to explain that the New Englanders modelled their gardens on English ones: 'In the first place, we were a brand new, unformed country when Elizabethans were enjoying their espaliers, pleached alleys, orchards, pleasure gardens, kitchen gardens.'

Colonialism and American Indian Gardens

This 'fact' that the native Americans had no gardens was a critical factor in John Locke's philosophy and in his support for the colonisation of America. Wars against Africans and native Americans were justified in Locke's view because these people were defending merely 'waste land', not property, as Martin Bernal explains in *Black Athena*: 'Locke had the curious but convenient belief that Africans and Americans did not practise agriculture and, according to him, the only entitlement to land came from cultivation.'

Seventeenth-century evidence, however, disproves Locke's belief. Sources other than gardening books need to be examined for records of indigenous American horticulture. In 1616 *A Description of New England* was published, written by Captain John Smith who was employed by the Company of Merchants. The author describes the coast of

Massachusetts as 'so planted with Gardens and Cornefields, and so well inhabited with a goodly, strong and well proportioned people'. He goes on to write of 'groves of mulberrie trees gardens' and 'two pleasant Iles of groves, gardens and cornefields'.

In a later account, *The Description of Virginia* (1625), Smith describes communities of Indians in which each household had its own land and garden: 'Their Houses are in the midst of their Fields or Gardens, which are small plots of grounds' and 'a little separated by groves of trees'. The women and children did the work, planting corn, peas and beans, and doing the weeding. They had 'plots of Onions' and also planted fruit trees such as 'Macocks' and 'Maracocks' which were like lemons.

Likewise Champlain, the French explorer, writes of some North American Indians being 'sedentary, fond of cultivating the soil, and having cities and villages enclosed with palisades'. He describes 'their settled habitation, the tillage and the beautiful trees'. Travelling by a river flowing into Lake Ontario, he writes: 'In several places along the banks, the trees would seem to have been planted for ornament. Vines and nuts are in great quantities, and grapes come to maturity there, but they leave always a sharp sour taste, which proceeds from want of cultivation; but those that have been cultivated in these parts are of pretty good flavour.'

In *The Voyages and Explorations of Samuel de Champlain 1604–1616* there are also references to Indian women growing beans, pumpkins, squashes, tobacco and sunflowers (the oil from which they rubbed on their heads). Everywhere he went there was Indian corn: 'They make gardens of it, planting three or four grains in a place ... Among the corn in each hill they plant three or four Brazilian beans, which are of various colours.' These kidney beans climbed the corn which grew to five or six feet high.

In 1643 Roger Williams also gives an account of Indian women gardening in New England, writing of tobacco that 'it is commonly the only plant which men labour in; the women managing all the rest'. He also records their communal way of working: 'When a field is to be broken up, they have a very loving sociable speedy way to dispatch it: All the neighbours men and Women forty, fifty, a hundred &c, joyne, and come in to help freely.'

In *A Key into the Language of America* Williams goes on to describe the cultivation of corn, beans, chestnuts, walnuts, acorns, cherries, grapes and currants. Of strawberries he writes: 'In some parts where the Natives have planted, I have many times seen as many as would fill a good ship within few miles compasse: the Indians bruise them in a Morter, and mixe them with meale and make Strawberry bread.'

Williams provides a detailed refutation of Locke's premise: 'The Natives are very exact and punctuall in the bounds of their Lands, belonging to this or that Prince or People, (even to a River, Brooke) &c. And I have knowne them make bargaine and sale amongst themselves for a small piece, or quantity of Ground: not withstanding a sinfull opinion amongst many that Christians have right to Heathen Lands.' He concludes by having the Indians say:

> We weare no Cloaths, have many Gods,
> And yet our sinnes are lesse:
> You are Barbarians, Pagans wild,
> Your Land's the Wildernesse.

According to Bruce Smith, in his recent book *Rivers of Change*, there was an agricultural economy in eastern North America 4,000 years ago: 'In all likelihood women first planted seeds, returning in the fall for the harvest.' U.P. Hedrick, in *A History of Horticulture in America to 1860* (1950), writes that 'all the tribes of North American Indians supplemented their common fare of fish and game with fruits and vegetables'. He quotes John Smith as saying that 'the Indians along the James River planted mulberry and locust trees, grapes, wild roses, and sunflowers.' He goes on: 'From a hundred less-well told accounts of Indian gardening in America east of the Mississipi, one may generalize and say that the gardening and cooking methods of all the Indian tribes were much the same, though some tribes were much more skilled in tilling the land than others.'

U.P. Hedrick notes the European surprise at first seeing the gardens in New York: 'To people who had never before seen a corn-stalk, a climbing bean, a pumpkin, a squash, or a gourd, an Indian garden must have seemed strange indeed.' He also refers to the fact that the New York Indians planted plum trees around their villages, copses of which could still be found, at the time he was writing, near the sites of old towns. These Indian gardens and orchards were all communal.

Trade in Plants

As for the Peruvian Indians, Hedrick (1950) quotes Spanish authorities: 'These early Spanish writers said that the New World gardens surpassed any similar ones in the Old World. Besides plants for food, medicine, and the arts, there were flowers in abundance. Acosta says the Peruvians offered them so many nosegays as they traveled about, that they were not able to carry them all. Some of these plants have been cultivated so long that botanists are unable to identify their wild ancestors. Before

Battata Virginiana ſue Virginianorum,& Pappus.
Potatoes of Virginia.

Woodcut of potatoes, from John Gerard's Herball *(1597).*

Columbus came to the New World, South American food plants had been carried north and east as far as Canada and New England.' And this is evidence quoted by a man who later goes on to call the American Indians 'savages'.

There is certainly plenty of evidence that early English gardening writers recognised the herbal skill of the American Indians. In his *Herball* (1597), for example, Gerard implicitly gives credit to the Peruvian Indians. He describes the newly imported *Mirabilis jalapa* or Marvel of Peru as an 'admirable plant' and a 'wonderfull herbe', but adds: 'We have not as yet any instructions from the people of India, concerning the nature or vertues of this plant: the which is esteemed as yet for his rarenesse, beautie, and sweetness of his floures, than for any vertues knowne; but it is a pleasant plant to decke the gardens of the curious.' The implication is that Indian knowledge about the plant would eventually be forthcoming.

Parkinson (1629) makes a similar point in his description of the Spider-wort, obtained from John Tradescant, who had brought it back from Virginia. He comments on the plant's possible virtues: 'There hath not beene any tryall made of the properties since wee had it, nor doe we know whether the Indians have any use thereof.'

Many plants were brought to England from the New World in the seventeenth century. *The American Physitian*, written in 1672 by William Hughes, is subtitled 'A Treatise of the Roots, Plants, Trees, Shrubs, Fruit, Herbs &c. Growing in the English Plantations in America'. The style of the book is not 'deckt up with fine Metaphysical Notions and Expressions, or stuft with hard or strange words', but written in 'plaine and easie Terms, such as I my self best understand: Nor was this written in a closet or Study, in the corner of a house, amongst many Books; but the most of it, some time since, was taken, with many other Observations, rather in travelling the Woods, and other parts, (when I had leisure at odd times to go on Shore, being then belonging to one of his Majesties Ships of War) especially in that praise worthy Island of Jamaica.' The author expresses the wish to go on one more voyage in order to bring back 'Roots, Seeds, and other Vegetables, to our Climate, for to increase the number of Rarities which we have here in our Gardens already'.

Hughes justifies writing the book: "Tis likely some may say, What need we trouble our selves with those things we cannot reach? To such I answer, That the most part of them here mentioned which grow not in England already, are brought over daily and made use of, either for Meat or Medicine, or imployed in several sorts of Trades, and the like.' One of these imports, which takes up a third of the book, is cacao, used to make 'the deservedly-esteemed Drink called Chocolate'. It had been first brought to England 20 years earlier and was sometimes drunk enriched with eggs, sack and spices.

In an earlier book called *The Compleat Vineyard* (1665), Hughes argues for the planting of vines. There had been plenty of vineyards in the past and 'some there are of this day both in Essex, and in the West of England, as also in Kent, which produce great store of excellent good Wine'. Despite this, however, he criticises English gardeners for not manuring and pruning properly: 'I have just cause to accuse the extream negligence and blockish ignorance of our people, who do most unjustly lay their wrongful accusations upon the Soil, which truly may be removed on themselves.'

Adolphus Speed, in *Adam Out of Eden* (1659), also argues for the proper cultivation and distribution of the land in this country. This would then avoid the need for emigration and colonialism: 'England affords Land enough for the Inhabitants, and if men did but industriously and skilfully improve and manure it, we need not go to Jamaica for new plantations.'

But by this time colonialism, for instance in Virginia and Massachusetts, was well under way. In *The Shaping of Black America* (1993) Lerone Bennett draws the connection between enclosures in England and colonial expansion in the New World: 'The situation was brazenly turbulent in England, where the upper classes were engaged in the bloody process of driving the peasants from the land.' The resultant 'beggars, vagabonds and thieves' were exported into servitude: 'It was in this setting of social nightmare that England embarked on its career of colonialism. The primary reason for this departure was the idea that England needed a dumping ground for its undesirables. As Francis Bacon put it in a state paper delivered to James I in 1606, colonization gave England "a double commodity, in the avoidance of people here, and in making use of them there".'

American Indian Herbal Knowledge

John Cowell, in *The curious and profitable gardener* (1730), acknowledges the skill and learning of the American Indians in his account of the Rev. John Clarke's travels 'about Virginia, Carolina, the Maderas, and other parts of America'. Cowell, a nurseryman in Hoxton, praises Clarke's method of collecting plants: 'When he gather'd the Seeds and Fruits, he was no less careful in setting down the Time of their Ripening, but chiefly was Curious in Learning from the Indians, and the Inhabitants, the Use of every Plant he collected, whether in Medicine, of for Diet, of for Dying or Staining of Colours, or for Fodder for cattle, or for Timber.'

Philip Miller also refers to the Indians' herbal knowledge. In *The Gardeners Dictionary*, under a species of milkwort called *Polygala senega*, he describes the use of the root to cure the bite of the rattlesnake: 'The Seneka Indians use this root, which they powder, and generally carry about them when they travel in the woods, lest they should be bit by the rattle-snake; and whenever this happens, they take a quantity of the powder inwardly, and apply some of it to the part bitten, which is a sure remedy.' He goes on to relate its benefit to the settlers: 'And of late years it has been used by the inhabitants of Virginia in many disorders ... so that the root of this plant, when its virtues are fully known, may become one of the most useful medicines yet discovered.'

In 1753 Robert Colborne's *The Plain English Dispensatory* was published. Colborne was an apothecary from Chippenham in Wiltshire and he acknowledges the supreme herbal skills of the Aztecs: 'The Americans appear to have acted the most prudently; and with respect to Physic, to have been the wisest People of whom we have any authentic Account. Montezuma Emperor of Mexico, took a particular Care to transplant into his garden all the choice Simples that benign Climate produced, where the only study of the Physicians was to attain to the Knowledge of their Names and Properties. They had Names for all kinds of Pains and Infirmities; and in the Juices and Applications of those Herbs consisted all their Remedies, with which they effected surprising cures.'

He describes the bark of the cinchona tree, used to cure malaria, as 'the most famous, the most celebrated, and most useful Drug that is yet known'. Native American knowledge is compared to European backwardness: 'The Americans have been able to discover to the Europeans the most effectual Remedies yet known, as the Peruvian Bark, Jalop, and others; for which we are indebted to the Experience of the illiterate Inhabitants of the new World; whilst all the boasted learning of the Europeans has been so little productive of Improvements in Physic; that, with respect to our own Plants, we know very little more of their Virtues, than what we have learned from Dioscorides, and some other of the Antients.'

By the nineteenth century this indebtedness tends to be ignored, just as the debt of Greek culture to Africa was being erased. George Glenny has a section of his *Garden Almanac* of 1851 entitled 'Hints for Emigrants'. He writes of Australia, South Africa and North America, giving details of the climate, natural resources and death-rates, but says nothing about any indigenous people. He advises that 'nobody should go out without all the useful garden implements, for he will have to learn the use of them whether he likes it or not'.

One of the few modern gardening writers to acknowledge American Indian horticulture is Harry Roberts, who was familiar with the earlier accounts of explorers. In *The Book of Vegetables* (1902) by George Wythes, Roberts writes: 'The Jerusalem Artichoke is a native of North America, and was cultivated there by the Indians. Champlain, writing in 1603, speaks of "roots which they cultivate, tasting like artichokes", and Gookin speaks of the Indians as putting slices of Jerusalem Artichokes into their soups.'

Another is Eleanour Sinclair Rohde in *The Old English Herbals* (1922). Most of her chapter on herbals of the New World consists of quotes from Nicholas Monardes' *Joyfull Newes* (1569), a Spanish account of Indian Herbal medicine, which was translated into English in 1577 by a merchant named John Frampton. She acknowledges the Indians' botanical skills: 'The book gives us many pleasant glimpses of the kindly courtesy of the Red Indians to their foes, and though, according

Indian gardens on Roanoke Island in 1586. Drawn by John White for Theodore de Bry's India Occidentalis *(1590–91), reprinted in U.P. Hedrick's* A History of Horticulture in America to 1860, *published in 1950.*

to some authorities, they would never tell the secrets of the herbs they used as medicines, we have Monardes's detailed accounts of how they showed the Spaniards the uses of them.'

In his startling book on Christopher Columbus, called *The Conquest of Paradise* (1991), Kirkpatrick Sale catalogues the general ignorance and arrogance of the European settlers in America, and the death and destruction they brought with them. He locates in the European culture of the fifteenth and sixteenth centuries a deep-seated antipathy to the wildness of nature: 'It is but a short step from the fear of the wild to the love of the tamed and from there to the imperative of human domination and control of the natural world – hence the images of the subjection and mastery of the untamed landscape that are so frequent in late-fifteenth-century culture.'

He argues that the most pervasive and revealing image of this control is the formal Renaissance garden: 'Here it is the hand of man and not the grace of nature that is ever-present: bushes and small trees trimmed in rigid geometric shapes to look like wedding cakes or perfume bottles, closely clipped hedges along geometric walks, blocks of flower beds in uniform colors, carefully edged lawns, and artfully distributed statues, benches, fountains, pools, and bridges.'

Sale claims that the American Indians were 'extremely competent cultivators who had worked out a horticulture that, even without domesticated animals, surpassed that of Europe'. They were skilled plant breeders, made extensive use of plants in medicine and had a rich botanical language. Some tribes, for example, had 40 words for different parts of a leaf, at a time when there was still no English world for petal. Above all, their style of gardening was different to that of contemporary Europe. Sale quotes Peter Martyr writing in 1504: 'They seem to live in the golden world, without toil, living in open gardens, not entrenched with dikes, divided with hedges, or defended with walls.'

The arrival of Europeans was devastating, particularly because of the diseases they brought with them. In *Ecological Imperialism* Alfred Crosby quotes John Winthrop, the first governor of Massachusetts Bay Colony and a lawyer by training, who notes on 22 May 1634: 'For the natives, they are neere all dead of small Poxe, so as the Lord hathe cleared our title to what we possess.'

Not only were the natives cleared from the land, but many indigenous plants were also destroyed. Crosby points out that over half the weeds and grasses in the USA, Argentina and Australia are European imports. He quotes Thomas Budd in the seventeenth century, writing from Pennsylvania: 'If we sprinkle but a little English hay-seed on the Land without plowing, and then feed Sheep on it, in a little time it will so encrease, that it will cover the land with English grass.'

THE LANGUAGE OF RACE

In the second half of the nineteenth century there was constant discussion about the English 'race'. During this period the legacy of the slave trade, Darwin's theory of the survival of the fittest, and growing imperialism, all led to the worry that, if Britain was to retain its power over the rest of the world, something had to be done about maintaining its assumed superiority. The threat of German economic competition and the discovery during the Boer War of how many working-class men were unfit to serve in the army caused concern about the deterioration of the race.

In *Gardens of Celebrities and Celebrated Gardens* (1919) Jessie MacGregor, however, ignores this evidence, asserting: 'The English race has always been ruddy and healthy, the men stalwart, the women fresh and fair.'

Charles Eley, in *Gardening for the Twentieth Century* (1923), writes of the yew tree: 'evergreen, of steady growth and great tenacity of life, it has been said to be a symbol of the British character.' He warns that it is poisonous to animals, but 'even this peculiarity may also be claimed to be a characteristic of the Anglo-Saxon race, in that no foreign intruder, bent on theft, has ever yet attempted to feast upon the Empire of Britain without regretting the adventure'.

The nationalistic concept of race is most evident in claims about the English innate love of gardening. Inigo Triggs begins his *Garden Craft in Europe* (1913): 'The love of gardens is an old characterisitic of our race.' W.J. Bean writes in 1914 that the love of gardening is 'deeply rooted in the English race'. George Taylor, being a Scot, extends this characteristic to the British as a whole. In 1919 he writes of 'the great love of Roses so inherent in every British soul'.

Marion Cran (1921) writes that 'in turning myself to win to beauty from the wild a patch of Surrey sand, I had only come into line with my Race, and obeyed the call of the blood'. Brenda Colvin agrees in *Land and Landscape* (1948): 'The people of these islands are innate gardeners and love to potter about in the garden, propagating and watching plants grow, especially flowering plants, for the sheer pleasure this brings them.'

Historical and geographical reasons are also put forward to explain English skill in gardening. In *Garden Design in Theory and Practice* (1912), Madeline Agar thinks the reason for English gardening success is the absence of war within the country. Writing from Amersham Common in Buckinghamshire, just before the First World War, she states: 'The love of gardening is distinctly a national trait, which long freedom from internal warfare has given opportunity to develop. Country people have manifested it from time immemorial.'

Canon Ellacombe (1895), on the other hand, puts it down to the weather: 'There can be no doubt that the interest of our gardens, and that which has made Great Britain a nation of gardeners, has been our fickle and comparatively cold climate.' He supports the protestant ethic of hard work, arguing that tropical vegetation is not interesting from a gardening point of view because nature and the climate do everything: 'It would take away all that to me constitutes the real interest of gardening, in its difficulties, and even its disappointments.'

Dion Clayton Calthrop too, in *The Charm of Gardens* (1910), maintains that the English love of gardening is due to the weather: 'We English are gardeners by nature: perhaps the greyness of our skies accounts for our desire to make our gardens blaze with colours.'

Eleanour Rohde often uses the concept of the English race in her books. In *The Old English Gardening Books* (1924), for example, she writes: 'The English garden was formulated in the sixteenth century and in a manner characteristic of our race, for there was no break with the past, all that was most attractive in medieval times being made still lovelier by Elizabethan principles of beauty and sense of form. There was a subtle pedantry and sweetness about the gardens of Tudor and Stuart days, but above all they were distinguished by their English characteristics of simplicity and homeliness.' Later, in discussing Thomas Tusser, she says: 'We are a conservative nation ... Tusser's careful lists of what the housewife should grow are full of the names of the lovable old-fashioned flowers we English folk cherish most.'

George Orwell considers this concept of Englishness in relation to horticulture in his essay 'England Your England', published in 1941: 'But here it is worth noticing a minor English trait which is extremely well marked though not often commented on, and that is a love of flowers. This is one of the first things that one notices when one reaches England from abroad, especially if one is coming from southern Europe ... We are a nation of flower-lovers.'

In his autobiographical book, *The Invisible Writing* (1954), Arthur Koestler quotes Orwell's description of the English. He also expresses relief at his escape from continental totalitarianism, and he compliments the English on being 'potterers-in-the-garden and stickers-in-the-mud'.

Writing soon after the Second World War, Walter Ingwersen (1951) sees gardening as a British instinct and comments on the change in post-war circumstances: 'The instinct to make gardens seems inborn in the British race, and in these days when we are all poor and our fine old gardens have fallen upon evil days we must do our gardening on a smaller scale and without a staff of trained gardeners.'

Racism

Often the concept of 'Englishness' develops into overt racism, as when Beeton (1862) calls Africa 'that land of monstrosities'.

In a poem on sugar cane, written in 1801, Frances Arabella Rowden attacks slavery and praises Wilberforce, but she also writes of the 'rude natives' of Mexico. In her poem on the banana tree, she describes Captain Cook being slain by a 'rude race of savage Indians'. Likewise

George Johnson, in *A History of English Gardening* (1829), refers to the 'bigotry' of the 'New Zealand savages'.

Anne Pratt, in *The Field, the Garden, and the Woodland* (1838), writes of the natives of Africa as 'sunk in ignorance', and describes the 'unenlightened' people of Arabia as having 'minds prejudiced against the truth'. Writing about India, in *Flowers and their Associations* (1840), she refers to 'that dreamy idleness so delicious to the Oriental'.

The anonymous author of *Garden Flowers* (1857) expresses in flowery language her concern that Africans eat iris bulbs. Despite the bulbs being nutritious, this seems to her to be a kind of sacrilege: 'Some species of this plant have large bulbous roots, and many of the African kinds constitute a large portion of the food of the Hottentots. They are eaten either roasted, boiled, or stewed with milk, and are said to be both palatable and nourishing. But it seems to be almost an insult to the Iris to descend from the contemplation of the beauteous colours of its flower, connected as they are with the prismatic bow of heaven and the romantic legends of an ancient mythology, to the subject of stewing and devouring its bulbous roots. Pardon, Flora, our mingling grosser fact thus rudely with thine airy wreath of fiction!'

Gardening is often equated with civilisation. In *The Book of Gardening* (1900) William Drury refers to the 'civilising and refining influences' of gardening and concludes: 'In fact, we are told upon excellent authority, that it is only among the most brutal and degraded races of savages that gardening is unknown.'

Similarly Alicia Amherst writes of the 'ignorant "Boers" or peasants' in South Africa who call all the spring flowers tulips. Amherst's book is based on a journey round the world in 1926–7 on behalf of the Society for the Oversea Settlement of British Women, and the Victoria League. It aims to give potential settlers 'a rough idea of the vegetation, so as to be able to picture to some extent the external characteristics of the chosen Dominion before setting out'. Amherst expresses the belief that a knowledge of plants might help bind the Empire together: 'To know something of the floral charm of the jungle, the forest, the hills and plains of the far-flung Empire could hardly fail to increase the interest and understanding which bind all British subjects together.'

Gardening can also supply convenient metaphors for those concerned about racial 'purity'. Rider Haggard's *A Gardening Year* (1905) is a 'gardener's diary for the year 1903', complete with digressions. He discusses the hybridisation of plants, for instance, and the dreadful human parallel: 'I believe that, theoretically, all Orchids can be crossed; at any rate, fertile marriage has taken place between the most dissimilar species, but it is certain that all should *not* be crossed, any more than a white woman should marry a Hottentot, or a Zulu mate with an Esquimau.'

AFRICA

Just as the colonists took their gardening methods and styles to the New World, so colonial gardeners in Asia and Africa constantly demonstrated their ethnocentrism by trying to re-create English gardens, even though the conditions were unsuitable. Many attempts were made, for example, to grow English lawns in the tropics. In *The Royal Botanic Gardens, Peradeniya, Ceylon* (1922) Stockdale, Petch and Macmillan comment on the difficulties involved: 'Visitors to Peradeniya are struck particularly by the beautiful lawns, a comparatively rare feature in gardens of the tropics. These lawns are the envy of other tropical gardens, but only persons who know can realise the difficulty of making and maintaining lawns in a climate where members of the vegetable kingdom vie with each other with such vigour for possession of the soil, and where animal pests, especially of the subterranean and creeping class, are so rampant.'

In *A Handbook of Tropical Gardening and Planting* (1910) Macmillan, who was curator of the Peradeniya gardens, is more specific about the 'enemies of lawns'. He writes of 'the pernicious termite or white-ant' and the need for an 'ant-exterminator', using a mixture of arsenic and sulphur, to destroy them. At the back of the book is an advertisement for this apparatus, called 'The "Universal" Destroyer'. The author also mentions one of the most invasive weeds in the lawns: 'Elephant's foot (Elephantopus scaber).'

This construction of English gardens abroad was often undertaken at the expense of indigenous flora. As early as 1840, in *Flowers and their Associations*, Anne Pratt expresses surprise at how settlers in South Africa neglected the wonderful native flowers: 'Not one of all the large tribe of magnificent heaths is admitted into a garden of the colonist, or has received so much of his notice as even to have acquired an individual name.' Instead they raised flowers such as hollyhock, tulip and hyacinth from seeds imported from Europe.

Neglect gave way to destruction, as Margaret Spilhaus records in *Indigenous Trees of the Cape Peninsula* (1950): 'Our forests disappeared principally because, from the arrival of the first settlers, they were ruthlessly exploited and never replanted.' In the Foreword J.C. Smuts gives the example of how 'timbermen and shipbuilders and repairers' reduced Hout Bay, which used to be 'one big forest area', to its 'present desolate character'. He concludes: 'It is one of the calamities of our Cape Flora that our indigenous plants have been systematically neglected in favour of imported plants.'

WHITE ANTS!

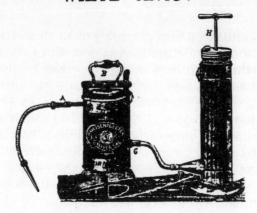

The ————
"Universal" Destroyer

As Recommended by Government Entomologists
in Ceylon, India, and the Straits Settlements.

The Guaranteed Apparatus for the Extermination of TERMITES
in their nests and heaps.

(SEE PAGE 485).

Full Particulars of Prices, &c., from the Sole Agents for Ceylon:

Gordon Frazer & Co.,
———— Colombo.

*Ant-exterminator used to help maintain English lawns in the Royal Botanic
Gardens, Peradeniya, Ceylon. Advertisement from H.F. Macmillan's
A Handbook of Tropical Gardening and Planting (1910).*

In *My African Garden* (1892) Donald McDonald explains how to produce an English lawn, cricket grounds, lawn tennis and croquet grounds. The native flora are acknowledged only in so far as they have been exported to Britain: 'Of its own productions in the way of flowers the region [Cape Colony], almost ever since it has been known to Europeans, has been a never-failing source of botanical novelty to the greenhouses and conservatories of Great Britain.' At the same time he wonders at the fact that potatoes, brought to Europe from South America, are now being grown in South Africa to supply the London markets.

McDonald describes some territories under the administration of the Royal Niger Company, stating that the 'success of their experimental operations, under the management of English gardeners, is having an important influence over the natives'. On other territories he comments: 'It only requires European enterprise to open up these valuable districts, which at present are mostly in a fearfully neglected state through the indolence of the opulent natives.' Nyasaland he considers to be even more in need of intervention: 'Gardening, however, can hardly be said to exist in a country that has only recently come within the pale of civilisation.'

The subtitle of McDonald's book is 'Hints on the Cultivation of English Vegetables and Flowers in South Africa and British and Foreign Possessions in and Adjacent to this Great Continent'. It contains an advertisement for Carters' boxes of tested English vegetable and flower seeds, which can be sent post free to all parts of Africa within the Parcel Post Union, with this related comment in the text of the book: 'There are few greater benefits which the settler can bestow than that of distributing the seeds of improved vegetables, and teaching the poor benighted beings how to grow them.'

Marion Cran, in *The Garden of Ignorance* (1913), writes: 'I never knew that African gardens were beautiful. No one ever told me so. I never read any garden papers or articles about them. They were as great a surprise to me as the peculiar blue of her hills, and the clear, close solemnity of her stars at night. People in South Africa love their gardens.' But the 'people' she refers to are the Boers and the English. The Africans she calls 'niggers' and 'natives', and she admires the 'quaint design' of the 'slave-bell towers': 'When a man had miles of farm, as those early pioneers often had, he needed a loud summons to call his natives home; hence those picturesque bell-towers to which the Dutch craftsmen had brought their skill and love of beauty.'

At Swanley College there was a colonial branch to train women to go to South Africa. In *A Third Pot-Pourri* (1903), Mrs Earle refers to its establishment: 'I have lately received papers with regard to establishing a Colonial branch of the Horticultural College at Swanley, Kent. This with a special view to the immediate demand for competent women in South Africa, in which country there is a present deficiency of 70,000 Englishwomen.'

In *Gardening for Women* (1908) Frances Wolseley expresses her eagerness to train female gardeners to cultivate the 'virgin soil' of South Africa. Skilled and well-instructed head gardeners were needed in the Colonies: 'There they have plenty of hands to do mechanical work, numbers of "coolies" to do menial jobs, but they want more intelligent directors and guides to industry.' The women would have a 'refining influence'

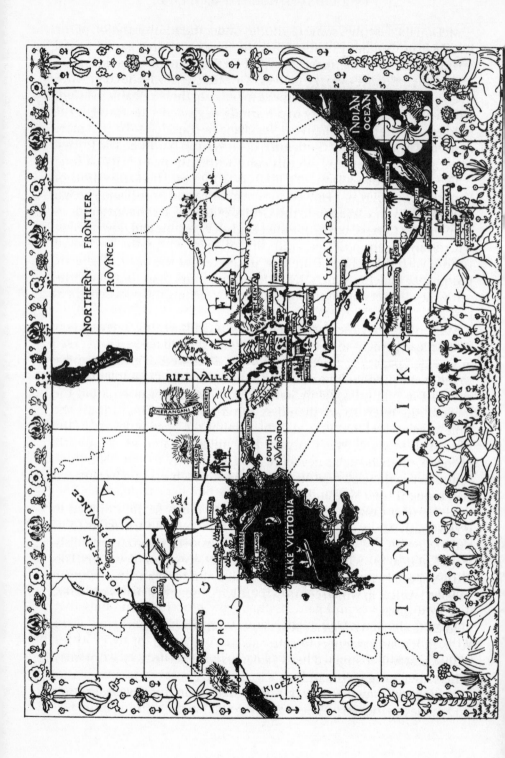

in the 'somewhat uncivilised surroundings', where they would super-intend the 'merely mechanical work of kaffirs'.

In the Preface to *A Book of Gardening for the Sub-Tropics* (1921) by Mary Stout and Madeline Agar, Charles Whymper manages in two short pages to be just as disparaging about both Jews and Egyptians, referring to the 'vast horde of Semites led by Moses into the desert'. He writes of 'the host of lovely and sweet-smelling plants than can be grown' in Egypt, 'so banishing from our minds the recollection of those perspiring, garlick-eating Jews amid the African deserts'. It is the white man's burden to make gardens in Egypt: 'The Anglo-Saxon is a peculiar person. One of his peculiarities is an intense love of home and garden; another is empire-building under a fiercer sun than his native land knows. It, therefore, seems right and proper that there should be a book to tell him, simply and completely, how his exile may be softened amid the sun-baked, sandy soils of his temporary home, by one of the means he would best love.'

Later in the book Mary Stout makes the usual complaint about the laziness of African gardeners: 'Native gardeners are extremely liable to overlook the first signs of pest attacks, being generally unobservant and unwilling to take trouble until the matter is urgent.'

In *Gardens of South Africa* (1924) Dorothea Fairbridge traces the history of colonial gardening in this part of the continent, beginning with the famous garden of the Dutch East India Company, planned in the seventeenth century by Johan van Riebeeck. She casually refers to the hundred slaves who were employed as gardeners and assumes that this was the origin of all South African gardening: 'As I walk through van Riebeeck's garden to-day, my thoughts go back to the little beginnings from which all South African gardens have sprung.'

She goes on to recount how certain free burghers made gardens 'in the teeth of troubles by floods, and of depredations by the angry little Hottentots whom they dispossessed'. Credit is later given to the Hottentots for their herbal remedies, but the main concern is that the British Empire should be 'self-supporting' in drugs, for 'three-quarters of the drugs used in South Africa were, up to August, 1914, imported from Germany'. There is also concern about the enemy within, because 'the Orange-groves and gardens that grow peacefully on lands that once were the Black Man's', she warns, 'may be the Black Man's again if the White Folk of South Africa let themselves forget the necessity for standing together, shoulder to shoulder, to hold the land for Civilisation'.

Opposite: Map of East Africa, from the second edition of Gardening in East Africa, *edited by A.J. Jex-Blake (1939).*

"Grand planting weather."

"He thought my skirt was widow's weeds."

Illustrations by the author, from Peter Ender's Up the Garden Path *(1944).*

Fairbridge also thinks that the Indians who came to Natal to work on the tea plantations 'present a race problem', but admits that they are 'very good gardeners'. She contrasts them with African gardeners: 'The native Zulu boys, though without the inherited instinct for gardening which marks the mali, are very neat-fingered and work well under instruction. They make good house-servants, too, noiseless and courteous, with a passion for rubbing up brass, and with a gentle mildness of manner that is almost uncanny in the descendants of Chakas's fierce warriors. At their present stage of garden knowledge it is useless to expect them to use their heads in regard to seeds and seasons, but their hands are far more deft than the fingers of the average white man, and they are very trustworthy. South Africa is fortunate in her supply of native labour, but you must be your own head gardener if you want success. You must also preside over all planting with a measuring line, if you have a native gardener, for he is as incapable of planting anything in a straight row as of playing the Moonlight Sonata.'

Another book which deals with colonial gardening is *Gardening in East Africa*, edited by A.J. Jex-Blake. It was published in 1934 and an enlarged edition came out in 1939. The Foreword talks of the love of gardening being a 'characteristic of British folk wherever they may be found', and the aim of the book is to help 'horticultural friends in distant parts of the Empire'. In Chapter XI, 'Flowering Trees and Shrubs', Lady Jex-Blake and Mrs L.H. Barradell state that 'serious gardening in Kenya is not much more than twenty years old'. References in other chapters are made to 'the wasteful husbandry of native races' and their unreliability as gardeners: 'The native gardener is, as a rule, an unskilled waterer, and constant supervision should be given to this most important operation.'

Although slavery was officially abolished in the first half of the nineteenth century, the second half of the century witnessed the European powers carving up Africa for their own benefit. The resulting colonial ideology is clearly reflected in gardening literature, for example in the illustrations to Peter Ender's *Up the Garden Path* (1944).

INDIA

The Indian Hand-Book of Gardening by Frederic Speede was first published in 1840. It begins a long line of colonial texts which disparage Indian gardening. 'Considering gardening as a mere art that may be performed by even the most ignorant labourer, manuals or books of instruction would be useless; yet this is the point of view in which it is almost universally held in this country, and hence the slow progress hitherto made in the cultivation of such produce of the garden as is generally held in estimation by the European portion of the community; left as it generally is, to the simple Hindoo mallee (or gardener,) it is not to be wondered at, that our bazars want, what are deemed the more delicate articles of vegetable production for the table.'

In 1864 *A Manual of Gardening for Bengal and Upper India* was published, written by Thomas Firminger, an Anglican clergyman stationed in Bengal. The author is scathing about horticulture in India 'Of the natives, those of the higher class, it would seem, have never manifested much fondness for it, nor taken much interest in the pursuit; while those, who follow it for a livelihood, have not found it sufficiently remunerative to devote to it more than the least possible of their time and thought.' Unlike Dorothea Fairbridge's complimentary remarks about the Indian gardener in South Africa, Firminger's view of the mali is expressed in typical colonial fashion: 'A garden left entirely to the hands of a malee, will invariably be found in that dirty, neglected state, so noticeable in the compounds around most European residences in India.' Of the malis around Calcutta he writes that they 'often prove neglectful, indolent, and cunning'. They cannot even understand 'the apparently simple operation of administering water to a potted plant in exact accordance with its wants'.

For Firminger this offers a justification of the class structure and the division of labour: 'It was hardly to be expected that to men in the humble sphere of the malee, much, if any theoretical knowledge could be imparted. The judicious application of the theory of gardening is not to be acquired but by men of a liberal education, and of a class far above that of mere labourers, such as our malees are.' When in 1855, however, the Agri-Horticultural Society of India established a school for native gardeners, the boys, when educated, simply went off to get better-paid jobs.

His book does include descriptions of many native plants, but Firminger is not very complimentary about the vegetables: 'It is only on rare occasions that these prove acceptable, where European vegetables can be obtained, though welcome as substitutes where they cannot.' Most are described as 'weeds' which the Indians use 'in their cookery merely as a vehicle for their curry-ingredients'.

It is not always remembered that the sealed glass boxes, which brought thousands of plants into England from the colonies, also took a similar number of plants back again, so that English gardens could be created. Firminger calls these Wardian cases 'unquestionably the best of all means of transmitting plants'. This is also noted in the 1918 edition, when reference is made to the seed company, Sutton and Sons of Reading, a branch of which had recently been established in Calcutta:

'The seed sold is nearly all imported, and few of the ornamental plants sold are indigenous.'

This is the sixth edition of the book, revised and edited by W. Burns, who includes a new section entitled 'Thieves', relating to the Indian gardener. He writes that, when theft occurs, 'it may be laid down for certain that it is either the act of the mali himself, or done with his concurrence'. The solution is drastic: 'A thorny hedge or barbed wire fence will assist to keep out thieves. It is an excellent idea also, if a visit of fruit thieves is expected, to leave several strands of barbed wire lying loosely about all over the spot which they will visit. This must be done personally, after dark.' Perhaps Burns had read the Rev. J.G. Wood's *The Natural History of Man*, in which the author writes: 'Certain it is that there are no more accomplished thieves in the world than those of India.'

'Grafting the Mango', from the fourth edition of G. Marshall Woodrow's Hints on Gardening in India *(1888). 'The grafter is Guja Bapoo of Aund, near Poona, one of my pupils in grafting, who has taught many of his fellow-countrymen.'*

In *Hints on Gardening in India* (1876) G. Marshall Woodrow refers to Firminger when justifying the writing of his book: 'Besides Firminger's expensive work, there is little else on the subject in print.' His work is aimed at British soldiers: 'These Hints were written for the use of the Soldiers of the British Army in India, to whom a beneficent Government not only offers the use of land, but yearly presents a supply of flower and vegetable seeds, and prizes for their successful treatment, with a view to providing for the men a pleasant and useful employment for their leisure hours. The wisdom of this act of grace cannot be doubted, as it not only furnishes healthful recreation and tends to relieve the monotony of the soldier's life in India, but the taste for gardening that is encouraged may supply the retired soldier with the means of earning a respectable living and thereby improve the status of the rank and file.'

In the sixth edition, published in 1910 as *Gardening in the Tropics*, the author assumes that it is part of the white man's burden to teach the natives how to garden. Despite the difficulties, he detects some recent improvement: 'Genuine progress in the cultivation of plants can scarcely exist where the educated races stand aloof and leave cultivation to the most ignorant section of the people. Fortunately, this condition is being gradually ameliorated, and even Brahmins may be indicated who have lived in honour and died rich from the pursuit of horticulture.' There are several designs for gardens in the book, all emanating from England. A design for a compound of ten acres contains a lawn and a tennis court, as well as 'a paddock, in which foals disport or sleek kine browse the dewy herb'. A plan for a public park of 100 acres, by A.G. Jackman of Woking, also includes a tennis court, along with 'open spaces for cricket and other games'.

A book called *The Indian Amateur Gardener* by Landolicus, originally published around 1880, provides another interesting insight into English colonial gardening in India. The fourth edition came out in 1936 and in it the author disparages the country: 'The indigenous fruits of India are very few indeed and, barring the Mango, are of not much importance.' He goes on to explain how to create English gardens, whether in the hill stations or in the plains, complete with tennis or croquet lawns and even cricket pitches. Above all, they should remind the English of home: 'Gardens around bungalows where Europeans live should be made to look as "homelike" as possible. Characteristic sweeping drives bordered with shrubs and flower borders, beds of flowers, bowers of roses, and verdant lawns should be the predominant ideas.'

Like McDonald's *My African Garden*, the book stresses the importance of the lawn, particularly for games and social occasions: 'In India good lawns fulfil many requirements – for nine months in the year they are in almost daily use for a variety of games, such as tennis, badminton and croquet, and are also the meeting places for social and other gatherings.' Detailed instructions are given on how to sow the lawn and maintain it. Watering an acre of lawn, for example, will require 875,000 gallons a year.

Donald McDonald is also the author of *English Vegetables & Flowers in India & Ceylon*. The first edition sold out in six months and the second revised edition was published in 1890. The Preface to the first edition

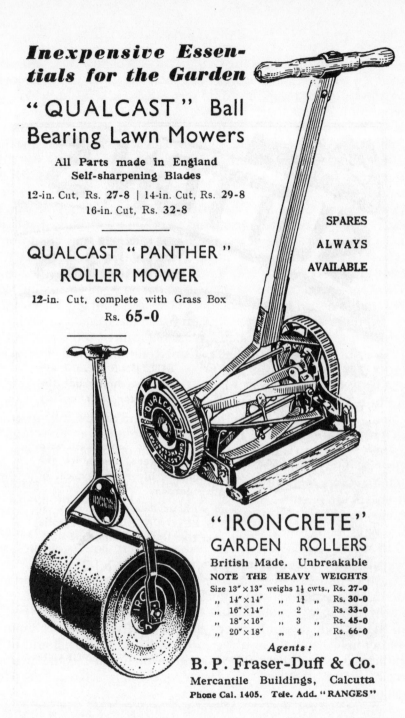
Advertisement for lawn-mowers and rollers to create English lawns in India, from the fourth edition of The Indian Amateur Gardener *(1936) by Landolicus.*

Advertising seeds and English gardens in India, from the fourth edition of
The Indian Amateur Gardener (1936) by Landolicus.

states that it is 'directed to those who find it necessary, through business or other occupation, military and civil, to make our great Eastern possessions their home for a period extending, more or less, over a number of years, and are desirous, so far as is possible, to cultivate Vegetables, Flowers, Bulbs, Roses and Fruits, as had been their custom in England. The Book is also intended to be of service to those Natives whose education to British ways has led them to be interested in the subject.'

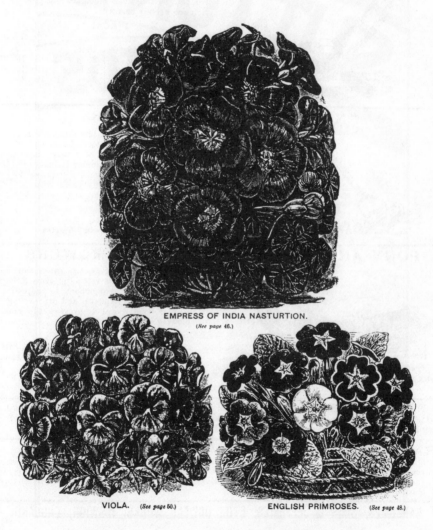

EMPRESS OF INDIA NASTURTION.
(See page 46.)

VIOLA. *(See page 50.)*   ENGLISH PRIMROSES. *(See page 48.)*

English flowers exported to India. From Donald McDonald's English Vegetables & Flowers in India & Ceylon *(1890).*

RANSOMES' LAWN MOWERS.
THE BEST FOR INDIA.

"NEW AUTOMATON" LAWN MOWER.

These Machines are intended for doing the highest class of work and producing the finest surface on Lawns for Cricket, Tennis, &c., and wherever closeness of cut and absolute freed m from ribbing are required. By close and frequent cutting these Machines will produce a rich and velvety surface.

PRICES.

	£	s.	d.		£	s.	d.
8 in. ...	2	15	0	18 in. ...	7	10	0
10 in. ...	3	10	0	20 in. ...	8	10	0
12 in. ...	4	10	0	22 in. ...	9	10	0
14 in. ...	5	10	0	24 in. ...	10	10	0
16 in. ...	6	10	0				

"NEW PARIS" LAWN MOWER.

These Machines are specially adapted for those who require a light working and low priced Machine. Being equally as strong and well-made as R., S. and J.'s more expensive mowers, they are unequalled by any similar Machines in the market, and unlike many of their rivals, will prove to be good and serviceable articles after many years' wear.

PRICES.

6 in., 30/-; 8 in., 35/-; 10 in., 40/-; 12 in., 50/-; 14 in., 60/-; 16 in., 70/-. Grass Boxes, 5/- to 7/6 extra.

PONY AND HORSE-POWER LAWN MOWERS.

In these Machines the grass can be delivered on either side at pleasure; they have a simple arrangement for adjusting the knives and concave, and are provided with a wind guard to prevent the grass blowing about.

PRICES.

Pony Machines, 26 in., £14; 30 in., £18. Horse-power, 30 in., £20; 36 in., £24; 42 in., £28; 48 in., £32.
Leather Boots for Pony, 25/-; Horse, 30/- per set.

N.B.—The Prices given above include delivery to English Shipping Port. To these must be added cost of freight and insurance; also the charge for packing, which varies from 3/- to 10/- for the Hand Machines, and from 17/6 to 27/6 for the Power Machines.

RANSOMES' LAWN MOWERS are specially suited for cutting the tough native grass which is used on many of the lawns in India; and wherever they have been introduced they have given the highest satisfaction. They can be ordered from R. S. & J.'s Agents in India, Messrs. Octavius Steel & Co., Calcutta; Messrs. Massey & Co., Madras; Mr. F. W. Shallis, 9, Marine St., Bombay.

RANSOMES, SIMS & JEFFERIES, LTD., ORWELL WORKS, IPSWICH, ENGLAND.

Commercial interests in growing English lawns in India. From Donald McDonald's
English Vegetables & Flowers in India & Ceylon *(1890).*

Many Indians, says the author, are being educated at universities in England, the consequence of which, when they return home, is 'the pleasing characteristic of an increasing disposition to render the surroundings of their bungalow or other dwellings cheerful with English Flowers and Plants'. He thinks that an interest in gardening 'may be the means of scattering a refining influence over their lives'.

McDonald writes of 'the superstitious native gardener' and gives this advice on bird-scaring: 'Employ the services of a youth to keep away the birds from growing and fruiting crops; keep his stomach well filled or he will do more damage than they can possibly commit.' He has a section on English lawns, which also deals with cricket, lawn tennis and croquet grounds, and at the end of the book there is an advertisement for English lawn-mowers.

In *Flowers and Gardens in India* (1893) Mrs Temple-Wright also states that 'a lawn is an absolute necessity'. It should be 'a little larger than a tennis-court, or suitable to hold a garden-party'. To keep it like velvet it needs to be regularly mown, swept, rolled and watered. She advises against growing creepers on the walls of the house, because they will harbour snakes and mosquitoes, and can look untidy.

Her summary of expenditure indicates the cheapness of Indian labour: 'The expense for keeping up this small garden will be five rupees a month to your mali for looking after and watering your flowers and shrubs. One extra rupee per month to your house bhistie for watering your grass-plot every evening, and eight annas per month extra to your grass-cutter for cutting your grass-plot once a week with the shears you will provide for him, and keeping your carriage-drive free from weeds.'

Again the stereotype of the mali appears: 'It is a foregone conclusion that your flowers will be stolen, and the deft fingers of the mali's wife will weave them into garlands to sell to devotees at the nearest temple.' She even includes a poem to the same effect:

> The mali trembles when he sees
> You making notes about your trees;
> And should your note-book disappear,
> He'll steal your plants without a fear!

By 1919 the book was in its seventh edition.

The colonial nostalgia for England is expressed by the anonymous author of *A Gloucestershire Wild Garden* (1903): 'Many years ago in India (ah, how many!) I used to picture to myself the home in England I hoped to form at some distant date, and visions of a house ensconced in woody depths, with gardens here and there in unexpected places, with lawns for tennis and croquet, with meadows for cream-yielding cattle, with water for ornament and use, and with a view over England's charming scenery, which under the circumstances of my visions loomed even more beautiful than the reality, if that be possible.'

The following year E.M. Eggar's *An Indian Garden* was published. The author gives an account of her garden of five and a half acres in Alipore, near Calcutta, containing mainly native flowers and shrubs, but also 'English home flowers'. She expresses the habitual complaints about her gardeners: 'These men, too, never can work properly unless under an overseer. It is their custom to labour with their hands only; some one else must supply the brains, and guide the fingers.' They never used the spade she bought them, because they only had their naked feet to push it into the ground, and they were incapable of driving the wheelbarrow straight: 'Every fresh gardening coolie we get has to be instructed in the art of using the English wheelbarrow, a perfectly new form of garden implement to them.'

She has problems with the rival religions. Hindus will not touch bonemeal because they think it contains human bones, perhaps from a relative or ancestor, 'so a Mahomedan boy has to dig it out of the sack and mix it in the earth. It does not seem to be of any consequence to the Mahomedan whether he is using his grandmother's bones to manure flowers with or not.' She describes herself sitting under two umbrellas, instructing the gardeners. In the rainy season of July and August she has three men pulling up weeds in the lawn by hand, and 'directly they have come to the end of the lawns they have to begin at the beginning, all over again'.

In *My Garden in the Wilderness* (1915) Kathleen Murray also writes about gardening in India. Like Landolicus, she describes attempts to create English gardens on foreign soil: 'Outside my dining room windows there is a south corner that is entirely English in design.' It contains hollyhocks, wallflowers, mignonette and sweet peas. There are copies of formal English gardens as well, with bedding plants.

She too complains about her hired hands: 'I have during the last week become extremely unpopular with the underlings in my garden, who have found themselves hustled and goaded and scolded into doing an appreciable amount of work. There is so much to be done that I feel as overwhelmed as the coolies do, with the exception that my dreams are haunted, as theirs certainly are not, with visions of all that still is left undone.' Her last servant had a 'supercilious attitude'; the present one has a 'cheerful unintelligence' and cannot be entrusted to pick the sweet peas.

As recently as 1951, we can find a similarly patronising account of the Indian gardener. In *My Garden's Bedside Book*, compiled by T.A. Stephens, there is a piece by B.H.B. entitled 'The Mali', which contains the following description: 'In India, a mali is the equivalent of a gardener, in fact gardener is the translation of the word. His methods, however, are not the same. No English gardener would use a pair of scissors to cut the lawn with. He would get bored very quickly. Not so the mali, he does not get bored. Time is of no concern to him, and he prefers to squat on his haunches and dig up the earth in a flower-bed with a piece of bent iron than stand up and use a hoe. Moreover, if you employ a mali, it is not necessary to have a garden of your own to get a supply of flowers.'

The idea of the lazy native is referred to in Edward Said's *Culture and Imperialism*, where he asserts that the 'natives' refusal to work was one of the earliest forms of resistance to the European incursion'. But in *The Myth of the Lazy Native* Syed Hussein Alatas also relates it more specifically to the attempt to impose capitalist labour practices. He writes particularly about Malays who often served the Europeans as gardeners: 'The image of the indolent native was the product of colonial domination generally in the 19th century when the domination of the colonies reached a high peak and when capitalist exploitation required extensive control of the area. The image of the native had a function in the exploitation complex of colonial times. This was the time when the capitalist conception of labour gained supremacy. Any type of labour which did not conform to this conception was rejected as a deviation. A community which did not enthusiastically and willingly adopt this conception of labour was regarded as indolent.'

Positive Images

After reading such disparaging colonial gardening literature, it came as a relief to turn to a book which actually celebrates the great tradition of Indian gardening. This is *Gardens of the Great Mughals* (1913), written by Constance Mary Villiers Stuart, from Beachamwell Hall in Norfolk, and illustrated with her own water-colours. She begins by commenting on the lack of existing books on the subject: 'Among the many books dealing with various branches of Indian Art, it is remarkable that none have so far been devoted to the subject of Indian gardening; although, in its traditional, artistic, and symbolic aspects, the Mughal Paradise Garden supplied the leading motive in Mughal decorative art, and still underlies the whole artistic world of the Indian craftsman and builder.'

The author goes on to describe the 'practical and imaginative beauty of Indian garden-craft' and asks why Italian gardens are so much admired and visited, while the great Indian gardens are ignored. 'Gardening in a horticultural sense still flourishes in India', she maintains, but stresses repeatedly that the decline of Indian gardening is due to the introduction of the English landscape garden.

The Shalimar gardens, north of Delhi, for example, deteriorated rapidly under the British in the nineteenth century. Similarly, new road building ruined other beautiful gardens in Delhi City. Traditional pergolas and cool shady alleys, 'under European influence, entirely disappeared from the Kashmir gardens'. The author is scathing about what replaced them: 'In place of the stately water-ways and avenues, the pergolas and gay parterres, the perfumed dusk of the Hindu pleasure-grounds, and the sunshine brilliance of the Mughal baghs [enclosed gardens], the incongruities of the Anglo-Indian landscape gardener reign supreme. It is easy enough to picture the change: the exposed private garden, a contradiction in its very terms; the public parks with their bare acres of unhappy-looking grass, their ugly bandstands, hideous iron railings, and forlorn European statues; their wide, objectless roads, scattered flower-beds, and solitary trees, and, worst of all in a hot country, their lack of fountains and running water.'

Villiers Stuart also rehabilitates the mali, when recounting how she planned her first garden in India: 'I remember how I argued at great length against the mali's (gardener) insistence that the walks should be raised above the garden level, unconsciously clinging, in my own mind, to the opposite English plan of the flat paths with their raised herbaceous borders. The mali won the day, though I was slow, I confess, to see the obvious fact that the walks, in an irrigated garden, must be necessarily raised for the water to pass under them.'

She also explains why he is often ridiculed: 'The Indian mali is often laughed at for his devotion to his "gumalis" and tubs, – though they are very practical in the plains, where the white ants are likely to devour everything in the ground, – for his crazy patchwork bedding, and his rows of untidy little pots. It is the small scale and multiplicity of these gumalis, and flower-beds, which prevents us seeing that they are only degenerate forms of two well-known Mughal motives – geometrical floral designs and plants in vases.'

Finally she wants to 'call the Indian master-builder and his malis to our aid' and concludes: 'It is not surprising to find Indians copying European styles even when their own are sounder and more suitable, as they naturally wish to imitate the arts of a nation which has proved itself to be strong in other ways. But in these latter days of aesthetic revivals, and more particularly of the rediscovery of the truth that the house and garden should form one harmonious whole, it is indeed strange that we should be so slow to learn from India.'

In an earlier book, *In My Indian Garden* (1878), Phil Robinson also regrets the demise of an old Indian garden. He recalls the 'black-shaded mango-trees' which used to grow in the garden of Khusru, once 'a kingly garden, royal in size and royal in its wealth of foliage': 'In remote corners were massed dark thickets of close-blossomed, heavy-fruited citrons. Robust shrubs of jessamine and oleander relieved in large colours the levels of green turf which were spread between.' All of this was transformed to reflect the contemporary English style: 'And now? Prim beds lie flat upon the ground, central in each a single blossomed Rose – a miracle maybe of its species – while on painted supports cling cobwebs of faint exotic flowers. Small plants, with the demeanour of the well-educated stand at even distances from one another, each keeping itself to its own hole ... A well-metalled road sweeps round between croquet lawns, to a band-stand made out of pickings from one of the old tombs.'

Another writer who recognises the ancient Mogul tradition is K.C. Ryves, who was brought up in a West Country parsonage, but then spent some time in India. In *Of Gardens East and West* (1921) the author admires the 'beautiful formal paths of fine brickwork in old Mogul gardens, such as the Shalimar, at Lahore; where the whole triumph of the garden lies in the harmonising of the rose and white of lotus, and the mellow reds and browns of the diapered brick walls, with the designed arrangement of tank and fountain and waterchute and the dark mass of watching trees'. She also praises Dara Shukoh's garden in Kashmir and writes: 'In this lovely land the spring flowers are a dream of delight, and the fruit-trees make a festival of blossom as daintily gorgeous as in the orchard-lands of England.'

Ryves criticises the idea of creating a 'little dream of England' for the 'short two months', while ignoring the other ten hot months when it becomes 'a place of dry and yellow grass, of ill-tended, unweeded borders' because of the lack of rain and the fact that it is too hot to garden. Instead she imagines a garden full of the odour of Indian plants, 'tuberose and moon flower, jasmine and champak, and the stealing scent of orange and citron'. She complains of the Western fashion not to plant cypresses: 'They are too slow of growth for this transitory Anglo-Indian life, and it is not our custom to plant for posterity.' Although the author recognises the longing 'for a vision of sweet English daffodils and primroses', she still concludes: 'The real garden indigenous to the country is, after all, a more serviceable one than that which we have brought with us out of the West.'

In *The Craftsman's Plant-Book* (1909) Richard Hatton celebrates another aspect of Indian culture. The book is about sixteenth-century herbals and the author is disparaging about Britain's contribution to their illus-trations: 'Great Britain seems to have contributed little or nothing to the illustrations of the famous herbals.' He goes on to compare a 'beautiful Indian drawing' of around 1570: 'Of the excellence of such

a drawing it is impossible to speak too highly. I doubt whether better drawings of plants and animals have ever been done.' Hatton, Professor of Fine Art at Armstrong College, Newcastle-upon-Tyne, concludes by asking: 'When, one ventures to ask, will people recognize that India had an art which rises superior to anything produced by other Eastern nations, and is unsurpassed, in its kind, by anything that Europe has to show!'

FRANCE

Renewed conflict with France broke out at the end of the eighteenth century and in the nineteenth century comparison is constantly made between French and English horticulture. The most usual criticism made of French gardening is that it is too formal by comparison with the freedom and informality of the English style, particularly that of the landscape garden.

At the end of the nineteenth century, however, Reginald Blomfield was vitriolic about the English landscape garden and wanted to reinstate French formality. Along with another garden architect, Thomas Mawson, whose book *The Art and Craft of Garden Making* came out in 1900, and with John Sedding, Blomfield attacked both the landscape garden and the new 'natural' garden championed by William Robinson. In *The Formal Garden in England* (1892) he praises the formal gardens of Elizabethan times and expresses the view that Le Nôtre, who designed Versailles, 'carried the art of garden design to the highest point of development it has ever reached'. The spread of the English landscape garden to the rest of Europe he views as a disaster: 'It is not an exhilarating thought that in the one instance in which English taste in a matter of design has taken hold on the Continent, it has done so with such disastrous results.'

He criticises the landscapist for seeing grass only as a background. For Blomfield grass is a very beautiful thing in itself: 'Grass-work ought to be designed with reference to its own particular beauty. The turf of an English garden is probably the most perfect in the world, certainly it is far more beautiful than any to be found on the continent, and even the French admitted this two hundred years ago.'

Arthur Young (1792), on the other hand, comes to the defence of French lawns. Like Celia Fiennes and Daniel Defoe before him, he travelled widely throughout England keeping a diary. In 1787 he started

Opposite: 'In the Jungle'. An Indian drawing, executed about 1570, from Richard G. Hatton's The Craftsman's Plant-Book *(1909).*

his travels in France, visiting many gardens. At Chantilly he finds an imitation of an English garden: 'The most English idea I saw is the lawn in front of the stables; it is large, of a good verdure, and well kept; proving clearly that they may have as fine lawns in the north of France as in England.'

Henry Phillips, however, puts this down to the work of British gardeners. In *Sylva Florifera* (1823) he writes: 'The few lawns that are kept in any tolerably decent order abroad, are generally under the care of Scotch or English gardeners.'

George Mills is more generous to the French in *A Treatise on the Culture of the Pine-Apple* (1845). He boasts of growing the 'largest Pine-Apple ever produced in this country, its weight being $15^{1}/_{4}$ lbs. avoirdupois', and praises English cultivation: 'It has often been told me by gentlemen, who have seen the Pine-apples growing in their natural state, that they never saw them so fine as those grown in this country.' Nevertheless he also admits : 'I saw Pine-apples as well grown in France as I ever saw them in this country.'

In *The Rose Garden* (1848) William Paul refers to the competition between France and England as to which was 'the acknowledged favourite of the two greatest nations in the world'. He admits that the French may be more prolific rose growers, but 'English cultivators produce far handsomer plants than the French'. In *The Tree Rose* (1845), on the other hand, A.H.B. writes that 'the French stocks are considered far superior to the English'.

Catherine Gore, writing from France in 1838, acknowledges French superiority in the cultivation of roses, but claims that they attain their highest perfection in England. She is keen, however, to establish the cosmopolitan nature of the rose: 'This imperfect sketch of the geographical history of the rose, may serve to prove that it has not its exclusive birth-place in the East; but that it is to be found in all countries of the globe, for the gratification of the whole human race.'

In *Cultural Directions for the Rose* (1863) John Cranston, from King's Acre Nurseries, near Hereford, also praises the French. Discussing the importance of hybridising and cross-breeding, he states: 'Little however has been accomplished by English amateurs or cultivators, which has often surprised me; with the French it has been otherwise; and to them we are indebted for nearly all our finest Roses.' He thinks the French have more energy and, after the 'fearful havoc' wreaked on roses 'during the severe winter of 1860 and 1861', he encourages the English to breed a 'more hardy race' of roses.

In *The Gardeners' Annual for 1863* Dean Hole is more nationalistic. He gives an account of some French florists visiting the Rose Show in the gardens of the Royal Horticultural Society. Apparently they were astonished at what they saw and believed that the roses must have been grown under glass. Hole claims: 'Our climate execrable can produce such roses as neither "warmer France, with all her vines", nor any other climate can. In whatever else they may surpass us, they do not do *these* things better in France.' He boasts that 'we can grow blooms that are larger and lovelier than theirs'.

W.D. Prior, on the other hand, in *Roses and their Culture* (1878), puts the two countries more on a level: 'In the present day England and France are the homes, par excellence, of cultivated Roses, before whose perfections all others must utterly yield.' The author was a nurseryman in Colchester and he sees the French climate as more favourable for breeding roses: 'The French have been the chief originators of fresh varieties, though a few eminent English rosarians have held them in successful rivalry.'

In 1868, after visiting France, William Robinson published his views on French horticulture in *Gleanings from French Gardens*. He is also more even-handed than Hole, arguing that English plant nurseries and private gardens are better than their French counterparts, but that the French lead in growing fruit, decorating their apartments and in the public parks and gardens of Paris. He also thinks their system of watering is superior, using hoses, with water laid on. In particular he praises French secateurs, against which there was a prejudice in England, where they preferred to use a knife. He says that every French fruit-grower uses secateurs and 'he cuts as clean as the best knife-man with the best knife ever whetted'.

French superiority in grafting is claimed in Charles Baltet's *The Art of Grafting and Budding* (1878), which is a translation of his French book. The Preface states: 'The art of Grafting and Budding has for many years been practised in France on such an extensive scale, and with such remarkable success, that gardeners of that country are now far in advance of all others in this branch of horticulture.' Grafting in England, however, had been going on for a long time. In *The Customs of London*, first published around 1502, Arnold has a chapter entitled 'The Craft of Graffying and Plantinge of Trees and altering of Frutis as well in Colours as in Taste'. There is also an extant, though incomplete, copy of an anonymous work published about 1520, entitled *The craft of graffynge & plantynge of trees*.

An amazing tribute to the French appears in *Gardening for Beginners* (1902) by E.T. Cook, who seems to have presaged Henry Ford's car assembly-line. He complains about English gardeners wasting a very large amount of time in watering: 'This is a point on which we might well take a lesson from the French market gardener, who as a rule will, compared with us, do the same amount of watering in less than half the time, and with much less labour. He arranges his beds so that he can use two cans, one in each hand.'

An anonymous publication from around 1520.

French market gardeners are also praised by C.D. McKay in *The French Garden* (1908): 'The French, in their careful, methodical, and practical way, make use of every inch of room, and instead of getting one crop out of the beds they get four.' The author has the 'idea of growing early lettuces and other vegetables in England', thus avoiding the need to import the 'produce of the gardens of Paris and of Holland.' This would be 'to the great advantage of the nation'.

In 1905 McKay organised a visit to Paris for a number of gardeners from Evesham. They examined the market gardens at Vitry, about six miles from Paris, but 'the gardeners of another district which it was proposed to visit had read of the proposed visit in the papers, and there was an inclination among them not to show their methods, as they feared their industry might suffer from new competitors'.

Not only did the French produce earlier crops but they packed them more carefully: 'In France the packing is usually done by women, who show great taste, care, and deftness in their work.' A retired French market-gardener came to Evesham for a few weeks to teach the English gardeners, after which the French system was introduced. The following year the *Evesham Standard* reported the great success of the scheme.

Another French import is mentioned by Louis N. Flawn in *Cloche Gardening* (1959). The author records the 'fresh impetus and many new ideas' which were introduced by the refugee Huguenots after their defeat at Dreux in 1562. He acknowledges the French derivation of the cloche or bell-jar and its influence on the invention of the continuous cloche by Major L.H. Chase in 1912. But he is concerned that we still use the French word: 'It has always seemed to be a pity that the French word "cloche" was applied to what is essentially an English product; nor does a continuous cloche bear the slightest resemblance to a bell.'

JAPAN

At the end of the nineteenth century the English developed an interest in Japanese gardens. Particularly influential was Josiah Conder's illustrated *Landscape Gardening in Japan*, written in Tokyo and published in 1893. In this book the author refers to a paper he contributed to the *Journal of the Asiatic Society of Japan* in May 1886, 'in which the theory of Japanese garden compositions was first laid before European readers'. He also points to the desire to imitate Japanese gardens: 'To those desirous of reproducing elsewhere a model garden after the correct Japanese fashion, this copiously illustrated volume should afford some aid.'

Illustration from Josiah Conder's Landscape Gardening in Japan *(1893).*

At the beginning of the twentieth century the interest in Japanese gardening grew, partly as a result of exhibitions in London of Japanese gardens reflecting the alliance made between Britain and Japan in 1902.

In *The Book of the Chrysanthemum* (1907) Percy Follwell, head gardener at Drumpellier Gardens, traces the history of the flower from its origins in China to becoming the emblem on the Japanese national coat of arms. He calls the Chinese a 'peculiar, self-contained race', attributing their declining horticultural skills to 'their seclusiveness', and writes of continually hearing about disturbances in China against Europeans and Americans. The relationship between Britain and Japan, on the other hand, is celebrated: 'Only recently the Emperor of Japan conferred the Grand Order of the Chrysanthemum on one of our Royal Princes, in acknowledgement of a similar compliment paid him by King Edward VII., who had deputed the Prince to invest the Emperor with the Order of the Garter, as a signal of friendship and goodwill.'

In 1908 Florence du Cane criticises the 'lamentable failure of the so-called "Japanese gardens" which it has been the fashion of late years to try and make in England frequently by persons who have never even seen one of the gardens of Japan'. In *The Flowers and Gardens of Japan* she praises the careful design of Japanese gardens, comparing them to English gardens, which are beautiful enough in summer, but laid bare in winter: 'I could not help thinking that if more thought were given to the planning of our English gardens there might be something more complete and satisfying to the eye than the meaningless gardens ... which too often surround our English homes.'

The revived interest in Japanese plants is commented on by Horace and Walter Wright in *Beautiful Flowers and How to Grown Them* (1909): 'That mightiest of all epoch-making movements of the twentieth century, the awakening of Asia, in particular the rise of Japan and her alliance with Great Britain, has given new interest to those plants which originally came to us from the Far East.'

The authors applaud the rise of Japanese nationalism and the defeat of Russia in Manchuria. In a chapter on the chrysanthemum they compare the Japanese national flower to that of the British: 'The Chrysanthemum is the Golden Flower, the national floral emblem, of Japan. With the island warriors whose martial prowess has been proved within recent years on the bloodstained fields of Manchuria it holds the place that the Rose does with the allied island race of the West. This fact must have interest for us. Second only to the Rose as a popular flower in Great Britain, the Chrysanthemum stands first with the highly trained, progressive, ambitious Pacific nation whose future is bound up so closely with our own.'

In 1910 the Japan–British exhibition took place at the White City. The Penny Guide to the exhibition comments on the 'striking similarity between the Japs and our own people. This manifests itself in manner, physical stamp, and shape of the head.' There were exhibits on the Japanese colonies of Korea, Manchuria and Formosa. As John Mackenzie notes in *Propaganda and Empire*: 'The exhibition was the means of Japan's admission to respectability in the imperial club.'

An American writer, Harriet Osgood Taylor, also refers to the growing power of Japan. She calls the Japanese 'of all people on this earth the fondest, as a nation, of flowers', and sees Japan as 'not only greatest in the Orient, but one of the greatest nations in the whole world'. In *Japanese Gardens* (1912) she is both romantic and optimistic: 'It is the survival of the Japanese garden, and all that the love of it still implies, which has saved Japan from being brutalized by improvement, from being crushed beneath the responsibility of the transformation into a great Power, that has redeemed her from the curse that money-making brings. In the overturning of old ideals, while love of beauty and living things remains, Japan, thank God, can never grow into one of the sordid countries that the West knows so well.'

A direct connection is drawn between gardening, culture and foreign policy, while paradoxically the author praises both peace and war: 'The day that Japan ceases to love her gentle-spirited gardens, and to rejoice in their peace and their healing restfulness to the soul, that day also

Japanese Garden of a Marquis, from Madeline Agar's Garden Design in Theory and Practice *(1912).*

will she lose her pity and her kindliness, her art and her poetry, and
with them her wonderful patriotism, her fearless courage, her strength
and power in war, her steadfast devotion and self-sacrifice.'

After the Second World War, in *Flowers for the House and How to
Arrange Them* (1951), C. Romanné-James spends some time admiringly
discussing Japanese culture, thinking that a natural love of flowers is
'apparently inborn in the Japanese'. Although she criticises Japan's
recent war-mongering, she makes this ironic comment: 'The West was
wont to regard Japan as *barbarous* while she indulged in the gentle arts
of peace, and only called her *civilized* when she first began a wholesale
slaughter, on Manchurian battlefields, with modern weapons of war!'

SCOTLAND

Another way in which English gardening writing can often be nationalistic is by ignoring Scotland and Wales or by subsuming them under
'England'. In the Preface to *Trees and Shrubs for English Gardens* (1902),
for example, E.T. Cook has the effrontery to include the Scots and
Welsh within the term 'English'. He hopes his book 'may do something
to make English gardens more beautiful and interesting', and then
adds: 'The word "English", of course, stands for the British Isles.'

Anti-Scottish sentiment is sometimes expressed in English gardening
books. An example is to be found in James Pink's *Potatoes: How to Grow
and Show Them* (1879) in which he claims that the potato 'made little
progress in Scotland on account of the bigotry of the people, who
argued that it was a sinful plant because it was nowhere mentioned in
the Bible'.

On the other hand, one gardening writer who certainly cannot be
accused of chauvinism is the Scot, E.H.M. Cox, who in 1935 wrote *A
History of Gardening in Scotland*. On the first page he writes: 'In truth we
were a barbarous people.' He maintains that gardening was little practised
in Scotland before the accession of James I and points to the fact that
no gardening books were produced before 1683.

At the end of the seventeenth century, however, the story changes:
'Pleasure gardens of this period differed little from those in England ...
Our gardens did not follow quite such a stilted pattern of formality; but
those who designed them deliberately set out to imitate English gardens,
which in turn followed the French, Italian and Dutch styles.'

Some of the best English garden designers of the day planned Scottish
gardens. London and Wise, for example, designed the garden at Hatton
House, south of Edinburgh, which Cox calls 'the greatest formal garden
in Scotland'.

More significant, however, was the movement of Scottish gardeners to England: 'Scottish gardeners even at this period were in charge of many of the greatest English gardens and were quite capable not only of acting as head gardeners but also of laying out and making gardens.' Cox argues that the reason for many Scottish gardeners emigrating to England was that the Scots country lairds could not afford the luxury of pleasure gardens and also paid their gardeners very badly.

The list of famous emigrant Scottish gardeners is impressive, including Philip Miller of the Chelsea Physic Garden, who preferred to employ his own countrymen as apprentices. One of these was William Aiton, who came south in 1754 and later designed the original Botanic Garden at Kew. He in his turn appointed as foreman William McNab from Ayrshire, who eventually became head gardener at Edinburgh's Botanic Garden. Miller's successor at Chelsea was his former Scottish pupil William Forsyth, after whom forsythia is named. He went on to become Superintendent of the Royal Gardens of St James's and Kensington.

Cox quotes from the *Autobiography of Dr. Alexander Carlyle* (1722–70) that 'most of the head-gardeners of English noblemen were Scotch'. He also mentions the resentment this sometimes caused, quoting Switzer's (1715) infamous lines about Scottish gardeners: 'There are likewise several Northern Lads, which whether they have serv'd any Time in this Art or not, very few of us know any thing of, yet by the Help of a little Learning, and a great deal of Impudence, they invade the Southern Provinces; and the natural Benignity of this warmer Climate has such a wonderful Influence on them, that one of them knows (or at least pretends to know) more in one Twelve-month, than a laborious, honest South Countryman does in seven Years.' He later refers to 'the Poison of these audacious Empiricks in Gard'ning'. John Rogers, who once met Miller at Chelsea, writes in *The Vegetable Cultivator* (1839): 'Miller was looked upon with jealousy by many English gardeners, on account of his father being a Scotchman; and he is supposed to be one of the Northern lads sarcastically mentioned by Switzer.'

By about 1760 Scotsmen were also making a success of nursery gardening around London and Cox describes the response: 'Then the English in retaliation rushed into print and attacked Scottish gardeners tooth and nail. They also tried to resuscitate an old Chartered Company of Gardeners under a Charter of James I. A resolution was passed at an early meeting that no apprentice from the north should be employed.'

At this time many Scottish gardeners went to Russia to work, particularly after the accession of Catherine the Great in 1762. Ironically they were employed to design English gardens, with which Catherine was so madly in love. George Johnson, in 1829, refers to a toast that was often given: 'The Three exports of Scotland – Gardeners, Black Cattle, and Doctors.'

In Scotland itself Cox records the increase in tree planting which the great landed proprietors undertook between about 1775 and 1850: 'The greatest of all was the "Planting Duke", the fourth Duke of Atholl. Between 1774 and 1826 he planted 14,083,378 Larches and 13,348,222 trees of other kinds, a prodigious quantity.'

Cox notes that, in contrast to England, there have been few outstanding gardeners among the clergy in Scotland. He also points to the walled garden as being most typically Scottish, but by the end of the Victorian period he claims that it becomes impossible to differentiate between Scottish horticulture and that of other countries: 'Our gardeners were just as interested in the books of Dean Hole and the English gardening papers as those south of the border: they were just as friendly or antagonistic to the efforts of William Robinson and Gertrude Jekyll to break away from the rut into which Victorian gardening had fallen.'

Elizabeth Haldane, in *Scots Gardens in Old Times (1200–1800)*, published in 1934, also has little to say of the period up to 1600, calling it a 'poor tale'. This is qualified, however, by a reminder that the record is incomplete because so little was recorded.

On the ubiquitous Scottish gardener, she quotes Tobias Smollett in *Humphrey Clinker* saying that almost all the gardeners of South Britain were natives of Scotland. She also cites George Eliot: 'A gardener is Scotch as a French teacher is Parisian.' As to the reasons, Haldane refers to Loudon's *Encyclopaedia of Gardening*, in which he praises British head-gardeners and adds: 'Those of Scotland are by many preferred, chiefly, perhaps, from their having been better educated in their youth, and more accustomed to frugality and labour.'

Patrick Neill gives similar reasons for his assertion: 'Scotland has long been distinguished for producing gardeners in greater numbers than any other country in Europe; and several of them have risen to the highest eminence in their profession.' Neill was secretary to the Caledonian Horticultural Society and in 1817 wrote *An Account of British Horticulture*, his contribution to *The Edinburgh Encyclopaedia*.

He points first to the early education of the children of the Scottish labouring class in parish schools. Also, as gardening apprentices, they were instructed in 'arithmetic, mensuration, drawing plans, and botany'. Then he refers to 'the hardy mode of life and sober disposition of the young men, which have generally gained them the esteem of English masters'. Finally their struggle with a very variable climate calls 'into action all the powers of the mind' and creates 'a habit of unceasing attention to the duties of the station'.

After the Napoleonic wars Neill led a visit to Flanders, Holland and France. The tour was proposed in 1815 to find out about horticulture in the territories controlled by France, which 'had, for many years, been inaccessible to British travellers'. In his *Journal of a Horticultural Tour* (1823) Neill concludes: 'We were led to form the opinion that our own style of gardening in Scotland is, generally speaking, superior to what we witnessed on the Continent: it may be true that we originally derived our horticulture from the Flemings and the Hollanders, but it seems equally certain that we have now, in many respects, surpassed them.'

E.S. Delamer, in *The Kitchen Garden* (1855), also acclaims Scottish gardening skill and, like Neill, puts it down to the weather. He argues that difficult gardening conditions serve as a stimulus: 'Thus, Scotch gardeners, as a body, are believed to owe their excellence to the ungenial climate they have to contend with at home.'

Referring to the first Scottish gardening book, *The Scots Gard'ner* (1683) by John Reid, Elizabeth Haldane (1934) says it was so popular that it went through several editions. Some of the Paisley florists of a century later must surely have read it, for she quotes newspaper accounts that 'not less than one-third of the whole reading done in Scotland was carried on at Paisley'.

In Margaret Waterfield's book *Flower Grouping in English, Scotch and Irish Gardens* (1907) there is a chapter by Graham Stirling entitled 'Some Characteristics of Scotch Gardens'. In it the author praises the long tradition of Scottish gardeners: 'No article on national gardens would be complete without a tribute to the shrewd intelligence and skill of the Scotch gardener, whose worth is acknowledged all over the world, and that not only in the present day, but from the earliest History of Horticulture.'

WALES

Where Wales is mentioned in gardening books, it is often assumed to be part of England! William Watson, for example, in *Rhododendrons and Azaleas* (1910) writes that 'a love of gardening has for centuries prevailed among the people of this country'. He then goes on to praise a Welsh gardener: 'Sir John Llewellyn, Bt., Penllergaer, in South Wales, has one of the largest and best grown collections in England, and Sir John is an authority on all that concerns Rhododendrons.'

As initially it seemed impossible to find a gardening book written by a Welsh author, I decided to seek the help of the Welshman who was then chair of 'Gardeners' Question Time'. This is the reply I received from Clay Jones: 'Strange as it may seem I seem to be the only Welshman who has written gardening books in the English language. I have four to my credit all of which were published in the 1970s. I'm sorry I can't be more helpful but despite exhaustive enquiries I must conclude that Welsh gardeners are reluctant to put pen to paper!'

John Byng (Lord Torrington) was far more vicious in his conclusion. He kept a diary of his tour to North Wales in 1793 and could hardly wait to get back to England. His entry for 16 August reads: 'There is a joy to enter England, a much better, and sprightlier country than Wales; – that – from curiosity, may be view'd; but it is gloomy, – all in dirt, and misery, – with insolent natives, and horrid provisions, – The two first wonders in England are the handsome women, and the gardens; for neither of these first beauties of nature are to be found in Wales: In Wales I never saw a flower! They are too lazy to think of them.'

His lack of knowledge about gardens is revealed when his route is examined. Less than a month earlier he had stayed in Llangollen, where in 1778 Eleanor Butler and Sarah Ponsonby had settled, having eloped from Ireland. These ladies of Llangollen, as they became known, designed a picturesque garden which, as early as 1782, became famous in England, attracting the attention of Queen Charlotte in 1785.

Ignorance about Welsh gardens is mentioned by Elisabeth Whittle in her recent book *The Historic Gardens of Wales*: 'It is important, therefore, to counter the popular misconception that Wales has but few historic parks and gardens, and only a handful that are of outstanding interest. Such a view has been expressed for at least two hundred years.' She may well have been thinking of Byng when she writes: 'In the late eighteenth century, for example, early tourists saw few flowers; and J.C. Loudon, the prolific garden writer, remarked of Wales in the early nineteenth century, that "There are no public gardens; but few commercial ones; and the number of gentlemen's seats is very limited."'

Not far east of Llangollen, just inside the Welsh border, is Bettisfield where Thomas Hanmer cultivated his famous seventeenth-century garden. He wrote a book about it in 1659, but it was not published until 1933. It was transcribed from the original manuscript by Ivy Elstob and has an introduction by Eleanour Rohde, who calls Hanmer 'one of the most distinguished horticulturists during the middle years of the seventeenth century'.

Hanmer was descended from Welsh kings and princes and his father was MP for Flintshire, so presumably he was familiar with the town of Flint, which, from John Speed's map of 1610, looks remarkably like a garden city. His father was also one of the leaders of the Puritan party, but at the age of twelve Thomas became a page at the court of Charles I and he was a royalist during the Civil War. He was a close friend of John Rea, author of *Flora Ceres and Pomona*, which Eleanour Rohde calls 'the most important book of garden interest published between the Restoration and 1700', and with John Evelyn, who asked him for advice when he was making his garden at Sayes Court.

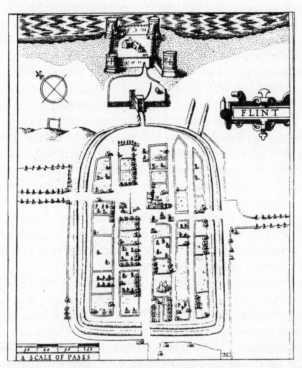

Town gardens in Flint, North Wales, from John Speed's map, 1610.

The Garden Book of Sir Thomas Hanmer is largely a description of various garden plants and how to cultivate them. It also contains a calendar entitled 'Remembrances of what is to bee done in a GARDEN every Moneth of the Yeare, and what plants are usually in FLOWER in each Moneth in England'. Hanmer neither refers to Wales nor mentions the fact that he is Welsh.

The fame of his garden does not seem to have lasted into the eighteenth century. In *A Tour of Wales* (1778) Thomas Pennant writes of his visit to Bettisfield, but does not mention the garden. He does, however, record seeing a picture of 'lady Hanmer, with a forehead-cloth, in an elegant white undress, studying Gerard's herbal'.

Following the Restoration, many formal gardens were created in Wales. One rescued from dereliction in the 1970s is Erddig, south of Wrexham, which Elisabeth Whittle calls 'one of the most significant surviving gardens of the early eighteenth century in Britain'. In 1799 the owner Philip Yorke opened it to the public, creating the first public park in Wales.

In mid-century the landscape garden spread to Wales and both Brown and Repton designed Welsh gardens. The most celebrated romantic Welsh garden in the eighteenth century is probably Hafod in Dyfed, the seat of Thomas Johnes who was MP for Radnor. Johnes had the house built in 1785 and between 1795 and 1801 he had over two million trees planted, winning six gold medals from the Society for the Encouragement of Arts, Manufactures and Commerce. His daughter Maria was also a talented botanist and gardener. In the end, however, he overstretched himself in improving his estate and was financially ruined.

In *An Attempt to Describe Hafod* (1796) George Cumberland gives an account of the gothic mansion 'situated on the side of a chosen, sheltered dingle, embowered with trees, which rise from a lawn of the gentlest declivity, that shelves in graceful hollows to the stream below'. There were hot-houses and a conservatory, and 'amid the recesses of the woods a flower-garden'. Cumberland claims that nothing in Switzerland or Italy was as fine as 'the scenery of this place'. He complains that after visiting Hafod he 'returned through our fine English scenes, as through a barren plain, uninterested'.

In *A Tour to Haford* (1810) James Edward Smith, who was President of the Linnean Society, also praises the 'velvet lawns, and thickets of shrubs and flowers' in the concealed flower garden, which extended for two acres, and he mentions a kitchen garden near the river. Of nearby Aberystwyth he writes: 'There is much garden-ground about this town ... In this warm sheltered situation the earliest vegetables are raised. The surrounding mountains are bleak and naked.'

John Rogers, who wrote his gardening books in the 1830s, was born in Richmond, Surrey, but his father was descended from an ancient family in Pembrokeshire with the name of Ap Roger. When he praises the nation's gardens in *The Vegetable Cultivator* (1839), he makes sure he refers to Britain, not England: 'In all ages, indeed, the successful cultivation of the garden has been coeval with a nation's greatest prosperity; and in the present day, the country in which it is most perfectly managed, is that most highly distinguished for its wealth and science. The British nation is indeed pre-eminent in this respect, and the British garden is superior to all others.'

Tourist guide books became popular in the nineteenth century. In 1860 William Peacock wrote one called *What I Saw in the Golden Valley*. He describes Symond's Yat and Coldwell Rocks in the Wye valley where he came across a clean and orderly cottage, in front of which a little garden 'breathed the delicious perfumes of its roses, peonies and gilliflowers'. Peacock was given hospitality by the couple who lived there: 'To what great ages the people in this garden of Eden attain! This afternoon, I encountered an Adam and Eve, who offered tea in their humble cottage; the wife 83, and husband 76. They had been married for fifty-three years; and the father of the old lady departed this life at the age of 95. Possibly this couple would not live out the charming gilliflowers, peonies, and sweet-william, which beautified the tiny garden in front of their little home; would not, peradventure, see the decay of their lilies, rosemary, and laburnums; yet was there, to all appearances, some years of life before them both.'

In the same year Peacock wrote *The Beauties of Llangollen and Chirk*, 'amid scenery the most beautiful and among people the most obliging. In no other part of the Principality is more civility to be met with than around Llangollen'. He describes a local garden: 'To my left hand is a garden prettily laid out with pea-rows, with lettuce and raddish beds, with onions, with potatoes, with fruit-trees a-many. Here are gooseberries and currants and raspberries; while, swaying their branches at the good-natured bidding of the summer breeze, grow the apple, the cherry, and the pear.'

The natural features of the Welsh countryside, which Gwyn Williams (1985) calls 'its bony surface ... all rocks and coarse grass', clearly have an effect on gardening in Wales. A.T. Johnson was an immigrant who created a garden at Ro-wen in Gwynedd which still survives. He also wrote about it in *A Garden in Wales* (1927) in which he tells of the 'dangerous features of our average Welsh winter', adding: 'Many half-hardy and tender subjects which flourish in western Scotland cannot be grown here without risk.' He describes Welsh poppies, Welsh anemones, Welsh Gromwell and Welsh ferns, while disputing whether they are peculiarly Welsh, and praises the little daffodils of the Welsh hills as the 'best and prettiest of all for naturalising'. He concludes the book, however, by saying that 'our English gardens' are 'the most wonderful in the world'.

H.L.V. Fletcher, on the other hand, praises the area in south-west Wales where he was brought up: 'The Pembrokeshire soil was good, the climate mild, the results of labour satisfying.' He describes the gardens as 'good' and he maintains that 'Pembrokeshire is a very good gardening country'. In *Gardening on a Shoestring* he also remarks on gardens in Herefordshire and Carmarthenshire.

In other gardening works there are occasional references to Welsh people's interest in horticulture. A.T. Johnson (1927), for example, mentions E.C. Buxton's garden in Bettws-y-Coed and also Hugh Davies's book *Welsh Botanology*, which appeared in 1813 and is subtitled 'A Systematic Catalogue of the Native Plants of the Isle of Anglesey in Latin,

Frontispiece, engraved by John Frederick Miller after a design by John Miller, from William Malcolm's A Catalogue of Hot-House and Green-House Plants *(1771), showing Britannia receiving fruits and flowers from Asia, Africa and America.*

English, and Welsh'. Hugh Davies was born and educated in Anglesey and found there several plants which had not yet been 'observed in Britain or any of its isles'. Davies, in turn, refers to a number of Welsh naturalists, including Edward Lhuyd, John Davies, Meddygon Myddfai, and L.W. Dillwyn, who in 1843 wrote *Hortus Collinsonianus: an Account of the Plants Cultivated by the Late Peter Collinson.*

Richard Pulteney (1790), in his book on English botany, also stresses the importance of Edward Lhuyd, who was born in 1660 and became Keeper of the Ashmolean Museum in Oxford in 1690, working there until his death in 1709. Lhuyd is more famous as a geologist and linguist, but in a letter, dated 14 September 1696, he describes botanising in the Snowdon Hills: 'I sent roots of what rare plants I met with, to the Duke of Beaufort's, my Lord of London's, and the Physic Garden at Oxford, and planted many of them at the Bishop of Bangor's garden, which is about 7 miles from these mountains.'

Another seventeenth-century Welsh botanist is Edward Morgan who was appointed to supervise the physic garden in Westminster. He produced a list of around 2,000 plants, which were cultivated in the garden, in a book called *Hortus Siccus*. Earlier, John Salusbury of Lleweni (1567–1612) cultivated his garden in Denbighshire, making notes on the plants he grew. He was particularly interested in the medicinal properties of herbs.

This interest in herbal medicine in Wales goes back at least a thousand years before Christ, to the priests and teachers of the people, known as the Gwyddoniaid, or men of knowledge. According to *The Physicians of Myddvai*, edited by John Williams in 1861: 'It is to these men that the art of healing is attributed, which they seem to have practised mainly if not wholly, by means of herbs.' Around 430 B.C. 'the art of medicine was protected and encouraged by the state'. Cicero and Pliny both write of the Gallic Druids' knowledge of the medicinal properties of plants, and in the ninth century Strabo describes the Druids as 'physiologists'.

PLANT HUNTERS

As early as 1660 Robert Sharrock writes of the 'advantage our Nation might have by propagation of exotique plants by seed brought new from severall Countryes beyond the Seas'. The Frontispiece to William Malcolm's *A Catalogue of Hot-House and Green-House Plants* (1771) shows Britannia receiving fruits and flowers from Asia, Africa and America, as if in tribute. The author writes that 'the collecting of Plants and Seeds from the various Parts of the Globe, and propagating them, has been my favourite Study'.

In *The Florist's Companion* (1794) John Hudson explains that, in order to obtain plants, 'the Alps and the Andes have been successfully scaled and the remotest regions of the earth adventurously traversed'. He begins the book by referring to the love and mercy of 'that Being, whose benevolence pervades the universe', but goes on to describe the savages encountered by the brave plant hunters: 'Men of the greatest nautical skill have navigated unknown seas, have penetrated the forests of both the Indies, have exposed themselves to the burning heat of the torrid and to the biting frosts of the frigid zones, undismayed by their savage and destructive inhabitants.'

In her botanical poems, published in 1801, Frances Arabella Rowden paints a picture of the colonies offering their riches to the imperial power:

> On Quito's shores, where Spain an empire holds,
> And the rich earth her golden stores unfolds.

Using sexual imagery, she describes the Spaniard Lopez taking the Mexican flower Lopezia back to Spain:

> 'Fair flow'r,' he cried, and clasp'd her in his arms,
> 'Let Spain's rich soil improve thy op'ning charms,'
> Then o'er the sea his trembling bride he bore,
> And smiling beauty grac'd his native shore.

In the nineteenth century the nursery firm of Veitch and Sons rivalled Kew Gardens in the number of plant hunters it sent around the world. *Hortus Veitchii* (1906) gives an account of 17 of them, describing the countries which they explored, for instance 'such practically virgin lands as California, certain parts of South America, Japan and Central China'.

Veitch writes of these countries that 'much of the region explored was virgin soil for a collector'. He continues with the same imagery when describing a plant hunter in West Africa: 'At that time travelling in Africa was difficult, and, owing to the hostility of native traders, foreigners were unable to penetrate far into the country.'

One plant collector who puzzled James Veitch was David Burke (1854–97), because 'Burke was one of those curious natures who live more or less with natives as a native, and apparently prefer this mode of existence'.

Another explorer sent out by Veitch was F.W. Burbidge who was born at Wymeswold in Leicestershire and became a gardener at Kew. His travels to Borneo are recorded in his book, *The Gardens of the Sun* (1880): 'The main object of my journey eastward was the collection and introduction of beautiful new plants to the Veitchian Collection at Chelsea.' He brought back 50 new species of fern.

Although he compares female orang-utans to the 'Coolie women of Hindustan', Burbidge is generally complimentary about the people in the interior of Borneo. He observes that women enjoyed perfect freedom with the men – although the women carried the heaviest loads – and he never saw a child beaten or chided. Some men were thoroughly domesticated, 'affectionately nursing their naked little babies at night, or in the daytime, while mamma had gone to the field for food, or the forest for fuel'. Their gardens are described: 'I noted neatly-fenced and well-kept gardens descending nearly to the water's edge. In these were sweet potatoes, cucumbers, maize, and "kaladi", or Caladium esculenteum. The women seemed to be the principal cultivators of these little plots.'

Unlike Landolicus in India, Burbidge praises the native fruits: 'The forests and gardens of Borneo are remarkably rich in native and naturalised kinds of edible fruits.' He gives a seemingly inexhaustible list, including mangosteen, durian, tarippe or trap-fruit, langsat, rambutan and jintawan, all of which he considers excellent. Others from Malaya include baloona, mambangan, tampoe, luing, Jack fruit and champada.

The final chapter of the book is entitled 'Notes on Tropical Travel', indicating some of the hazards involved: 'Always bathe in the morning. Care must be taken not to frequent alligator-infested streams.' As for danger from human sources, Burbidge believes: 'The strength of right and gentleness is the best of all protections for the traveller anywhere, and in any case the moral force of firearms is generally sufficient.' He recommends a good revolver, a good double breech-loading shot-gun and a Winchester repeater.

Finally he shows the link between plant hunters and economic botany, as well as other natural resources which could be exploited. He lists the animal, vegetable and mineral products of Borneo, but concludes that unfortunately the country is 'too far from the great highway of eastern commerce to attract any but the most sanguine of planters and capitalists'.

In *Kew Gardens* (1908) Hope Moncrieff points to a link that was often made between geography and racial energy. When discussing hot-houses and the origin of plants, he warns against the desire to live in the tropics: 'It is the sons of a temperate zone who are stirred into building palm houses or setting out to hunt for treasures of the tropics.' He also refers to 'the precious quinine, which by bold adventurers was stolen from Peruvian monopoly to thrive on Indian hills and elsewhere'.

In 1924 John Weathers notes that 'the discovery of America by Columbus in 1492 had a tremendous effect on Gardening', referring, for example, to the potato and tobacco. It is interesting to note here, however, the evidence collected by van Sertima showing the earlier widespread use of tobacco by Arabs and Africans: 'This habit of "oral" smoking, several medicinal and magical functions of the *tubbaq*, smoking words and smoking pipes, some with animal motifs and Mandingo totems, were transferred from the Africans to the Americans in pre-Columbian times.'

Despite using the word 'ransack', Weathers assumes that plant hunting means progress and that the areas to be explored are only natural, and not cultural: 'The whole world has now been well ransacked, but there are still regions in Africa, South America, and in Asia that have not yet been trodden by the foot of the white plant collector. In due course these regions will succumb to the march of progress and science, and our gardens may be enriched by flowers or fruits which are now luxuriating in primeval conditions.'

The Intrepid Horticultural Explorer

Plant hunting continued in the twentieth century and the image of the intrepid horticultural explorer became well established. Vita Sackville-West, in *Some Flowers* (1937), reminds us of it: 'We forget the adventures, the dangers, the hardships, which men have willingly experienced in order to enrich us casual purchasers of their spoils. We forget the preparation for expeditions, the struggle to engage native porters, mules, packs, and what not, the long trek over difficult tracks, the alarming nights and days, the frequent poises between life and death, the unique and thrilling moment when after all this cost of courage and endurance, the reward is suddenly found in a flower hitherto unknown to European eyes.'

She goes on to describe the Himalayan lily which Farrer brought back from Tibet. Like many colonialists, she sees the country as virtually empty of people, waiting to be exploited. She calls it a 'remote and lonely region, scarcely travelled and practically unmapped, where men are few, but flowers are many, a ravishing population put there as it were to compensate for the rudeness of life, the violence of the climate, and the desolation of the ranges'.

In 1927 J.W.C. Kirk's *A British Garden Flora* was published. The author was born in Zanzibar, where his father, a Scot who had been on Livingstone's expedition in 1858, was Consul. His father had introduced many plants from all over East Africa to Britain and the son followed suit. In the Foreword to the book, A.W. Hill, director of Kew Gardens, illustrates the connection between British colonialism and plant hunting: 'During his army service, which, before the Great War, included the

Part of Fred Stoker's garden in Loughton, Essex, drawn by H.A. Thomerson. From A Gardener's Progress *(1938).*

campaigns in South Africa and Somaliland, Colonel Kirk made interesting collections which are now incorporated in the Herbarium at Kew.'

One of the few gardening writers even to hint at questioning the morality of these plant hunters is Helen Nussey. In *London Gardens of the Past* (1939) she writes of John Tradescant the Elder: 'He is said to have joined a party of privateers with the object of securing (stealing) a certain kind of apricot which it was forbidden to export from Morocco.'

In *Plants for the Connoisseur* (1938) Thomas Hay, Superintendent of London's Central Parks, writes in celebratory terms of plant hunting in Asia and South America. He regrets that 'there must come a day when there will be nothing left in the way of virgin territory to explore'.

In the same year Fred Stoker praises the qualities of Joseph Banks who collected plants on Captain Cook's voyage to Australia. In *A Gardener's Progress* he writes: 'The name of Sir Joseph Banks, his support of scientific institutions and scientific men, his energy, learning and resolution are known to most. That he was President of the Royal Society for forty-one years is common knowledge, but the essential virtues of the man are not so generally realized. An account of their exercise is to be found in Cook's *First Voyage round the World*. Storm-bound in Tierra del Fuego, almost paralysed by intense cold, without food or protection, Banks's party would probably have been totally lost but for his own initiative, courage, endurance and generosity. By some of his contemporaries he was considered domineering. We may take it that his companions on the occasion just referred to thanked Heaven that he was.' Stoker fails to record those unable to thank Heaven, namely Banks's two black servants, who froze to death in Tierra del Fuego.

In similar vein, Stoker adds to the mythology surrounding Robert Fortune who collected plants in China. He first tells us about his uncle who told him that the correct way to deal with Chinese pirates was to shoot the steersman of the boat with a double-barrelled gun. Then he recounts Fortune's oft-repeated encounter: 'You may have read in Robert Fortune's *Tea Countries of China* how he beat off, single-handed, not a single junk but a small fleet by similar strategy and an identical weapon, though he had, by way of reserve, "put a pistol in each side pocket". A pistol in each side pocket! Not a modern automatic, mind you, nor a revolver, but an old-fashioned single-barrelled pistol much like those used to give the starting signal of a foot-race. What intrepid, matter-of-fact fellows the Victorians were! In their day the Marco Polo spirit – "We commended ourselves to God and then set forth" – still influenced conduct. A job was to be done. It was done. No need to make a song about it.'

According to E.H.M. Cox, the story of plant hunting in China is a 'tale of trying to kick through the hard brick wall of Chinese ultra-con-servatism in the old days'. In *Plant-Hunting in China* (1945) he writes of the plant hunters: 'All have borne themselves well and treated the natives fairly. It is an honourable calling, that of plant hunter, and a happy one.' Robert Fortune, who actually stole seeds and cuttings and disguised himself as a Chinaman to deceive the Chinese, is described as 'very successful in inspiring the Chinese with confidence in his honesty'.

This indiscriminate glorification of the plant hunters is not just an aspect of our colonial past. As recently as 1979, in 'The Hunt for New Plants', written for the Victoria and Albert Museum's exhibition catalogue, edited by John Harris, Kenneth Lemmon describes the enterprise of plant hunting in glowing terms: 'From about the middle of the sixteenth century a real taste for exotic or "outlandish" flowering plants, as they were called, began to prevail in this country. Also there was now growing up a race of gardeners who could take on the great challenge their noble masters thrust upon them with the arrival of seeds and slips of strange plants from foreign parts.' The author refers to the plant hunters opening up and mapping 'immense tracts of virgin territory' and bringing 'prosperity to hitherto unproductive lands'. He talks of China and Japan having 'opened their doors to travellers' when, in the case of the Chinese, for instance, it was their defeat in the Opium Wars which forced them to trade with Britain.

Lemmon goes on to praise Robert Fortune who succeeded, 'despite hostile natives', in transporting tea plants from China to India. Similarly he admires Richard Spruce who 'travelled the Amazon collecting seeds and plants of the cinchona tree (source of quinine) to send to India for its malaria stricken peoples'. In fact, as Hope Moncrieff reminds us, Spruce stole the seeds and exported them illegally. The quinine was used largely to protect the British army and workers on British plantations, rather than the Indian people in general. Its importance in helping to extend the British Empire is recognised by Edith Wheelwright in *The Physick Garden* (1934), though she uses different terminology: 'Quinine, together with the suppression of the mosquito has, of course, by checking the scourge of malaria, led to the advance of white civilization in many tropical areas of the world.'

One legacy of the plant hunters is their names. An example is provided by Bessie Buxton in *Begonias and How to Grow Them* (1946). The begonia was named by Charles Plumier after Michel Begon (1638–1710), a French botanist, then Governor of San Domingo. Buxton recognises that the flower was known before it was given this name, but leaves the impression that it only really began its existence when 'discovered' and named by Europeans: 'While Plumier must be credited with naming the new genus, other men had discovered the plants a century earlier. In 1649 Fr. Hernandez found a plant in Mexico that appears from the early drawings to have been a begonia. In 1688 Hans Sloane, exploring Jamaica, found a begonia which was later named B. acuminata, and now listed as B. acutifolia.'

An exception to this tradition of naming plants is mentioned by Mrs Francis King in *The Well-Considered Garden* (1915), when she refers to a lilac described as a 'rich red-violet'. It is 'Toussaint L'Ouverture', named after the famous black general who led a successful slave revolt against the French in San Domingo.

It is not surprising that English gardening literature reflects the ethnocentrism of English culture in general. What is strange is that today most people find the conjuncture of politics and gardening so incomprehensible. Yet clearly in eighteenth-century discourse, gardening and nationalism were explicitly combined. In the nineteenth century too, the link between gardening and colonialism was celebrated. Even at the end of the twentieth century the Empire lingers on.

Afterword

*'This I doe affirme upon good knowledge and certaine experience,
and not as a great many others doe, tell of the wonders of
another world, which themselves never saw nor ever heard of,
except some superficiall relation, which themselves have
augmented according to their owne fansie and conceit.'*
John Parkinson, *Paradisus* (1629)

*'One has to learn to manage even a Little Garden chiefly by
experience, which is sure teaching, if slow. Books and gardeners
are helpful; but, like other doctors, they differ.'*
Juliana Horatia Ewing, *Letters from a Little Garden* (1886)

Despite the incidence of racism, sexism and class bias in gardening literature, the golden thread which runs through most books is the stress on experience and openness to new knowledge. Readers can test what they read, both scientifically and aesthetically, through their own gardening. A continual dialogue takes place and there is generally little enthusiasm for authoritarian views.

According to John Gibson in *The Fruit-Gardener* (1768), the scepticism when confronted by authority, as well as the emphasis on first-hand experience, go back to the Reformation and the invention of printing, when the superstition of Rome was overcome: 'Then men began to read, to think, and to reason.'

In the seventeenth century Ralph Austen, like Culpeper, argued for using the 'Scale of Reason' and the 'Touchstone of Experience'. In *A Treatise of Fruit-Trees* (1653) he writes: 'Let not men think that Ancient and Learned Authors have discovered all Truths; or that all they have said is truth: they are but men and have their Errors ... It's not any great matter what men have thought, but what is the truth of the matter.'

This approach was eventually institutionalised and systematised, after the Restoration, by the Royal Society, whose precursor was the Invisible College. Robert Boyle wrote in 1646 of 'the principles of our

215

new philosophical college, that values no knowledge, but as it hath a tendency to use'. The Invisible College was founded around 1645 and met weekly in its members' homes. According to Boyle, its 'midwife and nurse' was Samuel Hartlib. A few years earlier Hartlib had invited Comenius to England to help found a college based on his theory of pansophic or encyclopaedic knowledge. Comenius, in his turn, had been influenced by Francis Bacon's idea of a philosophical academy or universal college devoted to the sciences.

From the 1826 edition of Culpeper's
The English Physician, *first published in 1652.*

At the end of the seventeenth century, in *Acetaria: A Discourse of Sallets* (1699), Evelyn summed up the purpose of the Royal Society. It was to extend the knowledge of nature 'beyond the Land of Spectres' which had confined men 'in a lazy Acquiescence' where they were 'fed with Fantasms and fruitless Speculations'. He wants to see 'solid and useful knowledge' arrived at by 'Investigation of Causes, Principles, Energies, Powers, and Effects of Bodies, and Things Visible', with the aim of improving them 'for the Good and Benefit of Mankind'.

This would take a long time, however, and Evelyn criticises those who think they know everything about gardening and who 'see not, that it would still require the Revolution of many Ages; deep, and long Experience, for any Man to Emerge that Perfect and Accomplish'd Artist Gardiner they boast themselves to be'. He acknowledges that his famous books, *Sylva* and *Kalendar*, are imperfect and 'both capable of Great Improvements'.

Since then many writers have put forward their long experience of gardening as their main credential. John Laurence's *The Clergy-Man's Recreation: Shewing the Pleasure and Profit of the Art of Gardening* (1714) is the result of 'Observations and Experience of above Twenty Years'. Likewise John Cowell had experience of gardening for 'above Thirty Years' when he wrote *The curious and profitable gardener* in 1730, and claims to 'have endeavour'd to bring that Art to as great Perfection as possibly I could'.

In his book on Blake, *Witness Against the Beast* (1993), E.P. Thompson argues that 'a great deal of the most notable intellectual energies of the eighteenth century lay outside of formal academic channelling. This was manifestly so in the natural sciences.' He includes in this informal tradition people such as Paine, Wollstonecraft and Cobbett: 'In this tradition experience is laid directly alongside learning, and the two test each other.' It is clearly a continuation of the seventeenth-century culture of people like Culpeper and Hartlib. In gardening books this tradition continued throughout the nineteenth and twentieth centuries.

After the author's name in the twenty-first edition of Abercrombie's *Every Man His Own Gardener* (1818) are the words 'sixty years a practical gardener'. Similarly Alice Martineau writes in the preface to *The Herbaceous Garden* (1913): 'I would commence by saying that many of the suggestions in this book are prompted by experiments and experiences gained in an old garden, worn-out and neglected when taken over, twelve years ago.'

During the Second World War Albert Gurie still stresses the importance of experience. As garden editor of the *News Chronicle*, Gurie had a wide readership and in *Vegetable Gardening* (1940) he appeals to everyone with a garden: 'No qualification is necessary to become a gardener other than the possession of a garden. But two things are needed to attain success at gardening – knowledge and experience. The latter often means a series of trial and error, yet if the lessons are learned and put into practice, success is assured.'

This democratic emphasis on experience, rather than an arbitrary insistence on authority, is the main characteristic which links most gardening books throughout the last four centuries. It points to the power which readers have to judge gardening books, not only from their own political standpoint, but from their gardening experience.

This analysis of gardening books has framed the literature in a particular perspective, but the works are there for anyone to read and judge its validity.

Bibliography

Abercrombie, John, *Every Man His Own Gardener* (W. Griffin, 1767; 21st edn, 1818)
Adamson, Robert, *The Cottage Garden* (Robert Reid, 1851; 2nd edn, Adam and Charles Black, 1856)
Agar, Madeline, *Garden Design in Theory and Practice* (Sidgwick and Jackson, 1912)
Alatas, Syed Hussein, *The Myth of the Lazy Native* (Frank Cass, 1977)
Allen, Grant, *Flowers and their Pedigrees* (Longmans, Green, and Co., 1883)
Allwood, Montagu C., *English Countryside and Gardens* (The Author, 1947)
Amherst, Alicia, *A History of Gardening in England* (Bernard Quaritch, 1895; 2nd edn, 1896; 3rd enlarged edn, 1910)
——, (Hon Mrs. Evelyn Cecil), *Children's Gardens* (Macmillan, 1902)
——, (Hon. Mrs. Evelyn Cecil), *London Parks and Gardens* (Archibald Constable, 1907)
——, (The Lady Rockley), *Some Canadian Wild Flowers* (Macmillan and Co., 1937)
——, (The Lady Rockley), *Historic Gardens of England* (Country Life, 1938)
Anderson, James (ed.), *The New Practical Gardener and Modern Horticulturist* (William MacKenzie, 1872–4)
Angus, W., *The Seats of the Nobility and Gentry in Great Britain and Wales* (The Author, 1787)
Anon, *The craft of graffynge & plantynge of trees* (Wynkyn De Worde, c. 1520)
Anon, *Soyle for an Orchard* (c. 1650 unpublished; privately printed in *Two Manuals of Gardening from English Manuscript Notebooks of the Seventeenth Century in the Library of Rachel McMasters Miller Hunt* (Pittsburgh, PA, 1952)
Anon, *A Book of Fruit and Flowers* (Thomas Jenner, 1653)
Anon, *The Trial of Robert Sweet at the Old Bailey before Mr. Justice Best* (Printed by L. Nichols, 1824)
Anon, *The Juvenile Gardener* (Harvey and Darton, 1824)
Anon, *The Young Lady's Book of Botany* (Robert Tyas, 1838)
Anon, *The Gooseberry Grower's Register* (P.G. Thomas Whittaker, and Br. Jacob Wolstencroft, Manchester, 1839)
Anon, *British Forest Trees* (Cradock and Co., 1843)
Anon, *Handbook of Town Gardening* (James McGlashen, 1847)
Anon, *Every Lady's Guide to Her Own Greenhouse* (Wm S. Orr and Co., 1851)
Anon, *Garden Flowers* (Thomas Nelson and Sons, 1857)
Anon, *My Kitchen Garden; My Cows, and Half an Acre of Pasture* (Bradbury and Evans, 1860)
Anon, *The Garden that Paid the Rent* (Chapman and Hall, 1860)
Anon (The Curator), *A Gloucestershire Wild Garden* (Elliot Stock, 1903)
Anon, *The Small Garden* ('The Poultry World', 1919)
Anson, E.R., *The Owner Gardener* (John Murray, 1934)
Archer, Thomas Croxen, 'On the Study of Botany', *Inaugural Lectures Delivered at the Liverpool Ladies' College* (Hamilton, Adams and Co., 1857)
Arkell, Reginald, *A Cottage in the Country* (Rich and Cowan, 1934)

Armitage, Ethel, *A Country Garden* (Country Life, 1936)
——, *Garden and Hedgerow* (Country Life, 1939)
Arnold, *The Customs of London, or Arnold's Chronicle* (John Doesborowe, Antwerp c. 1502; Rivington, 1811)
Arnold, Matthew, *Culture and Anarchy* (Smith, Elder and Co., 1869; Cambridge University Press, 1932)
Arnot, Samuel, *The Book of Bulbs* (John Lane: The Bodley Head, 1901)
Austen, Jane, *Mansfield Park* (T. Egerton, 1814)
——, *Emma* (John Murray, 1816)
Austen, Ralph, *A Treatise of Fruit-Trees* (Tho. Robinson, 1653; 2nd end, 1657)
——, *The Spirituall Use of an Orchard, or Garden of Fruit-Trees* (Tho. Robinson, 1653; 2nd edn, 1657)
——, *A Dialogue, (or Familiar Discourse) between the Husbandman, and Fruit-Trees; in his Nurseries, Orchards, and Gardens* (Thomas Bowman, 1676)
Austin, Alfred, *In Veronica's Garden* (Macmillan and Co., 1895)

B., A.H., *The Tree Rose* (Gardeners' Chronicle, 1845)
Bagenal, N.B., *Fruit Growing for Small Gardens* (Country Life, 1939)
Bailey, Liberty Hyde, *Cyclopedia of American Horticulture* (Macmillan and Co., 1900–1902)
Baltet, Charles, *The Art of Grafting and Budding* (Macmillan and Co., 1878)
Barron, William, *The British Winter Garden* (Bradbury and Evans, 1852)
Bartell, Edmund, *Hints for Picturesque Improvements in Ornamental Cottages, and their Scenery* (J. Taylor, 1804)
Barth, Henry, *Travels and Discoveries in North and Central Africa* (Longman, Brown, Green, Longmans, and Roberts, 1857)
Batson, Henrietta M. (Mrs. Stephen Batson), *Adam the Gardener* (Hurst and Blackett, 1894)
——, (Mrs. Stephen Batson), *A Book of the Country and the Garden* (Methuen and Co., 1903)
Beale, John, *Herefordshire Orchards, A Pattern for all England* (Roger Daniel, 1657)
Bean, William Jackson, *Trees and Shrubs Hardy in the British Isles* (John Murray, 1914)
Beeton, Samuel Orchart, *The Book of Garden Management* (S.O. Beeton, 1862)
Bell, M.G. Kennedy, *A Garden Timepiece* (Hutchinson and Co., 1925)
——, *The Joys of Bee-Keeping* (Herbert Jenkins, 1932)
Bennett, Fanny and Eleanour Sinclair Rohde, *A Vegetable Grower's Handbook* (Philip Lee Warner, 1922)
Bennett, Lerone, *The Shaping of Black America* (Penguin, 1993)
Bermingham, Ann, *Landscape and Ideology: The English Rustic Tradition 1740–1860* (University of California Press, 1986)
Bernal, Martin, *Black Athena* (Free Association Books, 1987; Vintage, 1991)
Berrall, Julia S., *The Garden* (Thames and Hudson, 1966)
Best, Clare and Caroline Boisset (eds), *Leaves from the Garden* (John Murray, 1987)
Biffen, Rowland H., *The Auricula* (Cambridge University Press, 1951)
Blackwell, Elizabeth, *A Curious Herbal* (Samuel Harding, 1737)
Blith, Walter, *The English Improover, or a New Survey of Husbandry* (John Wright, 1649; 3rd edn: *The English Improver Improved*, John Wright, 1652)
Blome, Richard, *The Gentlemans Recreation* (The Author, 1686)
Blomfield, Reginald, *The Formal Garden in England* (Macmillan and Co., 1892; Waterstone, 1985)
Boniface, Priscilla (ed.), *In Search of English Gardens: The Travels of John Claudius Loudon and his Wife Jane* (Lennard Publishing, 1987)
Bowles, Edward Augustus, *My Garden in Autumn and Winter* (T.C. and E.C. Jack, 1915)
Boyle, Eleanor Vere, (E.V.B., Mrs. Boyle), *A Garden of Pleasure* (Elliot Stock, 1895)
——, (E.V.B., Mrs. Boyle), *Seven Gardens and a Palace* (John Lane: The Bodley Head, 3rd edn, 1900)

Boyle, Robert, *The Works of Robert Boyle* (A. Millar, 1744)

Bradley, Edith and May Crook, *The Book of Fruit Bottling* (John Lane: The Bodley Head, 1907)

Bradley, Richard, *New Improvements of Planting and Gardening* (W. Mears, 1717; 5th edn, 1726; 7th edn, 1739)

——, *A General Treatise of Husbandry and Gardening* (T. Woodward and J. Peele, 1724; revised edn, 1726)

Bréhaut, T. Collings, *Cordon Trading of Fruit Trees* (Longman, Green, Longman, and Roberts, 1860)

Brett, Walter, *The Book of Garden Improvements* (C. Arthur Pearson, 1935)

——, (ed.), *Eggs from your Garden* (C. Arthur Pearson, 1940)

——, (ed.), *Garden and Allotment Pig Keeping* (C. Arthur Pearson, 1940)

Bright, Henry Arthur, *The English Flower Garden* (Macmillan and Co., 1881)

Brooke, Justin, *Peach Orchards in England* (Faber and Faber, 1947)

Brookes, Gilbert, *The Complete British Gardener* (Fielding and Walker, 1779)

Bryant, Charles, *A Dictionary of the Ornamental Trees, Shrubs, and Plants, Most Commonly Cultivated in the Plantations, Gardens, and Stoves, of Great-Britain* (J. Bowen, 1790)

Bunyard, Edward Ashdown, *The Anatomy of Dessert* (Dulau and Co., 1929)

Bunyard, George and Owen Thomas, *The Fruit Garden* (Country Life; George Newnes, 1904)

Burbidge, Frederick William, *Domestic Floriculture* (William Blackwood and Sons, 1874)

——, *The Gardens of the Sun* (John Murray, 1880)

Burgess, Henry, *The Amateur Gardener's Year-Book* (A. and C. Black, Edinburgh, 1854)

Butler, Charles, *The Feminine Monarchie, or A Treatise Concerning Bees, and the Due Ordering of Them* (Oxford, 1609)

Buxton, Bessie Raymond, *Begonias and How to Grow Them* (Oxford University Press, New York, 1946)

Byng, John (Lord Torrington), *The Torrington Diaries* (Ed. C. Bruyn Andrews; Eyre and Spottiswoode, 1936)

Calthrop, Dion Clayton *The Charm of Gardens* (A. and C. Black, 1910)

Castle, Lewis R., *Flower Gardening for Amateurs* (Swan Sonnenschein and Co., 1888)

Chamberlain, Edith L., *Town and Home Gardening* (J.S. Virtue and Co., 1893)

——, and Fanny Douglas, *The Gentlewoman's Book of Gardening* (Henry and Co., 1892)

Champlain, Samuel, *The Voyages and Explorations of Samuel de Champlain 1604–1616* (A. S. Barnes and Co., 1906)

Cheveley, Stephen William, *A Garden Goes to War* (John Miles, 1940)

Clarkson, Rosetta E., *Magic Gardens* (Macmillan Co., New York, 1939)

Cobbett, William, *The English Gardener* (Published by the author, Andover, 1829; Oxford University Press, 1980)

Colborne, Robert, *The Plain English Dispensatory* (The Author, 1753)

Collins, Charles, *How to Grow Tomatoes* (Horticultural Times, 1888)

Collins, Samuel, *Paradise Retriev'd* (John Collins, 1717)

Colvin, Brenda, *Land and Landscape* (John Murray, 1948)

Comenius, John Amos (Komensky, Jan Amos), *A Reformation of Schooles* (Leszno, 1638; Michael Sparke, 1642)

Conder, Josiah, *Landscape Gardening in Japan* (Kelly and Walsh, 1893)

Constantine, Stephen, 'Amateur Gardening and Popular Recreation in the 19th and 20th Centuries', *Journal of Social History* (Spring 1981)

Cook, Ernest Thomas, *Gardening for Beginners* (Country Life: George Newnes, 1901; 7th edn, 1920)

——, *Trees and Shrubs for English Gardens* (Country Life, 1902)

——, *Gardens of England* (A. and C. Black, 1908)

Cook, Moses, *The Manner of Raising, Ordering, and Improving Forrest-Trees* (Peter Parker, 1676)

Cooling, Edwin, *The Domestic Gardener's Assistant* (G. Wilkins and Son, 1837)

Coombes, Allen J., *The Collingridge Dictionary of Plant Names* (Hamlyn, 1985)

Cornelisson, Peter, *A Way Propounded* (The Author, 1659)

Cotton, Charles, *The Planters Manual* (Henry Brome, 1675)

Coventry, Francis, 'Strictures on the absurd Novelties introduced in Gardening', *The World* (12 April 1753)

Cowell, John, *The curious and profitable gardener* (Weaver Bickerton and Richard Montagu, 1730)

Cowper, William, *The Task* (J. Johnson, 1785)

Cox, Euan Hillhouse Methven, *The Evolution of a Garden* (Williams and Norgate, 1927)

——, *Wild Gardening* (Dulau and Co., 1929)

——, *A History of Gardening in Scotland* (Chatto and Windus, 1935)

——, *Plant-Hunting in China* (Collins, 1945)

Craig, Elizabeth, *Gardening with Elizabeth Craig* (Collins, 1940)

——, *Practical Gardening* (Collins, c. 1952)

Cran, Marion (Mrs. George Cran), *The Garden of Ignorance* (Herbert Jenkins, 1913)

——, *The Garden of Experience* (Herbert Jenkins, 1921)

——, *Garden Talks* (Methuen, 1925)

——, *The Squabbling Garden* (Herbert Jenkins, 1934)

Cranston, John, *Cultural Directions for the Rose* (Houlson and Wright, 1857; 2nd edn improved and enlarged, 1863)

Crocker, Emmeline, *Thirty-Nine Articles on Gardening* (Dulau and Co., 1908)

Crosby, Alfred W., *Ecological Imperialism: The Biological Expansion of Europe 900–1900* (Cambridge University press, 1986)

Culpeper, Nicholas, *A Directory for Midwives* (Peter Cole, 1651).

——, *The English Physician* (Peter Cole, 1652)

——, *The School of Physick* (Nathaniel Brook, 1659)

Cumberland, George, *An Attempt to Describe Hafod* (T. Egerton, 1796)

Cutherbertson, William, *Pansies, Violas & Violets* (J.C. and E.C. Jack, 1910)

——, *Sweet Peas and Antirrhinums* (James Clarke and Co., 1915)

Cuthill, James, *Market Gardening* (4th edn; Groombridge and Sons, 1870)

Darnell, A.W., *Winter Blossoms from the Outdoor Garden* (L. Reeve and Co., 1926)

Davies, Hugh, *Welsh Botanology* (The Author, 1813)

Dean, Alexander, *Vegetable Culture* (Macmillan and Co., 1896)

Defoe, Daniel, *Tour through the Whole Island of Great Britain* (G. Strahan, etc., London, 1724–6; Penguin edn, 1971)

Delamer, Eugene Sebastian, *The Kitchen Garden* (Geo. Routledge and Co., 1855)

Desmond, Ray, *Dictionary of British and Irish Botanists and Horticulturists* (Taylor and Francis, 1977)

Dillistone, George, *The Planning and Planting of Little Gardens* (Country Life: George Newnes, 1920)

Dillwyn, Lewis W., *Hortus Collinsonianus: An Account of the Plants Cultivated by the Late Peter Collinson* (Unpublished, 1843)

Divers, W.H., *Spring Flowers at Belvoir Castle* (Longmans, Green and Co., 1909)

Dowie, Ménie Muriel, *Things About our Neighbourhood* (Grant Richards, 1903)

Drury, William D. (ed.), *The Book of Gardening* (L. Upcott Gill, 1900)

du Cane, Florence, *The Flowers and Gardens of Japan* (A. and c. Black, 1908)

Dunbar, Janet, *The Early Victorian Woman: Some Aspects of Her Life* (1837–57) (George G. Harrap and Co., 1953)

Earle, Maria Theresa (Mrs. C. W. Earle), *Pot-Pourri from a Surrey Garden* (Smith and Elder, 1897; Dent, 1912; Century, 1984)

——, *More Pot-Pourri from a Surrey Garden* (Smith, Elder and Co., 1899; 5th edn, 1901)

——, A Third Pot-Pourri (Smith, Elder and Co., 1903)
——, and Ethel Case, Gardening for the Ignorant (Macmillan, 1912)
Eastwood, Dorothea, Mirror of Flowers (Derek Verschoyle, 1953)
——, The Story of Our Gardens (Gordon Fraser, 1958)
Eburne, Richard, A Plaine Path-Way to Plantations (John Marriot , 1624)
Edwards, John, The National Garden Almanack, and Horticultural Trade Directory (Chapman and Hall, 1854)
Eggar, Mrs. E.M., An Indian Garden (John Murray, 1904)
Eley, Charles Cuthbert, Gardening for the Twentieth Century (John Murray, 1923)
Eley, Geoffrey, And Here Is Mr. Streeter (Crosby Lockwood and Son, 1950)
Ellacombe, Henry Nicholson, In a Gloucestershire Garden (Edward Arnold, 1895; Century Hutchinson, 1982)
Ellis, Thomas, et al., The New Complete Dictionary of Arts and Sciences (The Authors, 1778)
Ely, Helena Rutherford, A Woman's Hardy Garden (Macmillan and Co., 1903)
Ender, Peter, Up the Garden Path (Herbert Jenkins, 1944)
Errington, Robert, Allotment Farming for the Many (Cottage Gardener Office, 1856)
Evelyn, Charles, The Lady's Recreation (1707; 2nd edn, 1718)
Evelyn, John, The French Gardiner (translation of a book by Nicolas de Bonnefons; John Cooke, 1658)
——, Sylva (Royal Society, 1664)
——, Kalendarium Hortense (John Martin and James Allestry, 1664)
——, Acetaria: A Discourse of Sallets (B. Tooke, 1699)
——, Directions for the Gardiner at Says-Court (ed. Geoffrey Keynes; Nonesuch Press, 1932)
——, The Diary of John Evelyn (1641–1706; Clarendon Press, 1955)
——, Manuscript on Bees from 'Elysium Britannicum' (ed. D.A. Smith; Bee Research Association, 1966)
Everett, Katherine, Bricks and Flowers (Constable, 1949)
Ewing, Juliana Horatia, Letters from a Little Garden (Christian Knowledge Society, 1886)

F., N., The Husbandmans Fruitful Orchard (Roger Jackson, 1608)
Fairbridge, Dorothea, Gardens of South Africa (A. and C. Black, 1924)
Fairbrother, Nan, Men and Gardens (Hogarth Press, 1956)
Falade, J.B., 'Yoruba Palace Gardens', Garden History, 18 (1), 1990
Felton, S., On the Portraits of English Authors on Gardening (J. Ridgway, 1828; 2nd edn, Effingham Wilson and Joseph Onwhyn, 1830)
Finch, Anne, Miscellany Poems, on Several Occasions (John Barber, 1713)
Firminger, Thomas Augustus Charles, A Manual of Gardening for Bengal and Upper India (R.C. Lepage and Co., 1864; 6th edn, rev. and ed. by W. Burns, Thacker, Spink and Co., Calcutta, 1918)
Fitzherbert, John, The Boke of Husbandrie (Rychard Pynson, 1523; corrected and amended by I.R., Edward White, 1598)
Flawn, Louis N., Cloche Gardening (W. and G. Foyle, 1959)
Flemwell, George Jackson, Alpine Flowers and Gardens (A. and C. Black, 1910)
Fletcher, Harry Lutf Verne, By Saint Phocas! (John Gifford, 1943)
——, Gardening on a Shoestring (Phoenix House, 1953)
Flint, Martha Bockee, A Garden of Simples (Charles Scribner's Sons, USA, 1900; David Nutt, 1901)
Follwell, Percy, The Book of the Chrysanthemum (John Lane: The Bodley Head, 1907)
Forsyth, William, Observations on the Diseases, Defects, and Injuries in All Kinds of Fruit and Forest Trees (The Author, 1791)
Foster-Melliar, Robert Aubrey, My Garden by the Sea (G. Bell and Sons, 1936)
Friend, Hilderic, Flowers and Flower Lore (W. Swan Sonnenschein and Co., 1884)
——, The Ministry of Flowers (W. Swan Sonnenschein and Co., 1885)
Fuller, Thomas, The History of the Worthies of England (London, 1662)

Fullmer, Samuel, *The Young Gardener's Best Companion* (The Author, 1781)

Fussell, George Edwin, *The Old English Farming Books* (Crosby Lockwood and Son, 1947)

——, *More English Farming Books* (Crosby Lockwood and Son, 1950)

Garton, James, *The Practical Gardener* (E. and C. Dilly, 1769)

Gaskell, S. Martin, 'Gardens for the Working Class: Victorian Practical Pleasure', *Victorian Studies* (Summer 1980)

Gaye, Phoebe Fenwick, *Week-End Garden* (Collins, 1939)

Gerard, John, *The Herball* (John Norton, 1597; Johnson, 1636; Bracken Books, 1985)

Gibson, John, *The Fruit-Gardener* (J. Nourse, 1768)

Gilbert, Samuel, *The Florists Vade-Mecum* (Thomas Simmons, 1682)

Glenny, George, *Glenny's Garden Almanac* (Houlson and Stoneman, 1848, 1849; C. Cox, 1850, 1851)

——, *Gardening for the Million* (17th edn, Houlson and Stoneman, 1849; 22nd edn, Houlston and Sons, 1875)

Goodsman, Charles Stephen, *The Concise Week-End Gardener* (John Crowther, 1940; 2nd impression, 1941)

——, *The Week-End Gardener* (John Crowther, 1941)

Googe, Barnabe, *Foure Bookes of Husbandry* (translated and increased from the book by M. Conrad Heresbach, Richard Watkins, 1577; revised by Gervase Markham, Richard More, 1631)

Gordon, George, *Dahlias* (T.C. and E.C. Jack, 1913)

Gore, Catherine Frances, *The Book of Roses; or, The Rose Fancier's Manual* (Henry Colburn, 1838; Heyden and Son, 1978)

Gothein, Marie Luise, *A History of Garden Art* (1913; English translation, J.M. Dent and Sons, 1928)

Graham, Dorothy, *Chinese Gardens* (George G. Harrap and Co., 1938)

Graveson, Samuel, *My Villa Garden* (Headley Brothers, 1915)

——, *Our Vegetable Plot* (Headley Brothers, 1918)

Green, David, *Gardener to Queen Anne: Henry Wise (1653–1738) and the Formal Garden* (Oxford University Press, 1956)

Greening, Edward Owen, *One and All Garden Books* (Agricultural and Horticultural Association, 1905–17)

Gunther, R.T., *Early British Botanists and Their Gardens* (Oxford University Press, 1922)

——, *Early Science in Oxford*, Vol. XIV 'Life and Letters of Edward Lhwyd' (printed for the subscribers, Oxford, 1945)

Gurie, Albert, *Vegetable Gardening* (News Chronicle, 1940)

——, *News Chronicle Gardening Book* (News Chronicle, 1952)

Hackleplume, *My Lady's Garden* (Watts and Co., 1921)

Hadfield, Miles, *Pioneers in Gardening* (Routledge and Kegan Paul, 1955)

——, *A History of British Gardening* (Hutchinson, 1960; Penguin, 1985)

——, Robert Harling and Leonie Highton, *British Gardeners: A Biographical Dictionary* (A. Zwemmer, 1980)

Haggard, H. Rider, *A Gardener's Year* (Longmans, Green and Co., 1905)

Haldane, Elizabeth S., *Scots Gardens in Old Times (1200–1800)* (Alexander Maclehose and Co., 1934)

Hale, Thomas, *Eden: or, A Compleat Body of Gardening* (T. Osbourne, 1757)

Hall, Alfred Daniel and M.B. Crane, *The Apple* (Martin Hopkinson, 1933)

Hall, George William, *Garden Plans and Designs* (W.H. and L. Collingridge, 1947)

——, *Garden Making for Amateurs* (Ernest Benn, 1953)

Halsham, John, *Every Man His Own Garden* (Hodder and Stoughton, 1904)

Hampden, Mary, *Every Woman's Flower Garden* (Herbert Jenkins, 1915)

——, *The Small Garden* (Herbert Jenkins, 1918)

Hampshire, John, *Specialisation in the Garden* (The Garden Book Club, 1943)
Hanbury, William, *An Essay on Planting* (S. Parker, 1758)
Hancock, Ralph, *When I make a Garden* (G.T. Foulis and Co., 1936)
Hanmer, Thomas, *The Garden Book of Sir Thomas Hanmer* (1659; Gerald Howe, 1933)
Hardy, Jack and S. Foxman, *Food Production in the School Garden* (Allman and Son, 1940)
Hardy, Thomas, *Jude the Obscure* (Osgood, McIvaine and Co., 1896)
Harper, William, *The Antiquity, Innocence, and Pleasure of Gardening* (The Author, 1732)
Harris, John (ed.), *The Garden: a Celebration of One Thousand Years of British Gardening* (New Perspectives, 1979)
Hartlib, Samuel, *A Description of the Famous Kingdome of Macaria* (Francis Constable, 1641)
——, (from Richard Weston) *Samuel Hartlib, his Legacie, or an Enlargement of the Discourse of Husbandry used in Brabant and Flaunders* (Richard Wodenothe, 1651)
Hatton, Richard George, *The Craftsman's Plant-Book* (Chapman and Hall, 1909)
Haweis, Mary Eliza, *Rus in Urbe: or Flowers that Thrive in London Gardens and Smoky Towns* (Leadenhall Press, 1886)
Haworth-Booth, Maude, *My Garden Diary* (John Murray, 1934)
Hawthorne, Hildegarde, *The Lure of the Garden* (Century Co., 1911)
Hay, Roy, *Roy Hay Talks About Gardening* (George Allen and Unwin, 1942)
——, *Gardener's Chance: From War Production to Peace Possibilities* (Putnam and Co., 1946)
——, *In My Garden* (Gryphon Books, 1955)
Hay, Thomas, *Plants for the Connoisseur* (Putnam, 1938)
Hayward, Joseph, *An Inquiry into the Causes of the Fruitfulness and Barrenness of Plants and Trees* (Orr and Smith, 1834)
Hazlitt, W. Carew, *Gleanings in Old Garden Literature* (Elliot Stock, 1892)
Hedrick, U.P., *A History of Horticulture in America to 1860* (Oxford University Press, New York, 1950)
Heeley, Joseph, *Letters on the Beauties of Hagley, Envil, and the Leasowes* (R. Baldwin, 1777)
Hellyer, Arthur George Lee, *The Amateur Gardener* (W.H. and L. Collingridge, 1948)
Henrey, Blanche, *British Botanical and Horticultural Literature Before 1800* (Oxford University Press, 1975)
Henslow, Thomas Geoffrey Wall, *Garden Development* (Dean and Son, 1923)
——, *The Cottage Garden* (Herbert Jenkins, 1941)
——, *Allotment Gardens and Management* (John Crowther, 1942)
Hill, Christopher, *The English Bible and the Seventeenth-Century Revolution* (Allen Lane: The Penguin Press, 1993)
Hill, John, *The Gardener's New Kalendar* (T. Osbourne, T. Trye and S. Crowder, 1758)
Hoare, Henry, *Spade Work: or, How to Start a Flower Garden* (Arthur L. Humphreys, 1902)
Hobday, Edward, *Cottage Gardening* (Macmillan and Co., 1877)
——, *Fruit Culture for Profit* (George Routledge and Sons, 1883)
Hobsbawm, Eric J., *Industry and Empire* (Weidenfeld and Nicholson, 1968)
Hogg, Robert, *The Dahlia: Its History and Cultivation* (Groombridge and Sons, 1853)
Hole, Samuel Reynolds (ed.), *The Gardeners' Annual for 1863* (Longman, Green, Longman, Roberts, and Green, 1863)
——, *A Book About Roses* (London, 1869; 20th edn, Edward Arnold, 1903)
——, *A Book About the Garden and the Gardener* (Edward Arnold, 1892)
Hope, Frances Jane, *Notes and Thoughts on Gardens and Woodlands* (Macmillan and Co., 1881)
Howe, Bea, *Lady With Green Fingers: The Life of Jane Loudon* (Country Life, 1961)
Hoyles, Martin, *The Story of Gardening* (Journeyman, 1991)
——, *Gardeners Delight* (Pluto, 1994)
Hudson, John, *The Florist's Companion* (William Preston, 1794)
Hughes, William, *The Compleat Vineyard* (W. Crook and John Playfere, 1665)
——, *The American Physitian* (William Crook, 1672)

Hunt, John Dixon and Peter Willis (eds), *The Genius of the Place: The English Landscape Garden 1620–1820* (Elek, 1975; MIT Press, 1988)
Hunter, Alexander (ed.), *Georgical Essays* (T. Durham, 1770–1772; enlarged edn, The Author, 1803)
Hyams, Edward, *English Cottage Gardens* (Whittet Books, 1970; Penguin, 1987)
Hyatt, Alfred H. (ed.), *A Book of Old-World Gardens* (T.N. Foulis, 1911)
Hyll, Thomas, *A pleasaunt Instruction of the parfit orderinge of Bees* (Thomas Marshe, 1568)
——, (Didymus Mountain), *The Gardener's Labyrinth* (H. Bynneman, London, 1577; Oxford University Press, 1987)

Ingwersen, Walter E. Th., *Wild Flowers in the Garden* (Geoffrey Bles, 1951)

Jackson, Robert (ed.), *Beautiful Gardens of the World* (Evans Brothers, 1953)
Jacson, Maria Elizabetha, *Botanical Dialogues* (J. Johnson, 1797)
——, *The Florist's Manual* (Henry Colburn and Co., 1816)
James, John, *The Theory and Practice of Gardening* (Maurice Atkins, 1712; Gregg International Publishers, 1969)
James, T., 'The Poetry of Gardening', *Carthusian*; reprinted in *The Flower Garden* (see below); also in Alfred H. Hyatt (ed.), *A Book of Gardens* (T.N. Foulis, 1910)
——, *The Flower Garden* (John Murray, 1852; originally published in the *Quarterly Review*, 1842)
James, William Owen, *Background to Gardening* (George Allen and Unwin, 1957)
Jarrett, David, *The English Landscape Garden* (Academy Editions, 1978)
Jarvis, Claude Scudamore, *Gardener's Medley* (Country Life, 1951)
Jarvis, Mary Rowles, *Three Girls and a Garden* (H.R. Allenson, 1912)
Jefferson, Thomas, *Garden Book 1766–1824* (American Philosophical Society, Philadelphia, 1944)
Jekyll, Gertrude, *Wood and Garden* (Longmans, Green and Co., 1899; Antique Collectors' Club, 1981)
——, *Colour in the Flower Garden* (Country Life, 1908; Antique Collectors' Club, 1981)
Jex-Blake, A.J. (ed.), *Gardening in East Africa* (Longmans, Green and Co., 1934; 2nd edn, 1939)
Johns, William Earle, *The Passing Show* (My Garden, 1937)
Johnson, Arthur Tysilio, *A Garden in Wales* (Edward Arnold, 1927)
Johnson, Francis, R., 'Thomas Hill: An Elizabethan Huxley', *Huntington Library Quarterly*, 4 (August 1944)
Johnson, George William, *A History of English Gardening* (Baldwin and Cradock, and Longman and Co., 1829)
——, *The Cottage Gardener's Dictionary* (William S. Orr and Co., 1852; retitled *The Gardener's Dictionary*, Bell and Daldy, 1872)
Johnson, Louisa, *Every Lady Her Own Flower Gardener* (W.S. Orr and Co., 1839; 14th edn, Piper, Stephenson, and Spence, nd)
Justice, James, *The British Gardener's Calendar* (R. Fleming, 1759)

Kemp, Edward, *How to Lay Out a Small Garden* (Bradbury and Evans, 1850)
——, *The Parks, Gardens, Etc., of London and Its Suburbs* (John Weale, 1851)
King, Louisa Yeomans (Mrs Francis King), *The Well-Considered Garden* (Charles Scribner's Sons, 1915)
Kingsley, Charles, *Madam How and Lady Why* (Bell and Daldy, 1870)
Kirk, John William Carnegie, *A British Garden Flora* (Edward Arnold and Co., 1927)
Kirkpatrick, H., *An Account of the Manner in which Potatoes are Cultivated and Preserved* (J. Johnson, 1796)
Koestler, Arthur, *The Invisible Writing* (Collins, with Hamish Hamilton, 1954)

Lamb, Christian, 'Knight to Empress', *The Garden* 116 (2), February 1991

Landolicus, *The Indian Amateur Gardener* (W. Newman and Co., Calcutta, c.1880; 2nd edn, 1888; 4th edn, 1936)
Langford, T., *Plain and Full Instructions to Raise All Sorts of Fruit-Trees that Prosper in England* (Richard Chiswel, 1681)
Langley, Batty, *New Principles of Gardening* (A. Bettesworth and J. Battey, 1728)
——, *A Sure Method of Improving Estates by Plantations of Oak, Elm, Ash, Beech and Other Timber-Trees, Coppice-Woods* (Francis Clay and Daniel Browne, 1728)
Laurence, John, *The Clergy-Man's Recreation: Shewing the Pleasure and Profit of the Art of Gardening* (Bernard Lintott, 1714; 6th edn, 1726)
——, *The Fruit-Garden Kalendar* (Bernard Lintot, 1718)
Lawrance, Charles Frederick, *The Book of the School Garden* (Evans Brothers, 1918)
Lawrance, Mary, *A Collection of Roses from Nature* (Miss Lawrance, 1799)
Lawrence, Anthony, and John Beale, *Nurseries, Orchards, Profitable Gardens, and Vineyards Encouraged* (Henry Brome, 1677)
Lawrence, William John Cooper, *The Young Gardener* (George Allen and Unwin, 1943)
Lawson, William, *The Country Housewifes Garden* (Roger Jackson, 1617; Breslich and Foss, 1983)
——, *A New Orchard and Garden* (Roger Jackson, 1618)
Leighton, Clare, *Four Hedges: A Gardener's Chronicle* (Victor Gollancz, 1935)
London, William, *A Catalogue of The most vendible Books in England* (London, 1657)
——, *A Catalogue of New Books* (Luke Fawn and Francis Tyton, 1660)
Loudon, Jane Wells, *Instructions in Gardening for Ladies* (John Murray, 1840)
——, *The Lady's Country Companion* (Longman, Brown, Green and Longmans, 1845; Paradigm Press, 1984)
Loudon, John Claudius, *An Encyclopaedia of Gardening* (Longman, Hurst, Rees, Orme, and Brown, 1822; revised edn, 1834)
——, *The Suburban Gardener, and Villa Companion* (Longman, Orme, Brown, Green, and Longmans 1838: 2nd edn entitled *The Villa Gardner* edited by Jane Loudon, Wm. S. Orr & Co. 1850)
——, *An Encyclopaedia of Trees and Shrubs* (Longman, Brown, Green and Longmans, 1842)
——, *On the Laying Out, Planting, and Managing of Cemeteries and on the Improvement of Churchyards* (A. Spottiswoode for the Author, 1843; Ivelet Books, 1981)
Lovell, Robert, *A Compleat Herball* (Richard Davis, 1659)

McDermott, Joe, 'Review of Ji Cheng's The Craft of Gardens', *Garden History*, 18 (1), 1990
McDonald, Donald, *English Vegetables & Flowers in India & Ceylon* (2nd edn, John Haddon and Co., 1890)
——, *My African Garden* (John Haddon and Co., 1892)
MacGregor, Jessie, *Gardens of Celebrities and Celebrated Gardens* (Hutchinson and Co., 1919)
McIntosh, Charles, *The Book of the Garden* (William Blackwood and Sons, 1853–55)
McKay, C.D., *The French Garden* (Associated Newspapers, 1908)
MacKenzie, John MacDonald, *Propaganda and Empire* (Manchester University Press, 1984)
Macmillan, Hugh Fraser, *A Handbook of Tropical Gardening and Planting* (H.W. Cave and Co., Colombo, 1910)
MacPhail, James, *The Gardener's Remembrancer* (T. Egerton, H. Symonds, and Richardsons, 1803; 2nd edn, Longman, Hurst, Rees, Orme, and Brown, 1819)
Makin, Bathsua, *An Essay to Revive the Antient Education of Gentlewomen* (Tho. Parkhurst, 1673)
Malby, Reginald A., *The Story of My Rock Garden* (Headley Brothers, 1912)
Malcolm, William, *A Catalogue of Hot-House and Green-House Plants* (J. Dixwell, 1771)
Maling, Miss E.A., *The Indoor Gardener* (Longman, Green, Longman, Roberts and Green, 1863)
Mansfield, T.C., *The Border in Colour* (William Collins, 1944)
——, *Of Cabbages and Kings* (Collins, 1945)

Markham, Ernest, *Clematis* (Country Life, 1935)

Markham, Gervase, *The English Husbandman* (John Browne, 1613; 2nd edn enlarged, Henry Taunton, 1635)

——, *The Second Booke of the English Husbandman* (John Browne, 1615)

——, *The English Hus-wife* (Roger Jackson, 1615)

——, *Farewelle to Husbandrie* (Roger Jackson, 1620)

Marshall, Charles, *An Introduction to the Knowledge and Practice of Gardening* (The Author, 1796; 2nd edn, F. and C. Rivington, 1798)

Martineau, Alice, *The Herbaceous Garden* (Williams and Norgate, 1913)

——, (Mrs Philip Martineau), *Gardening in Sunny Lands* (Richard Cobden-Sanderson, 1924)

——, (Mrs Philip Martineau), *The Secrets of Many Gardens* (Williams and Norgate, 1924)

Marx, Karl, *Capital* (1867; Penguin, 1976)

Maryon, Maud, *How the Garden Grew* (Longmans, Green, and Co., 1900)

Mascall, Leonard, *A Booke of the Arte and manner how to Plant and Graffe all sorts of Trees* (John Wight, 1569; 6th edn, Thomas Wight, 1592)

Massingham, Harold John, *This Plot of Earth: A Gardener's Chronicle* (Collins, 1944)

Maunsell, John Edmond Bush, *Natural Gardening* (Faber and Faber, 1958)

Mawson, Thomas Hayton, *The Art and Craft of Garden Making* (B.T. Batsford and G. Newnes, 1900)

Maxwell, Herbert Eustace, *Flowers: A Garden Note Book* (Maclehose, Jackson and Co., 1923)

Meen, Margaret, *Exotic Plants from the Royal Gardens at Kew* (London, 1790)

Meikle, Andrew, *Window Gardening for Town and Country* (George Routledge and Sons, 1870)

——, *The Cottage Garden* (George Routledge and Sons, 1874)

Middleton, Cecil Henry, *Your Garden in War-Time* (George Allen and Unwin, 1941)

——, *Digging for Victory* (George Allen and Unwin, 1942)

Miller, Joseph, *Botanicum Officinale; Or a Compendious Herbal* (E. Bell, J. Senex, W. Taylor and J. Osborn, 1722)

Miller, Philip, *Gardeners Dictionary* (The Author, 1731; 8th edn, John and Francis Rivington, 1768)

Miller, Wilhelm, *What England Can Teach Us About Gardening* (Hodder and Stoughton, 1911)

Mills, George, *A Treatise on the Culture of the Pine-Apple* (William Smith, 1845)

Milton, John, *Paradise Lost* (1667; Longmans, 1968)

Mollet, Andrew, *The Garden of Pleasure* (John Martyn and Henry Herringman, 1670)

Mollison, John R., *The New Practical Window Gardener* (Groombridge and Sons, 1877)

Moncrieff, Ascott Robert Hope, *Kew Gardens* (A. and C. Black, 1908)

Moore, Thomas, *The Elements of Botany for Families and Schools* (10th edn, Longmans, Green, and Co., 1865)

Mortimer, John, *The Whole Art of Husbandry* (H. Mortlock, 1707)

Morton, A.L., *A People's History of England* (Victor Gollancz, 1938)

Mott, Frederick Thompson, *Flora Odorata* (Orr and Co., C.A. Bartlett, and Brown and Hewitt, 1843)

Mumby, Frank Arthur, *Publishing and Bookselling* (Jonathan Cape, 1930)

Murdock, George Peter, *Africa: Its Peoples and Their Cultural History* (McGraw-Hill, New York, 1959)

Murray, Charlotte, *The British Garden* (S. Hazard, 1799)

Murray, Kathleen L., *My Garden in the Wilderness* (W. Thacker and Co., 1915)

Neill, Patrick, *An Account of British Horticulture* (Edinburgh, 1817)

——, *Journal of a Horticultural Tour* (Bell and Bradfute, Edinburgh, 1823)

——, *The Fruit, Flower, and Kitchen Garden* (A. and C. Black, Edinburgh, 1838)

Nichols, John Beverley, *Down the Garden Path* (Jonathan Cape, 1932) bibliography

Nicol, Walter, *The Scotch Forcing Gardener* (The Author, Edinburgh, 1797)
Notcutt, Roger Crompton, *A Handbook of Flowering Trees and Shrubs for Gardeners* (Martin Hopkinson and Co., 1926)
Nourse, Timothy, *Campania Foelix, or A Discourse of the Benefits and Improvements of Husbandry* (Thomas Bennett, 1700)
Nussey, Helen G., *London Gardens of the Past* (John Lane: The Bodley Head, 1939; 2nd edn, 1948)
Nuttall, G. Clarke, *Beautiful Flowering Shrubs* (Waverley Book Co., 1920)

Orwell, George, 'England Your England' (1941), in *Inside the Whale and Other Essays* (Penguin, 1962)

Pallister, Minnie, *Gardener's Frenzy* (Methuen and Co., 1933)
Papworth, John Buonarotti, *Hints on Ornamental Gardening* (R. Ackerman, 1823)
Parkes, Mrs William, *Domestic Duties* (Longman, Hurst, Rees, Orme, Brown, and Green, 1825)
Parkinson, John, *Paradisi in Sole, Paradisus Terrestris* (H. Lownes and R. Young, 1629; Methuen, 1904)
Paterson, Nathaniel, *The Manse Garden* (William Collins, Glasgow, 1836; G.T. Foulis and Co., 1926)
Paul, William, *The Rose Garden* (Sherwood, Gilbert and Piper, 1848)
——, *The Hand-Book of Villa Gardening* (Piper, Stephenson, and Spence, 1855; 3rd edn revised as *Villa Gardening*, Frederick Warne and Co., 1876)
Peacock, William F., *The Beauties of Llangollen and Chirk* (G. Vickers, 1860)
——, *What I Saw in the Golden Valley* (Thomas Coles, 1860)
Pennant, Thomas, *A Tour in Wales* (London, 1778)
Perkin, Harold, *The Rise of Professional Society* (Routledge, 1989)
Perry, Frances, *Water Gardening* (Country Life, 1938)
——, *The Herbaceous Border* (W.H. and L. Collingridge, 1948)
——, *The Woman Gardener* (Hulton Press, 1955)
Pettigrew, William Wallace, *Common-Sense Gardening* (Sunday Chronicle, 1925)
——, *Handbook of the City Parks and Recreation Grounds* (Manchester City Council, 1929)
——, *Municipal Parks: Layout, Management and Administration* (Journal of Park Administration, 1937)
Phillips, Henry, *Pomarium Britannicum* (The Author, 1820)
——, *History of Cultivated Vegetables* (Henry Colburn and Co., 1822)
——, *Sylva Florifera: The Shrubbery Historically and Botanically Treated* (Longman, Hurst, Rees, Orme, and Brown, 1823)
——, *Flora Historica* (E. Lloyd and Son, 1824)
——, *Floral Emblems* (Saunders and Otley, 1825)
Phillips, Patricia, *The Scientific Lady: A Social History of Women's Scientific Interests 1520–1918* (Weidenfeld and Nicolson, 1990)
Pink, James, *Potatoes: How to Grow and Show Them* (Crosby Lockwood and Co., 1879)
Platt, Hugh, *The Jewell House of Art and Nature* (Peter Short, 1594)
——, *Floraes Paradise* (William Leake, 1608; reprinted as *The Garden of Eden*, William Leake, 1653)
Pliny the Elder, (A.D. 23–79), *Natural History* (Penguin, 1991)
Pontey, William, *The Profitable Planter* (Sikes and Smart, 1800)
——, *The Forest Pruner* (The Author, 1805)
Powys, Caroline, *Passages from the Diaries of Mrs. Philip Lybbe Powys* (Longmans and Co., 1899)
Pratt, Anne, *The Field, The Garden, and the Woodland* (Charles Knight and Co., 1838)
——, *Flowers and their Associations* (Charles Knight and Co., 1840)
Pratt, Edwin A., *Pioneer Women in Victoria's Reign* (George Newnes, 1897)

Price, Uvedale, *An Essay on the Picturesque* (J. Robson, 1794)
Prior, W.D., *Roses and their Culture* (George Routledge and Sons, 1878)
Pulteney, Richard, *Historical and Biographical Sketches of the Progress of Botany in England, from its Origin to the Introduction of the Linnaean System* (T. Cadell, 1790)

Quin, Charles W. (ed.), *Garden Receipts* (Macmillan and Co., 1877)

Rack, Edmund, 'On the Origin and Progress of Agriculture', in Alexander Hunter (ed.), *Georgical Essays* (The Author, 1803)
Rackham, Oliver, *The History of the Countryside* (J.M. Dent and Sons, 1986)
Rea, John, *Flora, Ceres and Pomona* (Richard Marriott, 1665)
Reid, John, *The Scots Gard'ner* (Edinburgh, 1683)
Repton, Humphry, *Sketches and Hints on Landscape Gardening* (Boydells, 1794)
——, *Observations on the Theory and Practice of Landscape Gardening* (J. Taylor, 1803)
Richmond, Mrs I.L., *In My Lady's Garden* (T. Fisher Unwin, 1908)
Roberts, Harry, *The Book of Old-Fashioned Flowers* (John Lane: The Bodley Head, 1901)
——, *Keep Fit in War-Time* (Watts and Co., 1940)
——, *British Rebels and Reformers* (William Collins, 1942)
——, *English Gardens* (William Collins, 1944)
Robinson, Phil, *In My Indian Garden* (Sampson Low, Marston, Seale, and Rivington, 1878)
Robinson, William, *Gleanings from French Gardens* (Frederick Warne and Co., 1868)
——, *Hardy Flowers* (Frederick Warne and Co., 1871)
——, *The Garden Beautiful* (John Murray, 1906)
——, *Gravetye Manor* (John Murray, 1911)
Rogers, John, *The Fruit Cultivator* (James Ridgway and Sons, 1834)
——, *The Vegetable Cultivator* (Longman, Orme, Brown, Green, and Longmans, 1839)
——, *A Sketch of the Life and Reminiscences of John Rogers* (Henry March Gilbert, 1889)
Rohde, Eleanour Sinclair, *The Old English Herbals* (Longmans and Co., 1922; Minerva Press, 1972)
——, *The Old English Gardening Books* (Martin Hopkinson, 1924)
——, *Herbs and Herb Gardening* (Medici Society, 1936)
——, *The War-Time Vegetable Garden* (Medici Society, 1940)
——, *Uncommon Vegetables* (Country Life, 1943)
Romanné-James, C., *Flowers for the House and How to Arrange Them* (Williams and Norgate, 1951)
Ronalds, Hugh, *Pyrus Malus Brentfordiensis* (Longman, Rees, Orme, Brown and Green, 1831)
Roper, Lanning, *Royal Gardens* (W.H. and L. Collingridge, 1953)
Rose, John, *The English Vineyard Vindicated* (John Crook, 1666)
Røstvig, Maren-Sofie, *The Happy Man* (Basil Blackwell, 1954)
Rousseau, Jean-Jacques, *Julie: ou la Nouvelle Héloïse* (Amsterdam, 1761; Pennsylvania State University Press, 1987)
——, *Émile* (Amsterdam, 1762; Heinemann, 1956)
Rowden, Frances Arabella, *A Poetical Introduction to the Study of Botany* (published by subscription, London, 1801)
Rowe, W.H., *Tree and Shrub Growing* (Penguin, 1944; Faber and Faber enlarged edn, 1949)
Rowles, William F., *The Food Garden* (Headley Bros., 1917)
Royal Horticultural Society, *The Vegetable Garden Displayed* (Simpkin Marshall, 1941)
Rutter, John and Daniel Carter, *Modern Eden: or, The Gardener's Universal Guide* (J. Cooke, 1767)
Ryves, K.C., *Of Gardens East and West* (Andrew Melrose, 1921)

Sackville-West, Vita, *Some Flowers* (Cobden-Sanderson, 1937)
——, *Country Notes* (Michael Joseph, 1939)
——, *The Women's Land Army* (Michael Joseph, 1944)

Said, Edward W., *Culture and Imperialism* (Chatto and Windus, 1993)

Sale, Edith Dabney Tunis (ed.), *Historic Gardens of Virginia* (William Byrd Press, 1923; revised edn, 1930)

Sale, Kirkpatrick, *The Conquest of Paradise* (Hodder and Stoughton, 1991)

Salmon, William, *The English Herbal* (H. Rhodes and J. Taylor, 1710)

Sands, Mollie, *The Gardens of Hampton Court* (Evans Brothers, 1950)

Sanecki, Kay Naylor, *Wild and Garden Herbs* (W.H. and L. Collingridge, 1956)

Sedding, John D., *Garden-Craft Old and New* (Kegan Paul, Trench, Trubner and Co., 1891; 2nd edn, 1895)

Sharp, Jane, *The Midwives Book* (Simon Miller, 1671)

Sharrock, Robert, *The History of the Propagation and Improvement of Vegetables* (Thomas Robinson, Oxford, 1660)

Shaw, C.W., *The London Market Gardens* (London, 1879)

——, *The Kitchen and Market Garden* (Crosby Lockwood and Son, 1882)

Shaylor, Joseph, *The Fascination of Books* (Simkin, Marshall, Hamilton, Kent and Co., 1912)

Shebbeare, John (Battista Angeloni), *Letters on the English Nation* (London, 1755)

Shenstone, William, 'Unconnected Thoughts on Gardening', *The Works in Verse and Prose of William Shenstone*, Vol. II (R. and J. Dodsley, 1764)

Sieveking, Albert Forbes, *The Praise of Gardens* (J.M. Dent, 1899)

—— (ed.), *Sir William Temple Upon the Gardens of Epicurus, with Other XVIIth Century Garden Essays* (Chatto and Windus, 1908)

Simons, Arthur John, *The Vegetable Grower's Handbook*, Vols 1 and 2 (Penguin, 1945)

Simpson, John, *The Grape Vine: Its Propagation and Culture* (George Routledge and Sons, 1883)

Singleton, Esther, *The Shakespeare Garden* (Century Co., New York, 1922)

Smee, Alfred, *My Garden: Its Plan and Culture* (Bell and Daldy, 1872)

Smith, Bruce D., *Rivers of Change* (Smithsonian Institution, 1992)

Smith, James Edward, *A Tour to Hafod* (T. Bensley, 1810)

Smith, John, *A Description of New England* (Robert Clerke, 1616)

——, *The Description of Virginia* (Henrie Fetherstone, 1625)

Smith, Thomas, *The Profitable Culture of Vegetables* (Longmans, Green and Co., 1911)

Speechly, William, *A Treatise of the Culture of the Vine* (The Author, 1790)

Speed, Adolphus, *Adam Out of Eden* (Henry Brome, 1659)

Speede, G.T. Frederic S. Barlow, *The Indian Hand-Book of Gardening* (W. Thacker and Co., Calcutta, 1840)

Spilhaus, Margaret Whiting, *Indigenous Trees of the Cape Peninsula* (Juta and Co., Cape Town and Johannesburg, 1950)

Stamp, Winifred, *'Doctor Himself': An Unorthodox Biography of Harry Roberts 1871–1946* (Hamish Hamilton, 1949)

Stanley, Arthur, *The Book of the Garden* (Ivor Nicholson and Watson, 1932)

Stebbing, Maud Evelyn, *The Flower Garden and How to Work In It* (T.C. and E.C. Jack, 1917)

Steele, Richard, *An Essay Upon Gardening* (The Author, 1793)

Stephens, Theodore Alfred, *My Garden's Good-Night* (My Garden, 1939)

——, *My Garden's Bedside Book* (My Garden, 1951)

——, and Arthur Tysilio Johnson, *My Garden's ABC of Flowering Trees and Shrubs* (My Garden, 1946)

Steuart, Henry, *The Planter's Guide* (William Blackwood, Edinburgh, 1828)

Stevens, Thomas Hardy Goldsworthy, *Trees and Shrubs in my Garden* (George G. Harrap and Co., 1938)

Stirling, F. Graham, 'Some Characteristics of Scotch Gardens', in Margaret Waterfield, *Flower Grouping in English, Scotch and Irish Gardens* (J.M. Dent and Co., 1907)

Stockdale, F.A., T. Petch, and H.F.Macmillan, *The Royal Botanic Gardens, Peradeniya, Ceylon* (H.W. Cave and Co., Colombo, 1922)

Stoker, Fred, *A Gardener's Progress* (Putnam, 1938)

Stout, Mary, and Madeline Agar, *A Book of Gardening for the Sub-Tropics* (H.F. and G. Witherby, 1921)

Strabo, Walahfrid, *Hortus* (Hunt Botanical Library, Pittsburgh, 1966)

Strong, Roy, 'The Renaissance Garden 1500 to 1640', in John Harris (ed.), *The Garden* (New Perspectives, 1979)

Stuart, Constance Mary Villiers, *Gardens of the Great Mughals* (A. and C. Black, 1913)

Sudell, Richard, *Secrets of Successful Gardening* (Odhams Press, 1939)

——, *Intensive Culture* (John Crowther, 1942)

——, *A National Food Production Guide for Garden and Allotment* (Marshall Press, 1942)

Switzer, Stephen, *The Nobleman, Gentleman, and Gardener's Recreation* (B. Baker and C. King, 1715)

——, *The Practical Kitchen Gardiner* (Tho. Woodward, 1727)

Taylor, Adam, *A Treatise on the Ananas or Pine-Apple* (The Author, 1769)

Taylor, Ann, *Practical Hints to Young Females on the Duties of a Wife, a Mother, and a Mistress of a Family* (Taylor and Hessey, 1815)

Taylor, Geoffrey, *Some Nineteenth Century Gardeners* (Skeffington, 1951)

Taylor, George M., *Roses for the Home and Garden* (Garden Life, 1919)

——, *British Garden Flowers* (Collins, 1946)

——, *The Little Garden* (Collins, 1948)

Taylor, Harold Victor, *The Apples of England* (Crosby Lockwood and Son, 1936)

——, *Salad Crops* (HMSO, 1941)

Taylor, Harriet Osgood, *Japanese Gardens* (Methuen and Co., 1912)

Teetgen, Ada B., *Profitable Herb Growing and Collecting* (Country Life, 1916)

Temple, William, 'Upon the Gardens of Epicurus; or of Gardening in the Year 1685', *Miscellanea* Part II (Ri. and Ra. Simpson, 1690)

Temple-Wright, Mrs I., *Flowers and Gardens in India* (Thacker, Spink and Co., Calcutta, 1893: 7th edn, 1919)

Thomas, Graham Stuart, *The Old Shrub Roses* (Phoenix House, 1955)

Thomas, Harry Higgott, *Little Gardens and How To Make The Most of Them* (Cassell and Co., 1908)

——, *The Complete Gardener* (Cassell and Co., 1912)

——, *Gardening: A Complete Guide* (Cassell and Co., 1917)

——, (ed.), *The Manual of Practical Gardening* (Allied Newspapers, 1934)

——, *Gardening in Towns* (Methuen and Co., 1936)

Thomas, Keith, *Man and the Natural World* (Allen Lane, 1983)

Thomas, Owen and George Wythes, *Vegetable Growing Made Easy* (Country Life, 1913)

Thomas, William Beach, *Gardens* (Burke, 1952)

Thompson, Dorothy, 'Women and Nineteenth-Century Radical Politics: A Lost Dimension', in Ann Oakley and Juliet Mitchell (eds.), *The Rights and Wrongs of Women* (Penguin, 1976)

Thompson, Edward P., *The Making of the English Working Class* (Victor Gollancz, 1963; revised edn, Penguin, 1968)

——, *Customs in Common* (Merlin Press, 1991)

——, *Witness Against the Beast: William Blake and the Moral Law* (Cambridge University Press, 1993)

Thompson, Robert, *The Gardener's Assistant* (Blackie and Son, 1859)

Thonger, Charles, *The Book of the Cottage Garden* (John Lane: The Bodley Head, 1909)

Thornton, Robert John, *Temple of Flora* (The Author, 1812)

——, *The Medical Guardian of Youth; or, A Popular Treatise on the Prevention and Cure of the Venereal Disease* (3rd edn, The Author, 1816)

Tiltman, Marjorie Hessell, *A Little Place in the Country* (Hodder and Stoughton, 1944)

Tinley, George F., Thomas Humphreys and William Irving, *Colour Planning of the Garden* (T.C. and E.C. Jack, 1924)

Triggs, H. Inigo, *Garden Craft in Europe* (B.T. Batsford, 1913)
Trowell, Samuel, *A New Treatise of Husbandry, Gardening, and other Curious Matters relating to Country Affairs* (James Hodges, 1738)
Trow-Smith, Robert, *English Husbandry* (Faber and Faber, 1951)
Turner, James, 'Ralph Austen, an Oxford horticulturalist of the seventeenth century', *Garden History*, 6 (2), 1978
——, *The Politics of Landscape* (Basil Blackwell, 1979)
Turner, William, *A new Herball* (John Gybken, 1551; seconde parte, Arnold Birckman, 1562; Thirde parte, Arnold Birckman, 1568)
Tusser, Thomas, *Five Hundreth Points of Good Husbandry* (Rychard Tottell, 1573)

Unwin, Stanley, *The Truth About a Publisher* (George Allen and Unwin, 1960)

van Sertima, Ivan, *They Came Before Columbus* (Random House, New York, 1976)
Veitch, James H., *Hortus Veitchii* (James Veitch and Sons, 1906)
von Arnim, Elizabeth, *Elizabeth and her German Garden* (Macmillan and Co., 1898; Virago, 1985)

Wade, Edward, *A Proposal for Improving and Adorning the Island of Great Britain; for the Maintenance of our Navy and Shipping* (R. and J. Dodsley, 1755)
Wade, J.R., *War-Time Gardening* (C. Arthur Pearson, 1940)
Wakefield, Priscilla, *An Introduction to Botany, in a Series of Familiar Letters* (E. Newbery, 1796)
——, *Reflections on the Present Condition of the Female Sex* (J. Johnson, and Darton and Harvey, 1798)
Walpole, Horace, 'The History of Modern Taste in Gardening', *Anecdotes of Painting in England* Vol. 4, 1771; 3rd edn entitled *Essay on Modern Gardening* (Strawberry Hill, 1785)
Waterfield, Margaret, *Flower Grouping in English, Scotch and Irish Gardens* (J.M. Dent and Co., 1907)
Watson, William, *Climbing Plants* (T.C. and E.C. Jack, 1910)
——, *Rhododendrons and Azaleas* (T.C. and E.C. Jack, 1910)
Watts, Elizabeth, *Vegetables and How to Grow Them* (Frederick Warne and Co., 1866)
——, *Flowers and the Flower Garden* (Frederick Warne and Co., 1866)
Weathers, John, *A Practical Guide to School, Cottage, and Allotment Gardening* (Longmans, Green, and Co., 1908)
——, *My Garden Book* (Longmans, Green and Co., 1924)
West, Gilbert, *Stowe, The Gardens of the Right Honourable Richard Viscount Cobham* (Lawton Gilliver, 1732)
Whately, Thomas, *Observations on Modern Gardening* (T. Payne, 1770)
Wheeler, James, *The Modern Druid* (C. Davis and J. Clarke, 1747)
Wheelwright, Edith Grey, *The Garden of Pleasant Flowers* (Gerald Howe, 1932)
——, *The Physick Garden: Medicinal Plants and their History* (Jonathan Cape, 1934)
Whitehead, Stanley B., *In Your Flower Garden* (J.M. Dent and Sons, 1947)
Whitmill, Benjamin, *Kalendarium Universale: or The Gardeners Universal Kalendar* (James Lacey and John Clarke, 1726; 7th edn, J. Wilkie, 1765)
Whittle, Elisabeth, *The Historic Gardens of Wales* (HMSO, 1992)
Williams, Gwyn A., *When Was Wales?* (Black Raven, 1985)
Williams, John (ed.), *The Physicians of Myddvai* (D.J. Roderic, 1861)
Williams, Mrs Leslie, *A Garden in the Suburbs* (John Lane: The Bodley Head, 1901)
Williams, Roger, *A Key into the Language of America* (London, 1643)
——, *The Hireling Ministry* (London, 1652)
Wilson, Henrietta, *Chronicles of a Garden* (London and Edinburgh, 1863; 2nd edn, James Nisbet, 1864))
Winstanley, Gerrard, *Fire in the Bush* (Giles Calvert, 1650)

——, *A Declaration from the Poor Oppressed People of England* (Also signed by 44 others, 1649)

Wolseley, Frances Garnet, *Gardening for Women* (Cassell and Co., 1908)

——, (Viscountess Wolseley) *In a College Garden* (John Murray, 1916)

——, *Gardens: Their Form and Design* (Edward Arnold, 1919)

Wood, John George, *Our Garden Friends and Foes* (Routledge, Warne, and Routledge, 1864)

——, *The Natural History of Man* (George Routledge and Sons, 1868–70)

Wood, Samuel, *The Plain Path to Good Gardening* (G.T. Goodwin, 1871; 2nd edn, entitled *A Plain Guide to Good Gardening*, Crosby Lockwood and Co., 1876)

——, *The Ladies' Multum-in-Parvo Flower Garden* (Crosby Lockwood and Co., 1881)

Woodrow, G. Marshall, *Hints on Gardening in India* (1876; 2nd edn, Education Society's Press, Byculla, Bombay, 1877; 4th edn, Bombay, 1888; 6th edn entitled *Gardening in the Tropics*, Alexander Gardner, Paisley, 1910)

Wright, Horace J. and Walter P.Wright, *Beautiful Flowers and How to Grow Them* (T.C. and E.C. Jack, 1909)

Wright, John, *Horticulture* (Macmillan and Co., 1893)

Wright, Richardson, *The Story of Gardening* (Dodd, Mead and Co., New York, 1934)

Wright, Samuel Thomas, et al, *How to Grow Strawberries* (The Horticultural Times, 1888)

Wright, Walter P. (ed.), *Cassell's Pocket Gardener* (Cassell and Co., 1900)

——, *A Book About Potatoes and Other Vegetables* (Headley Brothers, 1917)

Wythes, George, *The Book of Vegetables* (John Lane: The Bodley Head, 1902)

Young, Arthur, *Travels, During The Years 1787, 1788, and 1789* (W. Richardson, 1792)

Young, Robert Fitzgibbon, *Comenius in England* (Oxford University Press, 1932)

Index